THAT MAN HEINE

BY LEWIS BROWNE

STRANGER THAN FICTION

THIS BELIEVING WORLD

THAT MAN HEINE: A BIOGRAPHY

That Man Heine

A Biography by

LEWIS BROWNE

With the Collaboration of

ELSA WEIHL

New York

The LITERARY GUILD of AMERICA

MCMXXVII

Printed in the United States of America by
J. J. LITTLE AND IVES COMPANY, NEW YORK

TO THE MEMORY OF ONE
WHO UNDERSTOOD HEINE:
ISRAEL ZANGWILL

CONTENTS

BOOK ONE

THE EXILE IN GERMANY

BOOK TWO

THE EXILE IN FRANCE

BIBLIOGRAPHY

INDEX

CONTENTS

THE EXILE IN GERMANY

CHAPTER
ONE

*"Already in my cradle was the line of
march laid down for all my life. . . ."*

I<small>N THE</small> year 1796 there wandered into the town of
Düsseldorf on the Rhine a young Jew whose name was
Samson Heine. He gave himself out as a trader from
Hanover: a good-looking, fair-haired fellow, gaily clad
in the latest French fashion, and apparently well-to-do.
With him, we are told, came a string of twelve mettle-
some horses, and until these were discovered to be his
stock-in-trade rather than part of his personal entourage,
they gave him an air not uncalculated to impress the
good Jews of old Düsseldorf. For those Jews were, as
a group, exceedingly humble and poor. Most of them
were but the pettiest of petty merchants: stunted, round-
bellied, bearded little men who sold groceries or old
clothes in dark and dusty shops, or else peddled needles,
thread, and balsams, from packs which they carried on
their backs. They were a despised and hated lot, a
pariah folk skulking in narrow alley-ways and haggling
in a garbled German all their own. They were for the
most part poverty-stricken, ill-clad, and outwardly un-
lovely. And therefore a personable young man, well-
dressed and "emancipated," who could come clattering

into town with a string of twelve fine horses, must have seemed to them a personage of no little grandness.

It is not known whether this Samson Heine came to Düsseldorf with the intention of remaining there. Quite possibly he had thought but to trade off his horses and then move on to the next town. For years he seems to have been a foot-loose young bachelor, a happy-go-lucky fellow with a fondness for change and chance and amorous adventure. He liked horses and hunting dogs, had a passion for cards, and was not blind to the charms of theatrical ladies. A generation earlier such traits would have been quite scandalous in a Jewish young man; but times had changed drastically since then. The hunger for release which had just set all France aflame with revolution, had been felt also in Teutonic lands. Even the stoop-backed Jews swarming in the foul ghettos there, had begun to feel the pangs of this hunger. They too had become restless and had begun to ache for escape. And the young among them, knowing no better, had thought to find such escape in Germanization. They had taken to aping the ways of the Christians, cultivating their vices and imitating their modes. That was what they called "emancipation." "In your own home you may remain a Jew," they said; "but in the world, be a man."

Samson Heine was of this new generation. In his beliefs he was still a son of the ghetto; but in his manners and vices he was a man of the world. A spell of soldiering in Flanders and Brabant had loosed him from the ghetto and had taught him more than a little of Gentile ways. Of course he had not done any actual fighting in the campaigns, for, being a Jew, he had naturally been made to serve as a quarter-master. But he *had* been in the army, and the army had not failed to leave its mark on his demeanor. One can hardly doubt that in those years of war young Samson experienced many a joy forbidden by the Holy Law. And even at thirty-two, when he stopped over with his twelve fine horses in the Rhenish town of Düsseldorf, he probably had not yet outgrown an appetite for such joys. So it is hard to believe he came to the little river-port with the intention of settling there.

But whatever may have been his original intention, settle there he did. A girl made up his mind for him, a Düsseldorf girl whose name was Peira van Geldern. She was the orphaned daughter of a Jew who had been a physician in the town: not a very pretty girl, nor very young, but apparently very clever. Certainly she was far superior to most of the young people around her, and perhaps that was why at the age of twenty-five, when she first laid eyes on the handsome young trader from Hanover, she was still unmarried. In those days Jewish maidens were usually betrothed before they were eighteen; and it was counted almost a disgrace not to be married by the time one was twenty. If, therefore, Peira van Geldern was still unwed at twenty-five, it must have been because she had not until then been able to find a suitor to her liking. It could not have been because no suitors had appeared. Though she was neither strikingly beautiful nor immensely rich, she did come of an excel-

lent family—a cardinal consideration in Jewish match-
making—and was more than ordinarily educated.
Many years later her great son described her as having
been profoundly read in philosophy and poetry, and
considerable of a Latin scholar to boot; but that was
probably a filial exaggeration. A letter written by her
before her marriage, and reproduced in facsimile in
Hirth's collection, reveals clearly enough that though
the girl was of a serious and thoughtful turn of mind,
she had no adequate knowledge even of German, let
alone of Latin. Her language was that Judeo-German
patois which was the mother-tongue of almost all Jews
in Northern and Eastern Europe until three generations
ago. And she wrote it, of course, not in German characters, but in Hebrew script!

But though Fräulein van Geldern may not have been
a blue-stocking, undoubtedly she was better educated
than most other Jewish girls in Germany in her day.
And certainly she was better educated than the handsome
young stranger who had suddenly turned up in town with
his string of twelve horses. She was easily his superior
in intelligence and character, too. She could come to
a decision more quickly, and maintain it more stead-
fastly. She had more energy, more will, more ambition.
But that did not keep her from setting her cap at the
young bachelor. Perhaps his good looks and gay rai-
ment blinded her to his intellectual mediocrity; perhaps
the courtesy of his manner compensated for the frivolity
of his speech. Or, more probably, the ominous passing
of the years had humbled her a little, and made her

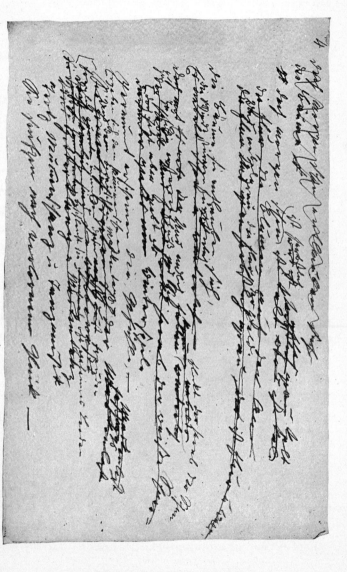

Fragment of Mss. of a poem by Heine.

fearful of delaying matrimony any longer. For she was
already twenty-five!

2

THEY were married early in February, 1797. If we are
to believe Gustav Karpeles, who has made the most la-
borious researches into the Heine genealogy, there seems
to have been some opposition to the match. The elders
of the congregation, having discovered that the rich-
looking suitor was in actuality almost penniless, apparently took it upon themselves to protect the orphan girl
against him. They therefore refused to recommend the
young man to the municipal authorities as a Jew worthy
of being admitted as a settler in the town. But the girl
spurned their protection. She came storming down on
the old rabbis of Düsseldorf, and, when she found them
obdurate, she appealed right over their heads to the
town council. For this young person was resolute, almost impossible to balk, once she had set her mind on
an object. She cajoled and petitioned for weeks on end
—and finally she triumphed. By express command of
the municipal authorities a permit was granted the Jew,
Samson Heine, to settle in the town of Düsseldorf. And
then he was made Peira van Geldern's husband.

Marriage worked vast changes in the young man.
From a happy-go-lucky cavalier he was transformed by
his wife into a settled and respectable burgher. She
made him forget his horses, and taught him to think of
velveteens instead. She set him up in business with her
dowry, renting a shop and stocking it with imported

English dress-goods. She made him keep far from the gaming table and the theatre, and thus allowed him no chance to indulge his old weaknesses. And he, having once made the plunge into virtue, seems to have tried to sink to the very depths, for he even joined the local *chevra kadisha*, the Jewish fraternity which visited the sick and buried the dead!

Perhaps in going to this particular extreme, Samson Heine went farther than his wife desired. She was not at all a pious young lady, this Peira who had just married him. On the contrary, she was quite militantly a rebel against the high wall of Holy Law which so long had kept the Jew pent-in and smothered. Indeed, in that direction she was far more emancipated than Samson himself. His emancipation revealed itself almost entirely in his manners, while hers showed itself in her thought. Through her father, who must have been a man of some learning, she had been brought under the influence of the French rationalists, and in a vague and blundering way she had become something of a Deist. But all that did not make her in the least tolerant toward what she considered sin. Though she may have entertained grave suspicions as to the validity of Rabbinic Law, she had no doubts as to the innate sanctity of the Jewish home. So, being the weaker character, Samson had to bow to her predilections. He tried to forget the inviting actresses of the local playhouse, and hardened his heart against the lure of dice and cards. Instead he kept diligently to his shop and slept dutifully at home— and in course of time became the father of four children.

3

THE first-born of those children was a boy. He was born on the thirteenth of December, in the year 1797, about ten months after the marriage of his parents. Harry he was named, in honor of a Mr. Harry who was an English merchant with whom the Heines did business. It was perhaps characteristic of the couple that they should give their child a foreign name instead of a native one like Heinrich or Hirsch; for they were inclined to be not a little affected. Certainly this was true of the young mother, and as a consequence she was probably rather lonely in little Düsseldorf. Even though a native of the town, she could have had but few truly intimate friends there. Being a Jewess, she could not come into any close social contact with the Christians; and being rather priggish, carrying herself with obvious consciousness of her intellectual superiority, she could not be very intimate with the Jews. So, in all probability, she lived very much alone, and all the intensity of spirit which might otherwise have been expended in social activities had to be directed solely toward her family. She made her home the world and her little son the pivotal point therein. Very early she seems to have determined that through this child she would redeem herself, that in his life she would, vicariously at least, achieve for herself the glories which fate had until then denied her. For Peira Heine, it must be remembered, was of no ordinary stock. The van Gelderns for generations had been Jews of importance, wealthy court factors enjoying inordinate privileges, or else learned physicians who were respected far and wide. In marrying Samson Heine she had made a match by no means brilliant; on the contrary, she had descended considerably in the social scale, for his family was quite mediocre. It was, therefore, not unnatural that Frau Heine should look to her child to redeem her. With the same determination wherewith she had tried to make her husband respectable, she now set out to make her son great. For she was not the sort who would let destiny become fulfilled of itself. She was too energetically ambitious a person merely to sit back and let things drift. She devoted herself diligently to child-study and to an examination of the most modern methods of pedagogy. She began to read voraciously and, as far as she could, deeply. She pored over Rousseau's "Émile," which by then was beginning to be known even in the smaller towns of Germany. And she tried to cultivate a taste for Goethe. With all her earnest, nervous, serious might she sought to equip herself for the task of guiding or dragging her son to success.

4

BUT three years after Harry was born, a second child, Charlotte, arrived; and of necessity the woman's preoccupation with her son then had to cease. At the age of four the little boy was sent to a nursery school conducted by some elderly German woman of the town, and there he was kept a day-pupil for about a year. But judging from his behavior Harry was not happy in this school. He loathed the teacher, and he was constantly striving to avenge himself on her because she slapped and birched him. One day he emptied the ink-well into her milk jug, and then proudly marched up and down the room, his little hands clasped behind his back in simulated innocence. Another time he filled the woman's snuff-box with sand, and when asked by her in fury why he had done it, he vehemently answered: "Because I hate you!"

But, save for such almost vicious expression of feeling, little Harry showed no precocity. At the age of five he was taken from the kindergarten and transferred to a private Hebrew school. No record has come down to us of the character of this Hebrew school, but if it was like the others in Germany at the time, it was far from an ideal educational institution. The curriculum did include the more elementary secular studies; but the major interests were of course the Bible and the Hebrew prayer-book. The language of instruction must have been the sorry Judeo-German of the ghetto; and the spirit was probably still that of the sixteenth century. The lads were seated on long wooden forms and taught to sway to and fro over their huge Pentateuchs while they chanted the Hebrew verses in a slow oriental sing-song. They read the Bible stories and the innumerable Rabbinic commentaries on them; and they learned the many ritual obligations incumbent upon all righteous Jews. Most assiduously of all they memorized the involved and largely meaningless daily prayers. It was essentially a parochial school, narrow, benighted, pitiful: a thing as anachronistic in a free-thinking world as the pitiful ghetto which had produced it.

Yet the years spent in that school were perhaps the most influential in the boy's life. In later days he rarely referred to them, and in his "Memoirs" he does not even mention them. But their mark, deep and ineffaceable, was on him nevertheless. Not merely did they provide him with a treasury of Bible lore on which to draw all the rest of his life, but also they inculcated in him certain mental mannerisms whereof he never freed himself to the day of his death. They scrawled a distinctive thought-pattern on the blank which was his child's mind; and though they scrawled it hurriedly, thinly, indistinctly, not all the other patterns acquired later in life could ever quite obliterate it. For during those two years the boy was brought as never before—and almost as never again —into immediate and exclusive contact with Jews. His playmates were all of them Jews, little circumcized boys who spoke German with ghetto accents, who piously wore fringed garments under their vests, and who reacted toward their little Christian neighbors with that commingled fear and contempt which is perhaps the most pervasive element in the psychology of the Jew. Hebrew prayers were dinned into his ears incessantly, and with them, Jewish plaints and execrations. Harry learned to worry about the dietary taboos and the Sabbath re-straints, and learned also to devise means of evading them. What the accident of birth had left tentative and merely probable, those two years in a Jewish *cheder* made certain and inevasible. The soul of little Harry Heine became definitely that of a Jew.

5

But then came a sudden change. After a couple of years under the tutelage of a Jewish *melamed*, the boy was all at once put at the feet of Franciscan priests. He still continued to receive religious instruction from a Jewish tutor, but only on Sundays and perhaps week-day afternoons. His secular instruction, however, he now received in the school attached to the monastery in Düsseldorf. And there an entirely different thought-pattern was traced on his mind. The change was of course a drastic one, and at first it must have been profoundly disturbing. In place of the familiar little bearded Jewish teachers, he now had periwigged priests over him; instead of listening to the chanting of Hebrew prayers, he now had to give ear to the conjugation of Latin verbs. In the dim dark cloisters not far from the classroom hung a great crucified Christ of grey wood, a gruesome thing the very sight of which would probably have moved his former teachers to step aside and spit surreptitiously. Yet little Harry had to walk by it every day, and even play in its shadow. Gone were most of the sights and sounds amid which he had been reared and in which he had learned to feel at home. The lad was in a new world now, a strange, cold, even inimical world to which he could not easily adjust himself. His

schoolmates were Christians, and many of them were
openly hostile to him. They made fun of him and on
occasion even pelted him with offal. Discovering that
he bore the affectedly foreign name of Harry, they immediately took to calling him "Haarüh," which was the
name of the town scavenger's donkey. Whenever they
saw the boy they mimicked the scavenger's voice, deri-
sively yelling "Haarüh! Haarüh!" The lad was tormented continually by that cry. In the classroom and on
the street he was so plagued by it that at last even any
passing reference to a donkey brought a blush to his
cheeks and a flood of tears to his eyes.

Of course, even had the boy not been a Jew he probably would have been the butt of his schoolmates' humor,
for he was undersized, weak, nervous, and in a queer
way affected. But being to boot a Jew, he was doomed
beyond all chance of escape. Because he belonged to
a despised minority, to the ghetto people, and was de-
fenceless against the mob, he was naturally marked out
to be its victim. No matter what he did, inevitably it was
found to be open to ridicule. One day, when he announced to his classmates with innocent pride that his
paternal grandfather had been "a little Jew with a big
beard," they all raised such a roar of mocking glee
that they earned the poor boy a thrashing from his master, who naturally blamed him for the disturbance.

The days of the lad were thus embittered beyond bearing in that Franciscan boys' school. He was quite helpless among his Christian classmates, too weak to fight
them, too proud to cringe. On at least one occasion he

was so driven to despair by the sound of their incessant "Haar*üh! Haarüh!*" that he broke down and complained to his mother; but she could offer him small comfort. No doubt she too had suffered enough in her school-days because of the mockery of the Christians, and knew well how vain it was to strive to escape it. So all she could counsel her son was: "Learn much and be discreet; then no one will be able to take you for a donkey."

But the advice was not easy to follow, for Harry was not an especially apt pupil. The curriculum in the school demanded endless conning of stupid paradigms, incessant memorizing of conjugations and declensions in German, Latin, Greek and French. And he had not the type of mind required for such dull labor. Even German grammar, as it was taught in his school, came to him none too easily. Reared in a Jewish home, and instructed for at least two years by ghetto teachers, Harry had never learned to be scrupulous about the gender or case of a noun. Prepositions had always been—and always remained—irritating little things unworthy of too great attention. So even in German, the language which he was destined to grace with the most beauteous of poetry and the most brilliant of prose, even in this he revealed himself no prodigy. As for French: in that he seemed almost stupid. He was quick enough in picking up the speech and indeed was soon able to use it almost as fluently as his mother-tongue. But he was nevertheless incapable of torturing it in the ways his master demanded. The boy was expected, for instance, to translate the German hexameters of Klopstock's "Messiah" into French Alexandrines: and the task was simply too much for him. As he himself cried out in later years: "that was a refinement of cruelty surpassing even the agony of the Passion, and not even the Messiah Himself could have borne it in peace!" Harry failed so lamentably to pass in this subject that his master declared him utterly void of poetic talent, and called him "a barbarian of the Teutoburg forest!"

It was therefore impossible for the boy to lift himself by mental superiority to a place where he could be safe from the jibes of his schoolmates. He could escape their thrusts only by fleeing their presence, by withdrawing into another world, a secret one, where no earthly tormentor could possibly follow. And perhaps before he was even in his teens the sensitive child discovered such a world. It was an older man, an uncle named Simon van Geldern, who showed him the way to that refuge. This Uncle Simon was a queer old fellow, a stoutish little Jew with a stern pallid face and a nose that was Grecianly straight but "by a third longer than the Greeks were accustomed to wear their noses!" He dressed in the old French fashion, wearing short breeches, white stockings, and buckled shoes: and he was never seen without a long pigtail that bobbed most comically from shoulder to shoulder as he tripped along through the cobbled streets. And his mode of living was quite as strange as his appearance. He had no fixed occupation, but gave himself up to all sorts of learned hobbies, and wrote long, dull letters about them to the newspapers. His humble little house was filled to the

attic with books and tracts and journals; and all day
long he fussed among them, ferreting out obscure bits
of information about which to write his tedious briefs.

But for all his oddity and crankiness, Simon van Geldern had a great and generous soul. He was often dismayed by the mischievousness of his little nephew, and
was sometimes moved to anger by the youngster's impudence. But nevertheless he treated him with great
indulgence. He gave the boy many fine and costly books
to read, and allowed him to roam at will through all his
library. He even let him rummage in the dusty attic
of the house, in that vast lumber room where were piled
many chests of papers and books and strange antiques.

6

THERE in the attic the unhappy boy found his world
of refuge. Even when he was an aged man he never forgot the glamor that attic had once held for him, or the
ineffable comfort it once had brought his aching soul.

"It was not a charming haunt," he wrote in his
Memoirs, "and its only inhabitant, a fat Angora
cat, was not scrupulously clean. . . . But my heart
was so young, so eager, and the sun shone so
brightly through the little dormer window that
everything seemed to be flooded in the light of fantasy. The old cat herself became to me an en-
chanted princess. Suddenly freed from her brutish
shape, she would reveal herself in all her former

beauty and splendor; and the whole attic would
change into a gorgeous palace. . . ."

Harry was free in the old garret, free to dream himself out of this world with all its intolerable mockeries
and irregular verbs. There under the sloping roof lay
the vestiges of another and more glamourous world.
Wonderful pictures of the planets and constellations
lurked mysteriously in dark corners; soldering irons,
retorts, globes, and other such astrological and al-
chemical apparatus cluttered the floor; ominously in-
comprehensible books by Paracelsus, van Helmont, and
Agrippa von Nettesheim, gathered dust and worms in
musty chests. And little Harry, his thin trembling
hands all black with dust, his wan eager face smudged
and grimy, burrowed into them ecstatically.

His most precious and exciting find was a tattered
note-book written by a certain grand-uncle who had become almost a legend in the family. The man must have
been one of those persons of extraordinary gifts and
tremendous temerity who, finding themselves forbidden
to rise to power by fair means, were driven to resort
to foul. Most families in Israel had produced such
spectacular individuals at one time or another: blazing
meteors that shot up out of the ghetto gloom, hung for
a dazzling moment asway in the sky, and then came
hurtling down into oblivion. But usually no records
were left to perpetuate their memory. In the case of
the van Gelderns, however, record did exist in the form
of that old note-book. Its author was usually referred

to in the family as "the Oriental," and many were the tales the old wives whispered of him, shaking their heads with simulated disapproval, but delighting to repeat the stories nevertheless. For years he had been an adventurer in the wild lands of Northern Africa. For a time he had even been a tribal sheikh there. He, a ghetto Jew from Düsseldorf, had actually become a robber-chieftain at the head of a band of cut-throat Bedouins! But, after years of adventuring in the desert, he had returned once more to Europe. He was admired at various princely courts for his knowledge of horse-breeding and his skill in riding; but the desert garb he insisted on wearing, and the dark air of mystery with which he carried himself, soon won him a greater reputation as an expert in necromancy. And as a necromancer he seems to have risen to a position of some prestige in eighteenth-century court circles. His triumph, however, did not endure. He became over-audacious and dared to mix pleasure with business. He was caught enjoying unconventional privileges in the boudoir of a very exalted lady, and only his horsemanship saved his head. He left all his possessions behind him, and fled for his life across the sea to England. And there, in disgrace and poverty, he spent his last days writing poetry in stilted French. . . .

Such in outline was the life-story of young Harry's great-uncle, and one can easily imagine how profoundly it affected the boy. Day after day he sat there in the attic and tried to decipher the Arabic and Coptic characters in the note-book, imagining that they told authen-

tically all the wild adventures the old women whispered
about. He gloated over those adventures. He recounted
them to himself so often that at last they became quite
his own. Crouching there against the grimy dormer
window, his little back bent, his bright eyes consuming
the frayed yellow leaves of the book, Harry felt no
longer a weak and timid schoolboy. Of a sudden he became a swift horseman in the desert, an imperious chief-
tain, a gallant courtier. His thin hands began to tin-
gle with strength, and his wan cheeks became flushed
and warm. He felt strong of a sudden, strong and full
of mad courage. And when night came and his tired
eyes closed in sleep, his mind still went on with the
fantasy. He would become then completely one with
the Oriental, wearing his robes, loving his friends, and
confounding, beating, crushing his enemies. Often even
in the clear light of day the boy was seized with the uncanny feeling that he no longer was himself but his de-
ceased great-uncle. At such moments he would catch
himself strutting as his temeritous ancestor might have
done, gesticulating with a fierce vehemence, and making
grandiloquent speeches in an improvised foreign tongue.
Sometimes the entrancing confusion would betray itself
even when the boy was at home among his family, or
in the town among his school-fellows. And then it would
get him into the most distressing of scrapes.

7

For a whole year or more young Harry remained
under the spell of his great-uncle's glamourous mem-

ory; and when finally he sank back into singleness of being, secret traces of the spell lingered in his soul. He remained forever after addicted to dreams, fleeing off to his fantasy-world at the least prick of barbed reality. Yet, significantly, he was never able to stay for long at a time in that fantasy-world. Inexorably he felt himself dragged back to reality, conscious that it was, after all, *the* reality. Even as a boy he never could remain long in the realm of sheer dreams. No matter how ineffably happy he might be there, he could never blind himself to the fact that it was, after all, a realm of illusion. For his mind held a strand of sanity which never parted, a stout strand but for which he might in time have degenerated into a mere *Luftmensch*, into an aimless, drivelling dreamer with light head swimming high in the clouds and legs dangling in air.

He was saved from that fate by an element of rationality inherited or at least learned from his mother. Frau Heine, as we have already seen, was a person of emphatic rationality. She was above all else a practical woman, a person strongly endowed with common sense, and formidably unquixotic. She did not in the least approve of indolent day-dreaming, and frowned upon Harry's fondness for the attic in her brother's house. She considered the boy's preoccupation with ancient tomes a sheer waste of time—perhaps even a dangerous indulgence. For she was completely a product of her hard-driven, calculating, middle-class environment, and had little conception of the worth of things not material. Poetry to her was largely nonsense, and

the poet no more than "a poor devil out-at-elbows who
supplied occasional verses for a few shillings, and in
the end died in a poor-house." The good woman very
vehemently did not want her son to grow into such a
creature. She did all in her power to shield him from
all poetic influences, snatching away every romance she
found in his hands, never allowing him to go to the theatre, keeping a vigilant eye on his friendships, and bitterly scolding the maids if they told ghost stories in
his presence. She wanted him to grow up to be a practical man, a personage of material, not artistic, might.
The crown she dearly coveted for his brow was one of
gold, not of laurel leaves.

8

AT first Harry's mother seems to have dreamed of a
military career for him. In an earlier generation such
a dream would have been quite absurd in a woman like
Frau Heine, for advancement in the army had then
been impossible for any Jew. But a new day had dawned
and now the old restrictions were no more. Napoleon
had opened to the Jews a new gate to the world of glory
and gold, the gate of the great god Mars. And the gate
was wide and inviting—far wider and more inviting
than that of Mammon, which until then had been the only
one open to Jews. Napoleon himself had shown how
far a man could advance through the gate of war. But
a little while earlier he had been no more than a Cor-
sican upstart; and now he was lord of a continent. So

it was not altogether extraordinary that Frau Heine should have dreamed of a great military career for her son. What alone was extraordinary was the pertinacity with which she attempted to prepare him for that career. Harry by this time had already passed from the Franciscan grammar school into the lycée, where considerable attention was paid as a matter of course to mathematics. His mother, however, was not satisfied, and insisted that the boy take private lessons besides. She arranged for additional courses to be given him at home, so that the poor lad's head was made literally to reel with logarithms and equations.

Yet, so far as we know, Harry did not openly rebel against his mother's driving. Perhaps it was because he did not dare, or else because he rather shared her dreams. It would not have been at all unnatural if he, a weakling and a timid child, should have revelled in the hope of becoming a mighty man of war. Such a hope could have cheered him beyond measure when he hid from his tormenting schoolmates. We know he was fascinated by the figure of Napoleon; indeed, he regarded the man as little less than a god. The armies of the Emperor had occupied Düsseldorf when Harry was still a child of nine; and many of the lad's happiest hours had been spent listening to tales about Napoleon from a blustering French drum-major who had been quartered in the Heine house. And once during those years Harry actually set eyes on the Emperor in person! The glorious memory never left him; even when he was a grown man he could recall it with warming vividness.

"When I think of the great Emperor," he wrote,
"then all is summer green and golden in my
thoughts. . . . I saw him as he rode with his
retinue down the middle of the Allée, and the shud-
dering trees bowed as he passed, the sunbeams trembled in fear and curiosity through the green leaves,
and in the blue heavens swam visibly a golden star.
The Emperor was wearing his modest green uniform
and his little cocked hat known the world over.
. . . Listlessly he sat, almost loosely; one hand
holding high the rein, the other gently patting the
neck of his little white horse. So he rode calmly
down the middle of the avenue . . . while with a
thousand, thousand voices the people cried: 'Long
live the Emperor!' "

But it was one thing to dream of becoming a great
general, and quite another to wrestle with geometry.
Harry had a good mind, but he did not like to whip it
to work. He preferred to let it wander lazily, discovering for him happy castles in Spain rather than new
proofs in Euclid. Even in music, the one artistic interest encouraged by his mother, he preferred to listen
rather than labor. For a while he was made to take
instruction in violin playing, but his nervous, flighty
mind could not adapt itself easily to the discipline of
"practice." He loved music intensely, for he had
already discovered its power to induce in him his dreams.
But he could see no remotest connection between the
horrendous abomination of violin scales, and the magic

called music. One day, so we are told, his mother was
amazed at the beautiful tones coming from the room
in which the boy was taking his violin lesson. The
playing was astoundingly expert, and for an instant the
gratifying thought leapt in her breast that her son had
not been neglecting his violin after all. But when she
opened the door, lo, it was the teacher who was playing!
The pupil was lying full length on the sofa, his eyes
closed, his lips smiling as in a dream. And when his
mother shook him angrily and began to upbraid him
for his laziness, the boy cried out: "Oh, why did you disturb me! I had almost finished imagining a whole
beautiful song!"

9

THAT was characteristic of the boy. He was forever
lying back on sofas and letting his imagination run
wild. Somehow he could not drudge. He resembled
his father in this, for Herr Heine, despite that he had
become a shopkeeper and a family-man, had remained
a lazy ne'er-do-well. One can well understand why
Harry was always more drawn to his father than to his
mother. He could feel in the man a deeper sympathy,
and win from him a more indulgent response. There
was nothing of the strenuously pertinacious about Samson Heine. On the contrary, he was obviously weak-
willed and lazy. And he was vain, too, always worrying
about his good looks and apparel. He liked to parade
about town in a showy uniform which his rank as an
officer in the Düsseldorf civilian guard entitled him to

wear. He possessed an unbounded love of life, sought after pleasure continually, and gave as little thought to the day that was past as to the day that was to come. Yet he was not a fool or a churl. He could divine instinctively what his wife could not perceive even after long cogitation. He could, as his son declared in later years, think with his heart, "the dearest heart conceivable."

And in all these respects his son was very like him. Harry, too, had an unbounded love of love, a vast longing to sink himself fathoms deep in joy. But he was thwarted. The world, that pathetic little world which sat by the waters of Düsseldorf and slaved, would not receive him. How could it? The boy did not *belong*. He did not fit into that world, nor into any part thereof. He was, to begin with, undersized and sickly. He could not fight with his schoolmates and pummel them into respecting him in the streets. Nor was he diligent enough a student to make them respect him in the classroom. Besides, he was a Jew—yet not sufficiently Jewish a Jew to find himself quite attuned to Jewish living. In the Franciscan school he had been so weaned from the religion of his ancestors that he would no longer conform to the laws of Moses. But at the same time he had not been converted to the religion of his neighbors, and he could not conform to the dogmas of the Church. His teachers were orthodox Christians only by profession; at heart they were largely free-thinkers. They were, most of them, French priests who had come under the spell of Voltairean skepticism, and who took no pains

to conceal it. Had they been devout believers, perhaps
it would have gone far differently with their pupil.
Encouraged by them, the little Jewish boy might have
been able to root himself in Catholicism, for he was of
himself attracted by the color and mystery in Catholic
ritual. But this, too, was denied him, for every impulse
to fling his harried young soul into the embrace of the
Church was checked by a schooled skepticism.

Nor could he root himself nationally. He was, after
all, a Jew; a child of a gypsy race. Today his parents
sojourned in Düsseldorf, but tomorrow they might move
to Danzig or Delhi. And even though they remained
in Düsseldorf—what was he then? A German? Hardly.
He had been born a German, but from the time he was
nine his native town had been French. He had sat at
the feet of French teachers, and had learned almost his
first oaths from a French drum-major. His mother had
remained a German in her sympathies, but his father had
served in the French civilian guard. So what could the
son be? . . .

10

THAT was the root-evil in the life of the lad—he did
not belong anywhere. Had he been natively of tougher
spirit, probably he would not have been conscious of
the evil. But natively he was excessively sensitive, and
the friendliest criticism, the most innocent jest at his
expense, seemed to him a malicious affront. Inevitably, therefore, he could not be at ease among the

people around him. He suspected them, subconsciously at least, of bearing him ill-will, or of despising him. He did have a few friends among his schoolmates, but somehow he could not feel utterly at one even with these. He was intimate with several Jewish boys, among them one who called himself an atheist, and who was nicknamed the "herring philosopher." His closest friend, however, was a Gentile boy named Christian Sethe, a strong, handsome, blue-eyed lad who belonged to a well-to-do family, and labored under none of the disadvantages which made life so hard for Harry. Temperamentally he was altogether of a different type. He was habitually deliberate, and carried himself with so serious an air that his schoolmates called him the "Councillor." Yet he seems to have cherished a great fondness for the nervous little Jewish boy, and always tried to protect him. Harry was a lovable and attractive youngster in spite of his many peculiarities. He was delightfully ingenuous and trusting—absurdly so at times. Yet he had an extraordinarily agile mind, and he always seemed to have some pert and funny remark on the tip of his tongue. He could be vastly entertaining, and was always ready for mischief. Probably it was for these reasons that the slow and rather sedate "Councillor" was so fond of the little fellow.

But the friendship between the two boys was never quite perfect, for their positions were too unequal. Harry was in every outward respect the inferior, and, being conscious of it, he could never lay the suspicion that the other might be patronizing him. As a conse-

quence, even with Sethe, his truest and most loyal companion, he could not feel utterly at one.

Among the girls of his class, Harry had no friends
whatsoever. Like most shy, weak, and undersized boys,
he was rather afraid of girls. He loved his little sister, Charlotte—but she, after all, was his own sister.
He could not imagine himself daring to reveal any affection for the sisters of his schoolmates. There was one
pretty little blonde-haired girl in the town, the daughter
of a local judge, whom secretly he quite adored; but,
so far as we know, he never exchanged a word with her.
Indeed, he stood in such awe of her that on one occasion, when he was reciting a poem at some school exercises, he actually fainted when he caught sight of her
in the audience!

The only girl with whom he did become fast friends
was one of a far different sort. Sefchen was her name,
and she lived in the squalor of the old quarter of Düsseldorf with her aunt, who was reputed to be a witch.
More than this we cannot say with any assurance, for
it is clear that the account of the girl given in the poet's
"Memoirs" is extravagantly colored. He wrote of her
as having been the orphaned granddaughter of the executioner of Goch, a wild child of "dishonorable" birth
who had been reared in loneliness in the executioner's
cottage hard-by the gallows of a forest country. But no
record has been found of any executioner of Goch, and
this detail may be entirely fictional. The poet wrote
his "Memoirs" during the last years of his life, and
his imagination had by that time played no little havoc

with his early recollections. As he then remembered Sefchen, she had been very slim and tall, with long streaming hair the color of blood, large dark eyes, and a pale beautiful face.

"She had that slimness of figure which is to be found in the quadroons of the West Indies . . . and her close-fitting dress was like the wet cloth of a statue. But no marble statue could vie with her in beauty, for she revealed life itself: every movement revealed the rhythm of her body, and, I fain would say, the music of her soul. . . ."

But it was not so much her beauty that won Harry, as her demeanor. She was not like the golden-haired girl, grand and aloof in her manner. She did not make him shy and uncomfortable, as did all the more respectable girls in Düsseldorf. For, after all, she was one of a lower order, a ragged orphan living in the old quarter of the town. She, too, was an outcast, a lonely waif who could find shelter only in a world of dreams. So he loved her and sought to be with her all the time. For the son of Herr Heine, the velveteen merchant, to be seen with the niece of the Old Woman of Goch, was little short of scandalous, and his conduct must have set more than one tongue a-wagging. Had the boy's mother learned of it, no doubt she would have put a stop to the affair immediately. But apparently only the father ever heard of it, and he, characteristically, did not trouble to interfere.

So young Harry was free to go to Sefchen whenever he cared. Day after day he stole out to her decrepit old house in the lower end of the town, and sat there listening to her weird songs. Sefchen knew many old folk songs, gruesome ballads about death and ghosts and avenging swords; and she was as pleased to sing them as he to hear. For both were able to find a vast joy in those runes. If we can believe the "Memoirs":

> "Once, when Red Sefchen was singing . . . and I saw the emotion that was in her, I was so moved that I suddenly burst into tears and we fell into each other's arms sobbing. . . . I asked her to write the verses down for me and she did so. She did not write them in ink, however, but in her blood!"

Probably the poet's romantic imagination bolted with him when he set down that recollection; but a grain of literal truth there may have been in his words. Whether Red Sefchen wrote in her blood or no, certainly she warmed the blood of young Harry. Just how intimate the boy and girl became there is now no saying, but it is more than likely that they did not indulge in more than kisses and furtive embraces. The proof of this supposition lies in the fact that years later the boy's whole attitude toward sex was still quite naïve and apparently virginal. Actually he may not have been at all in love with Sefchen. Social protest rather than erotic passion may have moved him to make those frequent

visits to her lowly house. For she was despised by the
world even more than he, since he, though a Jew, was
at least of respectable shopkeeper stock. As he wrote
in his "Memoirs":

> "Despite the infamy which fell upon those who
> came in contact with any of her outcast race, I
> kissed the lovely daughter of the executioner. I
> kissed her not only because of my own tender feel-
> ing for her, but also in scorn of the old social order
> and all its dark prejudices. . . ."

But it was not alone the rebel in Harry that attracted
him to Sefchen; even more it may have been the budding
poet. For a budding poet he was, indeed, despite his
mother's adjurations. He was fascinated by fairy-tales
and songs, and secretly he often tried to make up some
of his own. The only person, however, to whom he dared
show most of his efforts was Sefchen, for she alone
seemed to understand what he was about. She was herself somewhat of a poet, and much of Harry's inspiration came directly from the old ghost-stories and folk-
songs she knew. "She had certainly the greatest influence
on the poet waking in me," Heine declared in later years.
"My first poems, the 'Dream Pictures,' written soon after
this time, have a gloomy and horrible tinge very like the
bloody shadow which this relationship cast over my
young life and thought."

Indeed, so profoundly did Sefchen stimulate the boy
in this direction that in time she herself became to him

a poem. It is likely that the real Sefchen was not even remotely like the romantic creature his imagination made of her. She may have been no more than an ordinary, superstitious, red-haired peasant girl, thin because she was given too little to eat, and pale because that little was bad. But in Harry's eyes she was altogether the wondrous creature whereof all the poets sang. Looked at with sufficient imagination, her thinness, her pallor, and the color of her hair, fitted her completely into the current tradition of Romanticist poetry. She became a lovely wraith-like thing to him, a half-unreal lady whose large dark eyes seemed to hint imponderable mysteries. And no doubt he indited many verses to her glory.

11

LITTLE, however, is left of the poetry he wrote at this time; little even is known of it. That he did write is fairly certain, but apparently he destroyed his verses almost as soon as he set them down. His mother was to blame for that, for her antipathy to poetry must have made the boy ashamed of his efforts. Young Harry seems never in those days to have thought of himself as a coming poet. His mother had by this time given up her old dreams of making him a general, for the Emperor's star had begun to fall. The French armies had been withdrawn from the Rhineland, and Düsseldorf was once more a Prussian town. All the old restrictions against the Jews had been put into force again, and it had become absurd to hope for a military future for

the boy. There was now only the stock career of the
Jew open to young Harry Heine: he had to become a
trader. Curiously, we have no record that the boy
objected to being delivered up to such a future. Perhaps he felt it his duty to do whatever was now demanded of him by his parents, for things were going
badly with the family finances. Until that time Herr
Heine had been, for a Düsseldorfer, fairly well-to-do,
for he had profited by the general expansion of commerce which followed the French occupation. Indeed,
about five years after Napoleon occupied the town—
that is, in 1811 or 1812—Samson Heine's business had
so increased that he found it necessary to move across
the street to a larger establishment. But with the withdrawal of the French forces in 1813, his good fortune
came to a sudden end. Gone were the roistering grenadiers, with their huge appetites and spendthrift ways;
and gone also were hundreds of camp-followers who
had helped make the little port teem with commerce
and excitement. Of a sudden a vast depression crept
over the shops and stalls, and Düsseldorf became once
more silent and small. The Heines, left with a large
house and little business, now had to begin seriously to
retrench. They could no longer hope to support their
eldest son through a long course of preparation for some
exalted career. Instead they felt they must hurry him
through to some immediate means of earning a livelihood. So they withdrew him from the Franciscan ly-
ceum, where he had been lazily studying philosophy and
calculus, and put him into a business school.

The boy was then about seventeen, and he seems to have accepted the change with fair grace. Indeed, he even became diligent in this less academic school, and devoted himself whole-heartedly to the prosaic studies which were there required of him. One must remember he belonged to a folk which had been conceived in want and reared in need. It was almost an inherited wisdom in him that made him aware, however faintly, of the value of the practical. That this awareness was never able to last for long, or be overwhelming even when it did come to him, was a fact he had not yet discovered. He was still a mere boy, and had not yet arrived at any knowledge of his own character. At seventeen he merely knew he must somehow make a future for himself—and trading seemed the most feasible means of accomplishing his end. It may even have seemed also a glamourous means to him. All the world just then was talking of the Rothschilds, those erstwhile petty money-lenders of the Frankfurt ghetto who had suddenly reached out and swept the credit of a continent into their coffers. In later years the poet said his father was distantly related to the Rothschilds; but he was probably indulging in Semitic license there. "All Israel are brethren," runs an ancient Hebrew proverb, and in that sense only was Harry related to the Rothschilds.

But he did not lack a genuine blood-connection with millions. One of his own uncles, Salomon Heine, had become a man of stupendous wealth in Hamburg. He had come to the town years earlier with just sixteen groschen in the pockets of his leather trousers; and by

dint of vast diligence and inordinate ability he had succeeded in making himself one of the richest bankers in
all Germany. One cannot doubt that tales of this man's
phenomenal rise must have profoundly impressed his
young nephew in Düsseldorf. Certainly they must have
impressed the boy's mother, Peira van Geldern, that
proud, strong-willed, ambitious woman, who had rejected every suitor until she was actually twenty-six,
only to accept the ineffectual Samson Heine. She must
have been more than a little envious of her brother-in-
law's success, and one cannot wonder if she set her heart
with perhaps excessive determination on her son's achiev-
ing a similar success. Her own husband had turned
out a failure. He was still good-looking and debonaire
—too much so, she may now have thought—but he was
otherwise a mediocrity. If he had prospered during the
years of the French occupation, it had been only in a
small way. He had never been able to take full advantage of his opportunities and break his way through
to real wealth. In the scramble for power which attended the years of war, he had lacked either wit or
will—or both—to grasp much of the spoils. And now
that the scramble was over, he was left almost a ruined
man: an impoverished shopkeeper in a little sleepy
town on the Rhine. He was a failure; and for his ambitious wife that was all the more reason why their
son had to become a success. To her there was now
but one desire left: to make Harry a millionaire. . . .

THE EXILE IN GERMANY

CHAPTER
TWO

*"At the very first move I lost the queen
—but persistently I still play on."* . . .

II

In 1815, when Harry was eighteen years of age, his father took him south to Frankfurt to start him on the road to millions. It is suspected by many biographers that the boy's departure from Düsseldorf was not accomplished without some difficulty. Being eighteen, he was eligible for conscription, and just then, when Prussia was making its final desperate effort to destroy Napoleon, no eligible youths were being excused. So, quite possibly, his parents officially declared him to be only sixteen, registering the year of his birth as 1799— and Harry was so undersized that no one thought to dispute their word.*

And with his convenient birth-certificate to protect him from the military, young Heine came riding with his father into the great old city of Frankfurt. Employment was very soon found for him in a Jewish banking establishment. He was called a "volunteer" to spare him the indignity of the term "apprentice," and

---

* The earlier biographers all accepted either 1799 or 1800 as the correct date for Heine's birth. But since the publication of Karpeles's investigations, 1797 is generally agreed to have been the year.

he received board and lodging in the house of his chief. The boy must have been delighted at first with the prospects of his new life. Frankfurt was a great, strange city where he imagined he would be rid entirely of that village narrowness and spite which had made his boyhood years so bitter. He would be free here, he thought, and quite independent, with spending money in his pockets, and high hopes in his singing heart. One pictures him as he must have looked in those hours: a short, slight, rather pallid boy, his cap pushed far back on his curly fair head, his thin hands deep in the pockets of his velvet trousers, gazing in happy wonderment at the gaily painted houses of the ancient town. After little Düsseldorf with its fifteen thousand inhabitants, Frankfurt with its fifty thousand must have seemed to the boy a veritable metropolis. With its great Rathaus rising so proudly on the Römer hill, with its noisy marketplace, its statues and fountains and tree-lined boulevards, the city must have appeared to the lad almost incredibly grand. There were famous people there, great musicians and scholars and writers. One of these was pointed out to him in a café one day—none other than the famous Ludwig Börne, who then was writing theatrical criticism. It was Harry's first sight of a man who was destined to play a most tragic part in his own life—but that, of course, he did not yet know. At the moment the boy's only wish was that he might muster the courage to go up and present himself, for it had long been his secret ambition to meet a real author face to face. But he did not dare. All he could do was tell himself that soon,

very soon, when he had established himself in Frankfurt and become a great banker, he would be able to
meet Börne and all the other celebrities of the city.

But the boy quickly discovered that success would
not come as easily as he had imagined. He lost his
job in the bank within a fortnight, though for just what
reason we do not know. For a while he wandered about
without employment, and then he found a job with
a spice-dealer. But that berth, too, lasted only a brief
time, and what adventures he had after his second dis-
missal we do not know. Never even in his most garru-
lous moments later in life did he refer, save darkly, to
that whole Frankfurt period. Evidently it was one of
unspeakably bitter disillusionment, for it revealed to
the boy just how profoundly alien he really could be in
the world. Here in Frankfurt Harry was made conscious of his Jewishness with a vicious crudity that
must have shaken him to the core. For here the worst
restrictions were still enforced against the Jews, and
they were penned up in a ghetto as in the darkest medieval days. The Frankfurt "Jews' Quarter" had been
enlarged only once in many centuries, though the popu-
lation had increased manifold during that time. The
old houses were rickety and narrow, and the street was
scarcely wide enough for a wagon to turn in. Yet in
some cases four and even five families had to live in
a single house, and so many corpses had already been
crowded into the ghetto cemetery that the tombstones
were literally piled on top of each other. During the
night, and all day on Sunday, all Jews were locked into

this foul quarter. There they had to swarm like so many worms: a vast horde, sickly, sweated, and indescribably humiliated. Even during the week-days the Jews were not allowed to roam as they pleased through the town. They were prohibited by law from walking on the pavements of the main streets, and forbidden even to show themselves in any park or grass-covered square. They were treated altogether like curs, kicked and pelted by every ruffian in the town.

Such was the Frankfurt to which the sensitive Harry Heine was brought in 1815. Perhaps he did not at once discover just how vile it could be to him, for during his first days in the town he may have been able to wander about freely without being found out. His features were not too obviously those of a Jew, and his identity was still unknown in Frankfurt. Perhaps he was able to transgress the local laws against his folk during all the rest of his stay in the horrid place. But the constant fear of detection must have poisoned his every moment on the beautiful promenades of the town. He had known prejudice in Düsseldorf, and had suffered from it a-plenty. But there it had never been even remotely so barbaric as in Frankfurt. In the days of the French occupation there had been no legal discriminations whatsoever against the Jews, and even when the Prussians came back, no involuntary ghetto had been ordained. From infancy Harry had been made to feel that he was a Jew and inferior to his Christian schoolmates; but he had been made to feel it in subtle and sometimes almost undiscernible ways. Indeed, so unobtrusive had been the prejudice against him, that at one time the boy imagined he had quite lost his identity as a Jew. He became fascinated by Catholic ritual, and forgot almost completely the religion of his forefathers. As he himself wrote in his "Memoirs": "There was a time when I devoutly kissed the hand of every Capuchin whom I met on the street." He loved to follow all the holy processions and to decorate the altar before his father's house. Apparently he was then largely free of any conscious *Judenschmertz*, and but little was left of his childhood feeling that he was an outsider.

But in Frankfurt a lingering spark of the old feeling leapt into consuming flame. Here there was no chance left the boy of forgetting his birth and parentage. Here he was a Jew inescapably, a cur unfit even to walk on one promenade with the Christians. Here more obviously even than in Düsseldorf he could not *belong*. . . .

2

So he left. After less than two months of it he could abide Frankfurt no longer. He had by that time gone through two jobs and practically all the money in his possession. So with a bitter heart and an empty purse he beat his way back to Düsseldorf. There he remained for several months, idling about the town because he could not find employment. He must have presented a sore problem to his parents, for they could not decide what to do with him. He was intelligent and

able, yet incorrigibly lazy at the same time. He refused
to apply himself to tasks which he did not fancy, no
matter how profitable or necessary they might be. He
preferred rather to hide himself in the library of his
queer uncle, Simon van Geldern, or else to lie in the
woods and sing songs. He read continually, especially
historical novels and Romanticist poetry. And he wrote
poems from time to time. These were by no means distinguished verses, for they were patterned too closely
after the poetic fashion of the day. They prattled metri-
cally enough about the stock Romanticist virtues, about
love, patriotism, holiness, and heroism; but they lacked
entirely that poignant simplicity and wit which were
later to characterize his work.

For Harry was still a boy. Though he had been much
with himself during all the years of his life, he had
not yet found himself. He still looked to the world for
guidance and seemed eager to accept its ways. Because
at the moment it reviled the fallen Napoleon, he, too,
now turned against him. In the niche once occupied
by the Emperor, Harry set up the image of Blücher—the
"Homeric god-like Blücher," as he called him. Germany, not France, now seemed to the youth to be "pious
and worthy," and lustily did he sing of "a liberated and
holy German Empire." He wrote prettily also of the
Church, for devout Catholicism was another of the
fads of current poetry. He sentimentalized the Middle
Ages, picturing the period as gentle and incomparably
beauteous. Nor was he actuated by hypocrisy when he
repeated such cant and stock sentiment. After all, he

was still no more than eighteen or nineteen years of age, and he was not yet strong enough to dare doubt what the world accepted. Fouqué, Brentano, and Tieck were the favorites of the hour, and the boy read them with exemplary devotion.

And thus he dragged out his days in Düsseldorf, reading, dreaming, and penning mediocre poesy. He enjoyed but little companionship, and still less understanding. He had, so far as we know, only one close friend, his old schoolmate, Christian Sethe—and one close friend was not enough to destroy the tedium of life in the little town. Harry's disposition had not been improved by his experiences in Frankfurt. His sensitiveness had increased, and his humor had taken on a rather unpleasant edge. He had learned to be rather sarcastic in his speech, and quite malicious in his sallies. One wonders that even Christian Sethe should have cared to remain friendly with him. Evidently Sethe possessed more than ordinary understanding. He must have been able to perceive the wistful, love-hungry soul quivering beneath the shell of repellent sarcasm. Perhaps also he was able to glimpse signs of some strange greatness in the Jewish boy, evidences of some quality which made Sethe feel that, for all his own social superiority, he was yet the other's inferior. But if Sethe did see such signs, he was unique in Düsseldorf. Neither of Harry's parents had the faintest suspicion that their son might be a genius. His father treated him with little more than lazy indulgence, and from his mother he received only constant complaint.

It could not have been from choice, therefore, that Harry remained at home. There was no other place for him to go. His parents were not sufficiently well-to-do to send him to a university; and he himself was not ambitious enough to go away and find employment. So he loitered about in the little town, a lazy ne'er-do-well —and, for want of anything better to do, secretly he wrote poetry. . . .

3

BUT at last came relief: his rich uncle, Salomon Heine, signified his willingness to take charge of the boy. This Uncle Salomon, the millionaire banker in Hamburg, was the shining light of the whole Heine clan, its richest and most munificent member. He was a self-made man, quick, crude, intelligent, and at times explosively generous. He could be exceedingly bitter when crossed, and no less kindly when flattered. He was vain and despotic, mercenary and ill-tempered— and yet at the same time charitable and forgiving. He lived like a pasha, and moved in the highest social circles of the land. Even so great a personage as Prince Blücher considered it politic to accept an invitation to this Jew's palace at Ottensen! Yet he did not deny his poor relations, but supported even the most embarrassing of them during all the days of his prosperity.

One cannot wonder that young Heine, out-of-work and unhappy, leapt at the chance of going to Hamburg. For in Hamburg there dwelt not merely his fabulously rich uncle, but also his uncle's daughters. Harry had already laid eyes on Amalie, the eldest of those girls. She had stopped over in Düsseldorf for a brief visit shortly before the boy set out on his ill-starred journey to Frankfurt, and the memory of her radiant person had remained with him. She had then been a child of fourteen: slender, beautiful, and tremendously desirable to the passionate, friendless boy. And apparently it was the thought of Amalie that lured him more than all else to the great city on the Elbe. For in a sentimental, youthful way Harry considered himself in love with her. "I'm lured to the North by a golden star!" he wrote to Sethe as he set out for Hamburg. . . .

But the "star" was not there when he arrived. The beautiful Amalie was away in the country, and there was no chance of her returning for a month or more. It was not difficult to wait, however. Hamburg was a great and exciting city with more than enough wonders to keep the eager youth from brooding over his momentary disappointment. Besides, there was work to do, new friends to make, and a whole set of new adjustments to effect. The task merely of accustoming himself to the splendor of his uncle's establishment was enough to keep him preoccupied for a while. The banker revelled in ostentatious luxury. His estate at Ottensen on the Elbe was one of the most magnificent in the whole country-side. Statues gleamed in a formal garden that reached down to the banks of the river; nightingales sang in the trees; liveried servants moved silently about like so many well-trained wraiths. And the old town house on the Jungfernstieg was no less elegant. Everything about Salomon Heine was gorgeous and expensive, and the penniless youth from Düsseldorf was almost overawed.

Of course, Harry was not allowed much more than a look at those elegant establishments. He was not asked to make his home in them, but told to find lodgings somewhere in the town. This he did, and immediately thereafter he was set to work in one of his uncle's offices. He worked diligently, too. He rarely felt in the mood now to write verses, for he was too engrossed with his new activities, and with wondering when his cousin would appear. He seems to have been afraid to ask point-blank when she was expected, and therefore went about in a constant perturbation.

> "Mornings I arise and wonder
> Will she come today?
> Evening passes, still I ponder,
> Still she stays away."

She was in his mind all of the time. He had seen her but once in his life, and then only for a day or two; yet he had thought of her so steadily since then that by now she had become the most real and immediate thing in his life. The avid imagination of the young poet had taken hold of her image and so colored and refashioned it that it had become almost incredibly lovely and desirable. What was worse: his imagination had not rested with the mere elaboration of a memory, but had

gone on and elaborated also a hope. In Harry's mind
the future was already certain and determined. Amalie,
that beautiful dream-princess, was to be his bride! She
was to give ear to his impassioned verses, become enam-
ored of him who wrote them, accept his suit, and then
raise him to the throne by her side. It all seemed inevitable to the poor youth. Having dreamed of that consummation, it became to him inexorable. There were,
of course, horrid moments of doubt, when a sudden
draught of rationality made clear to Harry how absurdly
without substance was his dream. But such moments
came rarely, and their memory was not allowed to linger. Harry needed his dream too desperately to allow
it to be swept away. Indeed, after the first days of ad-
justment to the novelty of his Hamburg surroundings,
the dream became the only thing that made life endurable. It kept his heart high when his head was bent
over the ledgers in his uncle's office; it kept his soul
warm when he sat alone amid the drabness of his room
in the lodging-house. It was Amalie and the thought
of winning her that sustained him and made him toil
so diligently. For she had become the central passion
of his life. As he wrote to Sethe:

"Rejoice, rejoice—in four weeks I shall see
Molly. And my Muse will return with her. . . .
Old heart, how glad you are and how loudly you are
beating!"

So did young Harry Heine write as he waited tremblingly for her coming.

4

AND then at last she appeared. Probably the real
Amalie was not even remotely like the fair lady of the
poet's imaginings—but that never occurred to him.
To Heine, when at last he set eyes on her, she was all
he had ever dreamed—and more. His love-lorn heart,
already but too well prepared for surrender, capitulated to her at the first glance. And out of the fulness of
his love he began to sing as never before. Poem after
poem poured from his pen, all of them telling of his
great and consuming passion. Gone were all thoughts
of Sefchen or what other girls he may have known in the
world; no memory was there now of any "blossoming
rose on the blossoming Rhine." Gone too was all
interest in patriotism or the "Holy German Empire."
Now the youth could sing only of his *fromme Minne*, his
pious love, that fair child, Amalie—who was daughter
to the richest banker in Hamburg. . . .

Many biographers of Heine take it for granted that
he was already far from lacking in sexual experience
by the time he came to Hamburg. They give full cre-
dence to his youthful boastings, and quite believe that
his relations with Sefchen, and with perhaps a girl or
two in Frankfurt, were more than platonic. But when
one reads the lyrics written during these first months in
Hamburg, one rather wonders if the boy had yet ever
known the embraces of women. There is in those lyrics
a naïveté, a sexual innocence, that is almost childish.

Harry wrote altogether like a pious boy carried away
by the ecstasy of youthful love. He talked with horror
of the ladies of the half-world, of the little French
shop-girls with their easy virtue, and the blowsy street-
women with their hard eyes. His whole tone was that of
the Romanticists whom he had been reading for years,
and he indulged repeatedly in such stock expressions
as "bold knight" and "high altar." When, shortly after
her return, Amalie gave him a lock of her hair, it so
excited the youth that he mentioned the gift several
times in his letters. He actually placed the lock of hair
in a "sharp-pointed iron cross," and wore it around
his neck like some holy amulet!

5

BUT the days of his happiness were brief. Had he
not been so blinded by the glory of his own wish-dreaming, no doubt he would immediately have seen that
Amalie did not return his love. As it was, it took weeks,
months, for the dread realization to seep into his mind.
And then he was desolated. Wildly, almost madly, he
uttered his grief to his old boyhood friend, Sethe. "I
must have a Madonna," he cried. "Perhaps the heavenly Madonna will replace the earthly one for me.
I *must* make my senses drunk, and drown my endless
sorrow in the depths of mysticism!" For now at last
he saw that Amalie hardly thought of him. Her mind
was on the rich gentlemen of Hamburg, on the well-
dressed, pompous, socially acceptable business-men of

the town. Harry to her was no more than a poor relation, an amusing youth who could write flattering jingles,
but who nevertheless was only—a poor relation. She
was not curt or cruel to him. Apparently she rather
liked to have him near her at times, and always treated
him with cousinly affection. But she would not take him
seriously.

One can hardly wonder at that. After all, Amalie
was a daughter of Salomon Heine, a child of a millionaire living in Hamburg, and altogether true to her environment. She was sixteen, rich, pretty, and spoiled.
Her education had been fashionable and slight, and all
her values were those of the gilded ghetto which had
produced her. She was refined but not cultivated,
graceful but not gracious. Naturally she could see
no great worth in this boy who came bearing only gifts
of poetry. To her Harry was but a poor apprentice in
her father's employ. He had none of the graces which
she had been taught to respect. His hair was blonde
and waving, and his hands were extremely delicate and
white; but otherwise he was not particularly attractive.
He was thin, short of stature, and near-sighted. He
dressed neatly but cheaply, and seemed always shy and
ill-at-ease in company. Why then should she prefer
him to the fashionable men who crowded about her
throne?

And as the realization of her apathy became more
and more inescapable to him, the heart of Harry was
turned to gall. Gone was all the laughter of his first
days of love, gone all the happy sighing of the youthful

Minnesinger. A tone of sepulchral hopelessness echoed hollowly in all his words. He still wrote poetry—indeed, more now than ever before. As he confessed to Sethe in October, 1816:

> "She scorns my beautiful songs which I compose only for her . . . but nevertheless the Muse is dearer to me than ever. . . . I write a great deal, for I have time enough. . . . I do not know whether my present poems are better than the earlier ones. But this is certain: they are much sadder and sweeter, like pain dipped in honey."

These "sadder and sweeter" poems were probably the first of the sheaf which he later called his "Dream Pictures." They were strangely, almost morbidly gloomy —a "brooding sinking in a dream-world lighted only by fantastic gleams."

He still saw Amalie, and deep in him there still flickered the hope that some day her heart might change. "At the very first move I lost the queen," he told Sethe, "but persistently I still play on as though I might yet win her."

But it was a gruelling game to play, as is obvious from his lamentations to his friend:

> "To be away from her, to carry for years a consuming longing in your heart—that is the torture of hell. . . . But *to be near her,* and yet for eternal weeks to languish in vain for a sight of her—that is enough to make the purest and most devout soul flame up in mad, frenzied blasphemy."

But if Harry's soul flamed up, he gave no outward sign of it. Outwardly he remained still an obedient, hard-working apprentice whose sole thought was of advancement in the business. Perhaps it was because he hoped that advancement might better his chances with Amalie. By this time he had learned that Hamburg was Hamburg, and that in it only wealth was the gauge of greatness. . . . And in a little while Harry did receive advancement. Probably as a reward for his diligence his uncle offered to set him up in a business of his own. In 1818, two years after the boy's arrival in Hamburg, the firm of Harry Heine and Co. was established. He was twenty-one years of age, yet already he had become the proprietor—nominally, at least—of a cloth-merchant's establishment.

6

IF THE young man had hoped that his rise in the commercial world would affect Amalie's attitude toward him, he was doomed again to disappointment. Herr Heine, the established merchant, found no more favor in the girl's eyes than Harry, the penniless apprentice. And thereupon the youth's whole conduct changed. Two years earlier, when he first discovered that his affection was not returned, he had taken refuge in a gloomy dream-world. He had taken hold of his bruised and tortured heart and had wept over it in silence. But that was not possible now. His strength of will was exhausted and he could no longer bear his pain with fortitude, or ease it with the balm of hope. So he let himself loose at last, striving with all his being to drown his woe in a millrace of dissipation. He began to indulge in the pleasures of Hamburg night-life, and almost consciously he made himself, as he confessed in a letter, "mad, wild, cynical, utterly repellent."

He did not enjoy depravity, but he did not know how else to ease the ache in his heart. He wanted to forget Amalie. His Muse was exhausted after the emotional strain of creating the "Dream Pictures," and he no longer was able to write poetry. Instead he went out into the town and sought solace of those creatures who throughout the ages have been the sordid comforters of embittered men. He no longer strove to please his uncle, but on the contrary went about uttering witticisms at the latter's expense. "My mother read belles-lettres," he boasted, "and I became a poet. But my uncle's mother read about Cartouche, the robber—and her son became a banker! . . ."

He spent all his hours dawdling on the promenades and in the cafés of the town, and neglected his business shamelessly. Almost every afternoon he was to be seen strolling beneath the spreading limes shading the elegant Jungfernstieg, or else sitting in the sunny Swiss Pavilion and watching the girls pass by. He began to affect a Byronic pose, for just then Byronism was the fashion among poets all over Europe. He let his curling locks grow long, and wore his shirt wide open at the neck. He learned to lift his lip in a contemptuous smile, and took to repelling people with a savage gusto. He allowed himself to get into debt to tailors and other tradesmen, for he cared nothing now for so conventional a virtue as thrift. He scorned all the sacred bourgeois taboos, and sneered at all the good Hamburg philistines who upheld them. He considered himself above such creatures, a superior being, an artist.

In part, this was sheer posing. Actually this æsthetic young cloth-merchant was not nearly so convinced of his own superiority as he tried to make out. For all that he affected to look down on his rich relatives and their boorish friends, inwardly he feared them. That was why he uttered his scorn with such fierceness and intensity. At moments he really did believe he was above them, a creature of nobler clay and finer spirit— but he wanted them to confirm the belief by frankly admitting his superiority. And because they refused to make the admission, but instead snubbed him as an inferior, he was all the more moved to shout his scorn.

7

FINALLY matters came to a crisis. The firm of Harry Heine & Company began to fail, and hastily Uncle Salomon liquidated its affairs. Just one year the concern had lasted, and then it was no more. But it is hardly possible that Harry was dismayed by this turn of affairs. He had already tasted his first poetic triumph: he had seen some of his verses in print! The *Hamburg Wächter* had printed several of his lyrics, and the youth felt that at last he had found his real career. The fact that the *Wächter* was a minor journal, anti-

Semitic and of no standing, and that the poems, which had appeared under a pseudonym and for which he had received no pay, had attracted no notice, hardly affected the confidence of their author. It was enough for him that they had been accepted and published, that they had actually been revealed to the world in print. When he was told by his uncle that his business career was at an end, he felt only relief. By then he knew he had never really cared for the grubby work of barter. And he knew also that he had never cared for Hamburg. To him the town had come to seem but an ugly congeries of brick houses and stone hearts, a place where only gold and steaming food were counted of any worth. Here most certainly he could not *belong*. As he wrote years later, the Hamburg women seemed to him for the most part fat kine whose highest passions were of the stomach rather than the heart. And the men were "mostly short, with coldly calculating glances, low foreheads, heavy-hanging red jowls . . . and with hands in both breeches' pockets, as though ready to demand: 'How much must I pay?' " He was glad, therefore, utterly elated, to be able to get out of the hateful place.

But whither? What to do next? . . . It was Uncle Salomon who gave the answer. In later years the poet often wrote with no little cruelty of the millionaire; but it is difficult not to accord the man a measure of praise. Salomon Heine was indeed crude and often maddeningly despotic. He was a vain man who loved to be truckled to, a petty tyrant inordinately fond of flattery and sub-

servience. One cannot doubt that the ungracious way
in which he helped Harry was responsible for much of
his nephew's bitterness throughout life. But for all that,
one must give credit to the stingy millionaire for having
helped at all. Harry really had no claim on him, other
than the traditional Jewish claim of kinship. Seeing
that the merchant-prince despised the arts and saw no
earthly need for artists, it is a wonder he was willing to
give any aid whatsoever to a lazy fellow who seemed
to care for naught save scribbling verses and loafing in
cafés. Yet Salomon Heine did not wash his hands of
his nephew, but gave him another chance. The boy's
mother, still ambitious for his future, wanted him to
study law; and the uncle promised to support him at
the university until he received his diploma. The allowance the banker offered was not a large one, but it
seemed sufficient for the needs of a student; and the
mother was ready to help out with what money she could
obtain by pawning her few jewels. So Harry immediately packed his belongings, and departed from the
city. He was done with business, done with it forever.
He was free now to follow his Muse and be himself.
Aron Hirsch, head-bookkeeper for Salomon Heine, was
instructed to see that the young man got away safely,
and in the carriage this good man could not refrain from
upbraiding Harry for having thrown away his golden
opportunity. But Harry only laughed.

"You wait," he cried exultingly, "you'll all hear
of me yet! . . ."

THE EXILE IN GERMANY

CHAPTER
THREE

"I do not know whether my present poems are better than the earlier ones. But this is certain: they are much sadder and sweeter, like pain dipped in honey. . . ."

CHAPTER
THREE

"I do not know whether my present
poems are better than the earlier ones.
But this is certain: they are much sweeter and sweeter, like pain dipped in
honey. . . ."

At once he tried to make himself a part of the life of the university. He became a member of the local Burschenschaft, the fraternity of the student patriots, and very earnestly he sought to live up to its ideals of impeccable chastity and utter loyalty to the Fatherland. He found it hard to share in the most common activities of the group, for he did not like beer, and smoking made him sick. But he did enjoy the constant solemn talk

III

A NEW university had been founded at Bonn in the Rhine country, a liberal institution with a faculty distinguished for its culture and lack of pedantry. Several Düsseldorf boys, among them Christian Sethe, were already among its students, and it was therefore natural for Harry to decide on going there. After a month or two at home in Düsseldorf, where he prepared himself for the entrance-examinations, he set off for Bonn. He seems to have been in the highest spirits, elated over the ease with which he had mastered his studies, and confident once again that Amalie would be his. He told himself now that only his lowly station had been responsible for the girl's indifference toward him. Once he was actually a *Doktor Jurisprudenz*, and occupied the position of a barrister in Hamburg, she would look on him far differently!

He arrived in Bonn in October, 1819, and a week or two later took his entrance examinations. His performance was by no means brilliant. In history he was declared "not without all knowledge," his Latin was classed "poor," and his German prose, "queer." But nevertheless he passed.

At once he tried to make himself a part of the life of the university. He became a member of the local Burschenschaft, the fraternity of the student patriots, and very earnestly he sought to live up to its ideals of impeccable chastity and utter loyalty to the Fatherland. He found it hard to share in the most common activities of the group, for he did not like beer, and smoking made him sick. But he did enjoy the constant solemn talk about the "New Day" that was to dawn in the land, about the "Holy German Empire" to be, and about "Freedom," "Liberty," and a thousand similar noble ideals. He was still only twenty-two, and, though he had suffered much, he was far from cynical. Apparently he was as sincere in his devotion to the ideals of the Burschenschaft as any in the group. Probably he even exceeded the rest in his devotion, for he was, after all, a Jew. . . .

The Burschenschaften had originally been founded to reintroduce into German life the fine old Christian virtues which were imagined to have been supreme in medieval times. The earnest youths who joined these societies—and they were to be found in almost all the universities in Germany—swore to be as brave, pious, honorable, and chaste as medieval Christian knights. Of course, had those students been better acquainted with the actual facts of history, they would have realized that these oaths, for all that they seemed so portentous, in reality demanded very little of them. But the young men knew only the stock romantic fables concerning the knights of old. They made a veritable cult of the past, took to wearing old-German costume, and sought to bring to life again the old-German conventions. Among these conventions was a rapacious hatred of the Jew, a murderous loathing for that stiff-necked infidel who preferred death in the alley of some foul ghetto to life in the arms of the Church. Harry Heine knew this full well, and the knowledge must have caused him no little inward conflict. But outwardly he gave no sign of it. He was tremendously anxious that none of his fellow-idealists should suspect that he still counted himself a Jew. Now that he had at last been made a member of a group, he wanted with all his might to feel that he unqualifiedly *belonged*. He was sick of being always an outsider. Even though the Burschenschaft was Christian and anti-Semitic, now that he had joined it he was determined to be thoroughly a part of it.

2

ALL of Heine's studies were in German history and literature, and the only course even remotely connected with the profession for which he was supposed to be preparing himself, was one in old-German political law. He still thought of Amalie and still wrote lyrics to her; but more and more he poetized about his German Fatherland, and sang the glory of her holy past and future. Undoubtedly there were moments when he had misgivings as to the sincerity of his new enthusiasm. A contemporary reports that once, when some other Jewish student loudly asserted that he preferred Christianity to his ancestral faith, Heine, who was present, could not keep a contemptuous smile from playing on his lips. But he uttered no word of protest.

Despite such moments, however, Heine was happy at Bonn—happier, indeed, than he had ever been before in all his life. Of course, there were many students who laughed at him because of the Byronic way he dressed; and many there were who disdained him because he was born a Jew. But he also had his staunch defenders. Foremost among the latter was his old friend, Christian Sethe; but besides him Heine now had a number of other friends: Karl Simrock, Jean Baptiste Rousseau, Friedrich Steinmann, and a Prince von Wittgenstein. It was his poetic talent which won him their friendship, for as it happened, poetry was most earnestly cultivated by certain of the students at Bonn that season. Heine, who could boast that he had already had some of his verses printed, seemed to them a person of real distinction, and they all rather looked up to him. It was the fashion among them to write poems to each other; and from the care with which Heine's effusions were cherished we can see in what esteem his colleagues held him.

This recognition was probably the young man's chief source of joy. He received it not only from his fellow-students but also from his professors. There was one teacher in particular from whom he received encouragement—the great August Wilhelm von Schlegel. At the time Schlegel was the literary oracle not merely of

Bonn but of all Europe. He had been one of the founders of the Romantic School in Germany, and his inspired translation of Shakespeare had won him the esteem of the whole German-speaking world. For Heine merely to have been noticed by the great man would have been triumph almost sufficient; but actually to receive his praise must have been overwhelming. Many years later Heine declared:

"I shall never forget that sublime moment. Even now I can feel the blessed tremor that passed through my soul when I stood before his desk and heard him speak. I was wearing a white linen coat, a red cap, long fair hair, and no gloves. But Herr August Wilhelm von Schlegel was wearing kid gloves and was dressed in the latest Paris fashion. . . ."

Heine had been taught to believe that a poet was a wretch who wore a threadbare ragged coat, supplied verses for a few groschen upon the occasion of a christening or a marriage, and often spent his nights snoring drunkenly in some gutter. But here Heine saw a poet who was all elegance in person, who always had near him a servant in the baronial livery of the House of Schlegel to snuff the wax candles which burned in silver candlesticks on the desk! Little wonder the young man was overwhelmed.

But Heine was not spoiled by the praise he received. He labored incessantly over every word he wrote, never counting a poem finished until he had perfected its every line. He submitted his best verses to his master for criticism, and when they came back all marked and crossed, he brooded for hours over the corrections. Heine was absurdly generous in praising the effusions of his fellow-students; but he was remorselessly severe toward his own work. Day and night he labored over his verses. Even while he slouched through the narrow cobbled streets on his way to class, portfolio under his arm, cap of burning red pushed far back on his fair head, he would be thinking of rhymes and measures. And at night on his bed his mind would go furiously picking and choosing words long after his nervous frame ached for sleep. It was a glorious period. He was poor and not in the best of health. He knew there were many at the univerity who looked down on him because of his birth and nervous mannerisms. He was giving no thought to the studies for which he had been sent to Bonn. But what cared he? Didn't Schlegel, the mighty Schlegel, believe in him? What if once he had indeed been spurned by his beloved? Soon enough she would repent and beg to give him her hand. For was he not already the foremost young poet at Bonn? And was he not almost certain to become the foremost in all Germany soon? . . .

It was a period of vast hope and strenuous industry. For the most part he wrote lyrics, and they were of a freshness, an originality, of a simple and apparently effortless beauty, that easily distinguished them from the lame rhymings of the other young poets at Bonn. Persuaded by Schlegel, Heine did try his hand at the

sonnet form for a while, and was successful with it.
But he soon gave it up and returned to the lyric. Somehow the lyric was native to him. He could express himself in it with a freedom no other poetic form allowed.
And the more he labored with it, the more adept he
became. His rhymes began to be bolder and more
striking, and his whole tone became firmer and more
realistic. He no longer used the stock phrases of the
Romanticists; the phosphorescent light of the Catholic
mystery no longer gleamed in his lines. He forgot to
carol about knights and priests and magic spells, but
sang now of more real and immediate things. The words
he used were the shortest and simplest he could find,
humble folk-words such as he had heard from Sefchen
in old Düsseldorf. And he set those words together with
sharp directness: plainly, honestly—not in the preciously inverted fashion affected by the poets of the day.
It was the folk-song quality he was after, the quality he
had found in Sefchen's simple runes. He wanted his
verses to seem, as Louis Untermeyer has put it, "an unconscious part of the world's speech; as if they always
were—born when the language was." And thus, although belonging to what was called the Romantic
school, he was already breaking from it. Or perhaps
it would be truer to say he was shaking himself free
from that sickly vapor of preciosity which had come
over the Romantic school and had brought it to deca-
dence.

Romanticism had become feeble and anæmic. Too
weak to strike out lustily for itself, it now sat limp by

the roadside and cast languishing glances towards the past. It had taken to lisping about altars and censers and occult mysteries, and thus had drooped off into the comforting stupor of Catholicism and Toryism. There was abundant reason for this. Europe was tired. The frantic struggle to beat down Napoleon had left the nations spent and nerveless. And decadent Romanticism was no more than a piteous wail for the imaginary glories that war and revolution had swept away. Young Heine, however, could hardly join in that wail. The praise of. Schlegel had given him such courage that he wanted to shout rather than wail. Far from being tired or spent, he felt now ready to do battle for years to come. *He* was not afraid of reality; on the contrary, he was most eager to embrace it. As a consequence, even in these poems written when he was hardly twenty-three, Harry Heine already revealed those qualities of realism and simplicity which were destined to make him the foremost German poet of his day.

3

In study, talk, and continual writing, the months rapidly passed by. The second semester, however, was not as happy as the first. Somehow the friends he had made among the students did not seem so close to him as before. Even Christian Sethe seemed to shun his company. Perhaps it was because Heine was no longer so fervent in acclaiming the trumpery ideals of the student patriots; or perhaps it was because he had already exhausted the patience of his friends. Despite his happiness during his first semester at Bonn, Heine had never been thoroughly at ease there. We can see this from the intensity with which he devoted himself to his poetry. There had been something not unlike desperation in the way he poured out his heart. Much of his verse had been most poignantly sad. Its recurrent burthen had been that of unrequited love, and even when it broke loose and rocketed up in ecstasy, it still had seemed to carry an overtone of despair. Evidently the young man had still smarted because his beloved had once rejected him, and he had been unable even in his happiest hours to exorcise the bitterness in his spirit. Heine had remained a queer person—moody, fretful, and at the least hurt cruelly sarcastic. He had not yet outgrown the nervous conceit he had acquired during his latter Hamburg days, and he had still carried himself with an irritating air of self-conscious superiority. He had grown vain not alone about his talents but also about his appearance. He dressed with meticulous carelessness, and a contemporary reports that he had a way of stealthily coquetting with himself whenever a mirror was within range. And he had not lost his almost pathological sensitiveness. He was acutely aware of even veiled hostility, and mercilessly assailed those who did not show him favor. Years of antagonism and frustration had developed in him a scathing wit which he rarely took pains to hold in leash. The mocking shouts of the little Christian boys in Düsseldorf, and the long sad hours alone in the attic there; the horror of those months in Frankfurt, where he had been not merely a ghetto Jew, but also homeless, penniless, and out of work; the years of humiliation in Hamburg, where he had been not merely a pauper among millionaires, but in addition a poet among business-men; above all, his devastating rejection at the hands of Amalie: all these evils had left their mark on him. The sardonic curl of his lips may have been an affectation; but the sarcastic turn of his mind was real.

His fellow-students, however, were not able to understand this. They could not pause to ask why Heine was so sensitive. They merely realized he was queer and unpleasant, resenting the slightest mockery and lashing out on the least provocation. So one after another they withdrew from him. And the more they withdrew, the more irritable became his temper and the sharper his tongue. That, naturally enough, only served to alienate his fellow-students still further, until at last he found himself almost entirely without friends. And then there was no other way for him to give vent to his spleen save in his writing. He began to compose a long drama in blank verse, a bitter, drastic tragedy set in fifteenth-century Spain. The plot centered around a brave young Moorish prince who had lost his beloved to the Christians, had won her back for a moment, and then, with the girl in his arms, leapt to his death rather than surrender to his enemies. It was a crude melodramatic affair, full of murder, madness, and unbridled passion; but that was just why Heine delighted in working on it. Almansor, the young Moor, was in reality himself; and the cruel Spanish Christians were none other than his own German persecutors. In the writing of every line of the play he was giving utterance to his own pent-up bitterness.

When the summer vacation came, Heine was so wrapped up in "Almansor" that he could not bring himself to go home at once. Instead he went to the pretty village of Beuel, just across the river from Bonn, ostensibly to read law, but actually to continue working on the play. Only toward the end of the summer did he go back to his parents. They were now living, with their three younger children, in a village called Oldesloe, not far from Hamburg. Poor Samson Heine had gone bankrupt in Düsseldorf, and had moved as close as possible to his rich brother, Salomon. The plight of the little family was desperate. The daughter, Charlotte, was already twenty, and the problem of providing her with a dowry in order to marry her off, was becoming daily more pressing. And the two younger sons, Gustav and Max, were growing up and presenting added problems. It was to a sad and depressing household, therefore, that Harry returned for his holidays. His mother had become haggard and sharp of tongue, for her long and vain struggle to keep up appearances and cling to her ambitions for her children had almost worn her out. And his father had grown too dispirited to attempt any new mercantile venture. He seemed content to loiter in the house and live off his rich brother's charity.

4

HARRY was not sorry when the time came for him to
return to the university. He had been miserable during
his last months at Bonn, but certainly not nearly so miserable as in the poverty-stricken home of his parents in
Oldesloe. Besides, he had already decided he would
go to some other university this second year. At Bonn,
where the great Schlegel reigned, it had been quite impossible for Heine to keep his mind away from poetry;
and he realized he was being sent to the university
not to become a poet but a lawyer. So he thought he
would go instead to Göttingen, where there was no
Schlegel and no great enthusiasm for literature.

But even while he journeyed to Göttingen, his major
interest was still poetry. He travelled on foot, and all
the way his brain was busy with new verses. At Düsseldorf, which he revisited while on the walk, he composed
a magnificently stirring song. He was standing on the
allée, just where he had stood nine years earlier when
the mighty Napoleon had marched by; and under the
influence of the old memory he conceived the now world-
famous song called the *Grenadiers*. And at Hamm,
where he stopped over to visit one of the students he
had known at Bonn, he tried to persuade a publisher
to bring out a volume of the verses he had thus far
written. Heine's reason told him he should think only
of law—but his whole being lived for poetry.

Even when he got to Göttingen he could not tear himself from the arms of his Muse. He disliked the university almost from the day he arrived there. He found the professors were all pedants and the students mostly snobs. "I'm bored to death here," he wrote to a friend at Bonn. "There is nothing to do save grind. But I should not complain, for, after all, that is why I came here." Yet he did complain, for notwithstanding his firm decision to give himself utterly to the study of law, his major interest remained poetry. He spent hours on the still unfinished "Almansor," or on new lyrics and sonnets; and only in desperate spurts did he give himself to the studies for which he had been sent to the place. Most of the time he was gloomy and irascible. He had very few friends, for a group of young Hanoverian aristocrats set the tone of the whole university, and among them a mere Jew had no place. He did belong to the local Burschenschaft, but took very little part in its life. All sorts of radical ideas had begun to creep into his thinking. He no longer talked about his "pious Fatherland," and no longer posed as a virtuous knight sworn to bring on the "Holy German Empire." He had become disillusioned; he realized now just how tawdry and pretentious was the patriotism of the Burschenschaften. He had discovered that the fervent students who were forever talking of their consecration to Old Germany, were really only playing parts. They were for the most part boisterous youths with fifth-rate minds, who befuddled themselves with beer and tobacco and then sang themselves into a frenzy of chauvinism. Heine could not stand them.

What few companions he had were for the most part poets; but he found little joy even in their company, for they were young men of obvious mediocrity. And this lack of understanding and appreciative friends was perhaps the chief source of Heine's unhappiness. Only one of the professors, the historian, Sartorius, took any interest in the poet; the rest scarcely noticed his exist-ence. And Heine, because of his sensitive nature, lit-erally hungered for attention. He craved sympathy and encouragement, for, as he remarked in one of his letters: "human beings are the vainest of all created things, and poets are the vainest of all human beings." It was as natural for him to desire praise as it is for the flower to want sunshine—and because he was denied it at Göt-tingen, his talent seemed to wither and fade away. Everything seemed to go against him that winter. He tried to find a publisher for a collection of his poems; but without success. "Almansor," the tragedy, was still unfinished. He was pinched for money, for in a few months he had gone through most of his year's allow-ance. Worst of all, disquieting rumors were reaching him that Amalie was about to be betrothed to some rich man from Prussia. All manner of imaginary torments beset the poet, and he wandered about in a constant state of distress and irascibility.

5

THEN suddenly things reached a climax. Late in December Heine was insulted by one of his fellow-

students during an altercation in a restaurant. In a
rage he issued a challenge to a duel with pistols, heed-
less of the strict law forbidding it. The university authorities intervened immediately, prevented the duel,
and, after a trial, sentenced Heine to suspension for half
a year. At the same time his Burschenschaft expelled
him, apparently because he was suspected of having
broken his vow of chastity. Whether this specific charge
was brought or no, we cannot now determine. Heine
was ill at the time, so ill, indeed, that the authorities
permitted him to remain at Göttingen for a week or two
after he received the *consileum abeundi*. And, according to Fürst, certain spiteful persons spread the
damning rumor that Heine had contracted a venereal
disease.

Heine made no attempt to exonerate himself. He may
have been really guilty; but, more probably, he did not
think it worth while to establish his innocence. He was
sick of the Burschenschaft and disgusted with Göttingen.
It was with vast relief that he found himself now ousted
from both. As soon as he was sufficiently recovered to
be able to travel—and had obtained the wherewithal
from his uncle—he left. He did not, however, go directly back to his parents in Oldesloe. Instead he went
to Hamburg, and in such distress and excitement that
one can readily surmise the reason. Evidently definite
word had reached him that his beloved was betrothed
to another, and in a mad frenzy he had rushed off to see
her. But, once in Hamburg, he did not even present himself. Instead, as he declared in a sonnet, he merely

stood in silent misery beneath her window all night long, and wept in his broken heart. For what use was there of presenting himself now? For five long years he had loved and desired her; five long years he had dreamed that some day she would be his. And now it was all ended. Reams and reams of paper had he filled with jewelled praise of her loveliness; scores of lyrics had he penned to make known his passion for her. And she had scorned him—*him*, the poet whose verses even Schlegel had praised. She had jilted him to accept Herr Friedländer, the banker!

Brokenly he betook himself to the humble house of his parents in Oldesloe, and there he sat for months in a daze of wretchedness. As far as we know, his whole family was now living off the bounty of the rich Uncle Salomon. Harry's father was a broken man—nervous, melancholy, and reft of all will. His mother went about with complaint forever on her lips. His sister sniffled with catarrh, and his two brothers wrote bad verses. There was very little money in the house, and even less cheer. On every side Heine saw naught save dejection, and the spirit in him was bitter beyond words. He still wrote, of course: poetry was his only relief. He poured out his heart in a veritable torrent of bitter lyrics and sonnets. Day after day he repeated in verse his fierce resentment at the scurvy trick life and love had played him. The sorrow which had filled his heart in earlier days was now a frenzied despair, and the irony with which he had written before, now became the most cutting mockery.

The harmless Herr Friedländer, who had won the hand of Amalie, became the butt of the poet's cruellest jibes. Heine probably had never laid eyes on his rival, yet he hated him remorselessly. He caricatured and made sport of the poor fellow in lyric after lyric, picturing him as a filthy dwarf in dapper clothing, as a "sour philistine," and a "wealthy old blight." Nor did he spare Amalie, either. Heine felt she had been false to him, that she had betrayed his love and accepted another merely because the other was rich and a person of station. From all indications, Amalie had never encouraged the poet, and certainly had never promised to be his bride. Only once, years earlier, had she kissed him, and then most probably in a cousinly fashion. She had never confessed any love for him, and never, so far as we know, had she written to him after he left Hamburg. But all that made no difference to the wretched youth. It was enough that in his fantasy-world he had imagined her his bride. In his mind she could not possibly escape the blame for his sickening disappointment. Despite his gaucherie and sarcasm and poverty and moodiness, despite everything, he felt she *should* have chosen him. After all, was he not a poet? . . .

It is terrifying to consider what would have happened had Amalie indeed accepted Heine. In all probability his great love for her would have lasted hardly a year, for he would very soon have discovered how far different she was from the girl of his imaginings. Then immediately there would have begun a struggle which would of necessity have had to end in disaster. Either Heine would have permitted Hamburg to conquer him, and would have become a miserable "successful" personage in the city; or else he would have flaunted Hamburg, broken with his wife, and been driven from the place as a rogue. Happiness could never have come to them, for they were too irreconcilably different in their attitudes toward life. She was the daughter of a Hamburg millionaire, a pretty, spoiled, fashionable débutante— and he was an incorrigible poet.

But Heine did not realize this. Having so long cherished a hope, he could not lightly forget it. His whole being was tormented by the thought that his beloved had forsaken him, and the verses he wrote were filled with horror and despair.

> "My blood is boiling, foaming, mad
> Because of an evil dream I've had. . . .
> It was a wedding revelry,
> The guests were seated smilingly.
> And when the happy pair I spied—
> Alas! My darling was the bride. . . .
>
> I saw the bridegroom fill his glass
> And drink, and with a gesture pass
> The wine to her. She drank and laughed—
> And, woe! It was my blood they quaffed.
>
> The bride then took an apple, and
> Put it into the bridegroom's hand.

He took a knife and cut it straight—
And woe! It was my heart they ate." *

Thus did he write now, with infinite bitterness and
venom.

"My songs, they say, are poisoned.
How else, love, could it be?
Thou hast, with deadly magic,
Poured poison into me."

And all love seemed to him evil:

"The angels call it Heaven's desire,
The devils call it Hell's own fire,
And man, he calls it—Love!"

Evil, all existence became to him evil, hateful, rotten.
And in such a mood he dragged out the dreadful weeks
at Oldesloe.

6

BUT then came a change. Spring arrived and hope
began to burgeon once more in the poet's breast. For
the third time he girded himself to study law, determined, it seems, to win his doctorate and establish himself in the world despite all the frustrations that had
come to him. This time he went to Berlin, hoping the
university there would prove less unpleasant than the

* The translation of this, as of most of the other poetic quotations
in this biography, is by Mr. Louis Untermeyer. His volume, "Poems
of Heinrich Heine," contains translations of the poet's most characteristic verses, and also a preface which is one of the most discerning
essays ever written on the subject of Heine's poetic tendencies.

others he had attended. Berlin was the intellectual as well as political capital of the land, a great and rich city, yet not narrowly commercial like Hamburg or Frankfurt. Heine liked the place from the day he arrived. The faculty at the university included men like Schleiermacher, Schopenhauer, and Hegel: great scholars who could recognize originality and loved to encourage it. Stimulated by his professors, Heine began to read and learn as never before. He had the quick and acquisitive mind apparently characteristic of his people, and he loved knowledge for its own inutile sake. Eagerly he threw himself into the study of history, philosophy, and literature, taking courses in logic, Aristophanes, German history, metaphysics, and even Hindu literature.

He paid only desultory attention to law. He did not trouble even to become acquainted with the leading professors in that department. Despite all the firm resolutions he had made in Oldesloe, once he arrived in Berlin he could not possibly interest himself in jurisprudence. He found the whole subject tedious, and he realized now as never before that he would not die a lawyer. Just how he would make a living he did not know. He began to think of diplomacy as a career, or of journalism. But he still continued to subscribe himself a student of law, for he knew that otherwise his allowance from Uncle Salomon would be cut off. He quite sincerely expected to devote himself to his law studies—when examination time approached. For the present, however, he wanted to study other and more congenial subjects. He found philosophy under Professor Hegel irresistible. The cold, sharp dialectic of the great thinker cut like a scalpel through the fatty tissues of Romanticism which still clung to the young poet's soul. It hacked away pitilessly at his soft sentimentalism, and, though Heine winced and swore because of the pain it inflicted, he could not desist from asking for more.

It is doubtful whether he ever really understood Hegel's theory of life, but nevertheless he was profoundly influenced by it. He became more rational than he had ever been before, more critical and sober in his judgments. His old tendency to flee into a dream-world at the least prick of reality began to lose its hold on him. He became more courageous, more willing to face the sharp, harsh exigencies of life. And he became quite consciously radical in his whole attitude toward life. The fondness for Catholicism which had marked him from early boyhood began to pass, for he no longer craved the opiate of mysticism. "I myself am just now a mystic," he wrote mockingly a year or two later, "for I must follow the advice of my physician to avoid all effort at thinking!" . . . All his life he had allowed his emotions to rule him, and they had led him into confusion beyond bearing. Now, instead, he began to give the rein to his intellect.

Heine was profoundly impressed by Hegel's personality and tried assiduously to cultivate his friendship. The young man paid little attention to his fellow-students, and took no part in their life. He did for a while keep

company with a group of young poets who gathered
regularly in Lütter and Wegener's wine-cellar; but he
could not stand their pace for long. He was weak physically. His stomach was easily upset and his head ached
intolerably at the least nervous strain. He tried hard
to share in the earnest dissipations of the crowd, but he
could not drink well and he still turned sick at the smell
of tobacco. So after a short time he forsook this little
group of serious drinkers and took to looking for company in other places. He was not long in finding it.
His reputation as an emergent poet won him entrance
into one or two of the best-known salons of the city, and
finally he actually managed to attract the interest of the
great Rahel von Varnhagen.

Madame Varnhagen, a Jewess by birth, was the leading woman in the intellectual life of Germany in that
day. When Heine first met her she was about fifty years
of age, small, sickly, and not beautiful. Yet her home
was the gathering place of the most brilliant men of the
time, and her influence in the world of thought and literature was paramount. She was a most extraordinary
person, quick, intelligent, and gifted with almost unbounded generosity of soul. She had no prejudices, and
believed implicitly in the right of the individual to set
his own standards and live his own life. She had un-
limited admiration for men of genius, chief of all for
Goethe. Indeed, her incessant praise of that poet's work
helped not a little to establish his position in the literary
world. She brought him to the attention of all Germany,
and made him the most talked-of poet of the generation.

One can easily understand, therefore, how happy was young Heine when he succeeded in winning the interest of this great woman. She was exactly as old as his mother, but he fell in love with her almost at once. According to Wolff, she became closer to him throughout the rest of his life than any other woman in the world. He began to frequent her home regularly, and not merely because he could meet there the greatest men of the day —Schleiermacher, Hegel, Chamisso, and any number of persons of lesser importance. Far more it was because *she* was there, "the little woman with the great soul." For she, Rahel von Varnhagen, "the most intellectual woman in the universe," gave him that for which he had ever hungered: appreciation. She had almost intuitively perceived the genius in this sickly, near-sighted, awkward youth. She saw beneath his alternating shyness and noisiness; she was able to overlook his eccentricities and occasional fits of childish vanity. And gently, tenderly, she sought to bring out of him all that treasure of beauty and love which she knew must be buried in his soul. There were moments, of course, when she almost lost her temper with him. His inordinate vanity tried her patience severely. In company he either sulked contemptuously or else tried to show off his brilliance too insistently. He always wanted to be the center of the stage, and seemed to think every word he uttered was clever and deserving of attention. But she realized that this over-assertiveness on his part was not sincere. She could see that it arose directly out of a dread in his soul that perhaps he was indeed a mediocrity.

She knew that the successive rejections and rebuffs which had come to the youth all through his life were primarily responsible for his nervous conceit. And therefore, despite his demeanor, she encouraged him to visit her home.

Nor was Rahel von Varnhagen the only important woman in Berlin to take an interest in Heine. There was also Elise von Hohenhausen (*geboren* von Ochs), and her friend, Helmina von Chézy: both women of great social prestige. The latter knew little about Heine's poetry, but she was convinced he must be a genius because of the way his "brown eyes swam enthusiastically in moist brilliance." But Elise von Hohenhausen, who was herself somewhat of a poet, admired the young man for less irrelevant reasons. She spoke of him as "the German Byron," and that was heady praise indeed, for Byron was then the most dramatic literary figure in all Europe. As we already know, Heine had long been imitating Byron, twitching his lip sardonically, letting his hair grow, and knotting his kerchief in an attractively careless manner. Now he loudly proclaimed himself a "cousin" of Byron, and even tried to emulate the Englishman as a philanderer.

But in the latter, at least, he was without success. Heine could not be gallant among ladies. He was still too inexperienced, and their very presence in a room usually made him feel ill-at-ease. It is impossible to speak with any certainty of the poet's relations with women during this period. His worst weakness was for boasting. Like many another poet, he liked to talk about his sins, whether they were real or imaginary. Actually he seems to have been quite silent and uncomfortable in the presence of most of the ladies he met. Only in his poems and later in his reminiscences was he the great Don Juan of the Berlin salons.

7

HEINE really had no time for dissipation. He was intensely industrious during those months in Berlin, writing and studying almost incessantly. Now he tried his hand at prose for the first time, contributing three lengthy articles about Berlin to the *Rheinisch-West-fälischer Anzeiger*, a journal published in Hamm. There was little originality in these letters, for they were written in the standard journalistic style of the day: superficial, gossipy, and at times somewhat insincere. This was largely because the reactionary government exercised a strict censorship over the press, and showed no tolerance to journalists who dared to talk of the king as seriously as of a fashionable chef. Young Heine's letters were perhaps fresher and more spontaneous than most of the feuilleton products of the time, largely because he wrote with enthusiasm and frank pleasure. But there was in them only the barest trace of the tang, the dash and courage, the pungency, which in later years made him the most brilliant prose-writer in Germany.

The *Briefe aus Berlin* were, however, only a minor product of this period. Heine's major interest was still in poetry, and he labored diligently at his verses during all his months in the capital. Shortly after his arrival in Berlin he presented himself at the office of a certain F. W. Gubitz, editor of one of the chief literary journals in the country, the *Gesellschafter*. "I am entirely unknown to you," the pale young man declared abruptly, "but I want to become known through you." And then he held out a sheaf of poems. Gubitz took them, and immediately accepted one for publication. He wanted to print a second, but insisted that certain minor changes be made in it. Again and again he returned it to the poet, until at last the demands of the editor were satisfied. Heine naturally resented this "gubitzing," but the *Gesellschafter* was an important journal, and in order to appear in it he was ready to swallow his pride. He knew that any appearance in this paper brought his work to the attention of the best public in Germany. So, abiding by Gubitz's corrections, he had the delight of seeing more and more of his work in print.

Finally a book of poems appeared. It was Gubitz who arranged for the publication, and the thin little volume appeared from the press of Maurer's Book Shop. "Poems of H. Heine" (*Gedichte von H. Heine*), it was called, and the author got thirty free copies (he was promised forty!) as payment in full for the work. But the poet did not complain on that score. It was enough for him that at last his poems had appeared in book form. Immediately he sent a copy to the great Goethe, and with it this letter:

"I might have a hundred reasons for sending Your Excellency my poems. But I shall give only one: I love you. I believe this is a sufficient reason. My efforts in poetry are, I know, of little worth; yet it may be that here and there will be found passages which reveal what I may in time be capable of producing. For a long time my mind was divided as to what is poetry. I was told: 'Ask Schlegel.' He said to me: 'Read Goethe.' This I have done in all reverence. And if in the course of time I shall produce something worth while, then I shall know to whom I am indebted for it. I kiss your blessed hand which has shown me, and the entire German folk, the way to Heaven."

He sent a second copy to the poet and critic, Adolf Müllner, but the enclosed letter was not nearly so humble in its tone as that to Goethe:

"If I have become a poet, then it is the fault of your excellent 'Schuld.' It was my favorite little book, and I was so fond of it that I paid it the honor of giving it as a present to my beloved. . . . When a great building is being erected, splinters fall; and such are the poems I am now taking the liberty of sending you. I am not doing this because I esteem you so highly; I take good care not to give that impression. Nor do I send my poems in gratitude for the delightful evenings I owe to you; for, being a human being, I am naturally ungrateful, and, being a German, I am habitually ungrateful to

poets. And in any case, there can be no question
of gratitude between us, for I believe that I myself
am now a poet! I am sending you, Sir, the enclosed volume of poems simply because I wish to
see a review of it in the *Literary Journal*. I shall
gain much if the review turns out well—that is to
say, if it is not too bitter. For I have wagered at
a literary club, that Councillor Müllner will review
me fairly, even though I subscribe myself one of
his antagonists!" . . .

Then Heine sat back, and anxiously awaited results.
There was a slight agitation in the literary circles. Several of the leading journals reviewed the book favorably,
and the editor of a literary almanac included Heine in
a list of the foremost young poets. There was some excitement in the Berlin salons, and not a little envy in
Lütter and Wegener's wine-cellar. Heine had actually
become in a small way famous.

But the poet was not satisfied. He had had dreams
of a flaring and sensational success, had hoped that his
little book would bring all Germany to his feet. Instead
there had been only a small flutter in the local salons,
discriminating reviews by Varnhagen and the poet Immermann, a mention or two in various of the minor literary journals, and a few letters. But nothing more.
At home there had been little rejoicing. Perhaps there
was even complaint, for the publication of the volume
showed that Harry was still trying to be a poet, instead
of dutifully preparing himself for a reputable profes-

sion in life. And worst of all, Goethe, the great Goethe who sat in Weimar and was the literary god of the land, had not even deigned to acknowledge receipt of the volume!

Had Heine been less wild a dreamer, had he been more restrained in his expectations and more sober in his judgments, he would have found little reason to complain at the reception of his first work. But he was young and a poet and a Jew—a combination little calculated to encourage patience or restraint. So, despite the publication of his book, he was still far from happy. This was partly due to his disposition, which seemed to drink in misery as the fields drink in the rain. ("He must have been unhappy," Heine once wrote of Lessing, "for he was a man of genius.") In larger part, however, Heine's distress was due to very tangible causes over which he had no possible control. In the first place, he was not well. Nervous headaches racked him day after day. At times they grew so bad that he had to lock himself in and refuse to see a soul. In the second place, he was poor. The allowance from his uncle was not sufficient to support him in Berlin, and his parents, themselves reduced to semi-pauperism, could not send him a penny. Once, through the good offices of Dr. Gubitz, he managed to get an advance from a Berlin banker named Lipke, who was a friend of Heine's uncle. And later, through Lipke, he succeeded in eliciting a promise of more generous help—four hundred thaler a year for two years—from his uncle. The promise was afterwards broken; but even had it been kept, Heine would not have had enough for his needs. Even though he economized strenuously, living in an attic over a baker-shop, he still could not make ends meet. He was constantly borrowing and trying to pay back, constantly fretting and struggling and worrying about rent and tailor bills and restaurant checks.

8

FORTUNATELY he had friends, and one cannot doubt it was their presence that held him in Berlin. He had remained nine months at Bonn, and four at Göttingen; but in Berlin he stayed fully two years. And this was because in Berlin as nowhere else he felt he could *belong*. He was not an outsider in the capital, for here he could find asylum among the people who were, after all, his only real kin: the Jews. At Bonn and Göttingen he had kept severely away from them. There he had belonged to the anti-Semitic Burschenschaft; and at least for a while had been attracted to Catholicism. But here in Berlin he ceased to pose. With relief he sank back and let himself be what, in essence, he had always been —a Jew. It was not difficult in Berlin, for here were to be found Jews of quite extraordinary quality. They were not merely the richest bankers and merchants, as in Hamburg; here they were also among the first intelligences, the leaders in the cultural life of the metropolis. And though many of these called themselves "religionless," and some even called themselves Christians, a significant

few did proudly insist they were still Jews. Of the last
the leader was the distinguished young scholar, Edward
Gans, whom Hegel considered his foremost disciple.
Associated with him were Moses Moser, Leopold Zunz,
Ludwig Marcus, and a number of other brilliant young
men who dreamed of bringing about a renascence of
Jewish culture. They had organized a society called the
Union for Jewish Culture and Learning (*Verein für
Kultur und Wissenschaft der Juden*), and dreamed of
giving to their Jewish brethren that understanding of
their religion and knowledge of their history which
would make them once more a noble, proud, and godly
people. And Heine, who had met these men soon after
coming to Berlin, and who at first had hardly sympa-
thized with their ideas, was in time won over by them,
and even joined their society.

But before he could become active in the Verein it
was already midsummer, and it was time for him to go
off for his holidays. He did not go home, however, but
instead journeyed to Poland to spend a few weeks at the
home of a fellow-student, a Count Breza. There Heine
saw the compact masses of Israel, the hordes of long-
coated Jews and bedraggled Jewesses swarming in the
filthy towns and villages. Yet he was not repelled by
the sight. Somehow he felt that just these hapless, downtrodden, uncouth wretches would ultimately deliver his
whole race. He sensed in them a quality which made
them far more to his liking than the sleek and fatted
Jews he knew in Germany. Subconsciously he felt a
profound kinship with them, for they, too, sang out of

the depths of their pain, and they, too, dreamed amidst humiliations. So he wrote:

"The Polish Jew with his filthy fur, his infested beard, his garlic-laden breath, and his jargon, is still dearer to me than many a German Jew in all the majesty of his government bonds!"

And as soon as he returned to Berlin he threw himself into the work of the Verein with all his energy. His whole attitude toward life changed, and instead of sulking in salons or moping in his bed-chamber, he took to devoting himself to concrete little activities. He became secretary of the Verein, and for a while gave a good deal of thought to the feasibility of organizing a women's auxiliary. He led a class in Jewish history in the school conducted by the society, and tried to conjure up ways of intensifying the Jewish spirit in the homes of his pupils. Indeed, for a time he became a veritable Jewish evangelist!

9

AND with this new enthusiasm came a total repudiation of all the reactionary ideals to which he had once been dedicated. He laughed aloud at the patriotism of the Burschenschaft youths, and refused to regard their professions of piety with more than cynical contempt. He had found them out. He saw now that those strutting nationalists were a menace, for they sought to hold back the coming of true freedom and enlightenment. Not they, he realized, but their opponents, the radicals,

were the real champions of the "New Day." And therefore he now openly went over to the radicals. He published an article on political conditions in Poland which
was unmistakably subversive; and in his conversations
he proclaimed even more freely his opposition to the
established order.

His reaction was decidedly normal under the circumstances. An individual who is an artist, or a Jew, or
in some other way peculiar, quite naturally leans toward
radicalism. He has an inordinate sympathy with unpopular causes because he is himself unpopular. It is
not surprising, therefore, that Heine, who was an artist
and a Jew, should have been impelled to become a radical. Had there been an organized revolutionary party
then in Germany, no doubt he would soon have become
one of its most fervent supporters. Indeed, after a little while Heine's only interest in the Verein itself was
his belief that it might indirectly stimulate liberal ideas.
His enthusiasm for the express aims of the society was
short-lived. He remained an intimate friend of Gans,
Moser, Zunz, and the rest of the leaders in the Verein;
but he soon ceased to take part in their activities. His
excuse to them was that he was too ill to devote himself
to the work, that his incessant headaches made it difficult
for him to do even his university work adequately. There
was a measure of validity in the excuse. He did suffer
excruciatingly with migraine, and he was finding it hard
to keep up with his prescribed work in law. But there
were profounder reasons for his withdrawal from the
activities of the Verein. For one thing, he was too

much of a realist to be able to blind himself for long to the vanity of those activities. He soon discovered that Gans and his colleagues did not quite know whither their movement was moving. They hoped to tear from their fellow-Jews those stained and blood-soaked rags of medievalism wherewith they still clothed their nakedness. The Wall of the Ghetto had been destroyed, but the far older Wall of the Holy Law still stood almost intact. And the young intellectuals in Berlin thought they must demolish this Wall of the Holy Law to set all Israel spiritually free. To such a program Heine could take no exception. But what cooled his ardor was the obvious inadequacy of the would-be wall-breakers for the task they had undertaken. They were all scholars and philosophers. They had no contact with the masses of Israel, had no knowledge of the wants and weaknesses of those humble shopkeepers and peddlers and artisans swarming in all the towns and villages from London to Ekaterinoslav. They did not pause to find out what was the life of their poor even in Berlin itself. Instead, Gans went about in fashionable salons and made grandiloquent speeches, while Zunz and the rest busied themselves with historical research. Consequently, all their efforts were doomed from the start to be utterly futile. "Highly gifted men tried to save a long-lost cause," Heine wrote later in life; "but all they could succeed in doing was dig up the skeletons of old champions. . . ."

But even this was not the root cause for Heine's defection from the Verein. The basic reason was that in

his heart he could not really feel himself a Jew—at
least, not completely and instinctively a Jew. He was
just enough of one not to be acceptable to the Christians—but no more. Most of his rearing in Düsseldorf,
and all his youth at Bonn and Göttingen, had so
estranged him from his own folk that he could not feel
himself essentially at one with them. It was not merely
that he was hypercritical in his judgment of the Jews,
hyper-sensitive to their faults. (All intelligent Jews—
like all unintelligent non-Jews—suffer from that ailment.) Rather he lacked all spontaneous sympathy
with their faith. As he himself confessed: "I have not
the strength to wear a beard, to fast, to hate, and out of
hate to be forgiving."

So he could not long remain an enthusiastic worker
in the *Verein für Kultur und Wissenschaft der Juden.*
After the first few months he began to neglect the work
and absent himself from the meetings. He promised
to write an article on the *Judenschmertz,* the "Jewish
Sorrow," for the journal of the society, but he put it off
from week to week until finally he forgot about it
entirely.

And with the waning of his interest in the Verein,
gloom came over him again. Once more he felt he had
been frustrated, cheated in some inexplicable fashion of
his birth-right. He was again an outsider. . . . Perhaps this, his failure to find himself a place in Jewry,
was as great a frustration as any he had yet suffered.
The rancor with which he now began to speak of Judaism
and the Jews, bears out the supposition. He could not

forgive the religion of his forebears that it failed to satisfy him. He was left now with nothing positive to which to cling. In 1822 he could still declare: "No one can really be an atheist, but according to one's nature one must believe in a Higher Being." But six months later he wrote, "I am now the born enemy of every positive religion!" He discovered quite falsely that atheism was a distinct teaching of Hegel, and went about poking fun at all believers. He still called himself a Jew, but —"only out of antipathy to Christianity." Had there been an established radical movement in the land, his difficulties would have been ended. But the reactionaries had stamped out every vestige of insurgence, and what few revolutionists still lived in Germany, were scattered and inarticulate. So there was no group for him to join; he was still unable to belong anywhere. . . .

10

SAD days followed. Heine tried to find salvation in poetry and wrote almost incessantly. But even poetry failed to allay the smart in his soul. It rankled in him that he did not receive the acclaim he knew he deserved. A host of little critics continued to assail his work, calling it insincere and flashy and unpoetic. His originality, his deliberate refusal to write preciously and sentimentally, like an orthodox Romanticist, angered those little critics. They could not quite understand him, and so they derided or denounced him. And he, abnormally sensitive, took their dispraise to heart. He began to feel there was a veritable conspiracy against him. "I know," he wrote to Karl Immermann, one of the few established poets who had given his poems any praise, "I know that a regular society has been formed to provoke me by spreading offensive reports and publicly slinging mud." There was some justification for his feeling. Recurrent fragments of scandal and gossip concerning his private life were emanating in a steady stream from Bonn, and these were making things hard for him in Berlin. He could not and would not deny the tales; rather he became defiant and repeated them himself. He felt he had a right to live as he pleased, and refused to accept censure from any source. He was certain in his own heart that his conduct, far from bringing him to the gutter, as his anonymous slanderers prophesied, would yet lead him to the peak of Parnassus. And to prove his conviction, he wrote with a frenzied fervor which showed itself all too clearly in his work.

He had already completed the tragedy, "Almansor," putting into it, as he declared, "my whole self, with my paradoxes, my wisdom, my love, my hate, and all my madness." And he had also completed a second play, "William Ratcliff." This second piece he later described as "a little grey northern tragedy . . . the résumé of my period of poetic storm and stress." According to his own account, he wrote it

"under the limes at Berlin during the last three days of January, 1821 [he must have meant 1822], when the sun was shining with a certain lukewarm kindliness upon the snow-covered roofs and the sad leafless trees. I wrote it straight off and without even a rough draft. While I was writing, it was as though I heard above my head a rustling like the beating of the wings of a bird. When I told my friends, the young poets of Berlin, about it, they looked at each other wonderingly, and one and all assured me that such a thing had never happened to them when they were writing."

This "William Ratcliff," written in such a gust of poetic energy, was even more morose and blood-curdling a drama than "Almansor." The scene was laid in Scotland—Sir Walter Scott had exercised a considerable influence upon Heine—but the plot was in large part autobiographical. In it the hero, finding he cannot have his beloved even though he has already murdered two rivals for her hand, stabs her, kills her father, and then shoots himself—a melodramatic dénouement which revealed quite clearly the murderous desires seething in Heine's own heart.

"Almansor" and "Ratcliff," together with a number of what he called his "malicious-sentimental poems," already had been accepted by an obscure publisher, and were soon to appear in book-form; but Heine hardly hoped for a friendly reception. The feeling that he was being persecuted was still strong in him.

"The coteries of toads and vermin in this place," he wrote to Immermann, "have already presented me with the dirty marks of their attention. They

have already got hold of my book before it is
actually published, and from what I hear, they are
going to . . . bring it into contempt in a way
which rouses my whole being and fills me with
sovereign disgust."

So there was little to cheer him. He had been in
Berlin already two years, and though he had written
much, he had made almost no progress in his law studies.
He had no money, and his uncle seemed unwilling to
send him more. He owed small sums to any number
of friends, and could hardly borrow further. A book
was on the way, but he could hope for no more—
and no less—monetary gain from it than he had obtained
from his first volume. He had lost most of the friends
he had won during his first year in the metropolis; and
he had made many enemies. His article on the political
situation in Poland had brought down on him the censure of the Prussian Government. His poetry had received several scathing criticisms, and he was finding it
difficult to get a producer for either of his two plays.
He was reft of any high cause to espouse, and he could
find no great faith to live by. Judaism had failed him.
And Christianity seemed to him now "like a bed-bug,
the stench of which poisons the very air." Worst of all
he was ill. "Pains like hot lead run through my head
and agonize me. . . ."

He could not stay on in Berlin. He felt it was imperative that he get away to some health resort, and even
more imperative that he see Uncle Salomon to wheedle

some more money out of him. So early in May, 1823,
he packed his books and papers and fled. But before
leaving he wrote a significant farewell letter to Rahel,
one of the few persons left in Berlin upon whose loyalty
he still could count. The letter, brief as it was, spoke
volumes:

> "You treated me, a sick, bitter, morose, poetic,
> and insufferable human being, with a kindliness
> and goodness which I certainly have not deserved
> in *this* life. . . ."

And with that word uttered, he forsook Berlin.

THE EXILE IN GERMANY

CHAPTER
FOUR

*"Now I understand thoroughly the words
of the Psalmist: 'Lord God, give me my
daily bread that I may not blaspheme
Thy name!' . . ."*

CHAPTER
FOUR

"Now I understand thoroughly the words
of the Psalmist 'for ... God, gave me my
daily bread that I may not blaspheme
Thy name!'..."

He went back to his parents. Two nights and a day he was jolted in a crowded stage-coach before at last he reached the end of his journey. But then it was only to find new miseries awaiting him. Things were still going badly with his parents. They had lived at Oldesloe and had continued begging Salomon Heine for help until at last that worthy, in a burst of generosity, had driven over to Lüneburg and found them a decent house there. Lüneburg was near enough to Hamburg for the banker to be able to watch over the impoverished family, yet far enough away to keep them out of sight. There he had settled poor Samson Heine and his wife, promising at the same time to provide the daughter with a dowry, and the two younger sons with an education.

The returned student took an immediate dislike to the place. Lüneburg was to him "the Capital of Boredom." The Christians there refused to be friendly with him because he was a Jew; and he refused to be friendly with the Jews because they seemed to him stupid. So, as he complained in letter after letter to his friends in Berlin, he was forced to live in complete isolation. "I come in contact with no single human being. I have made the acquaintance only of trees." His headaches, while less intense than in Berlin, now seemed to be more protracted. His second volume, the "Tragedies and Lyrical Intermezzo" (*Tragödien nebst einem lyrischen Intermezzo*), had appeared and had been reviewed as adversely by the critics as he had feared. Even in his own family circle the book won no appreciation whatsoever. "My mother," Heine wrote to his Berlin friend, Moses Moser, "reads my plays and songs, but does not like them particularly; my sister just puts up with them; my brothers do not understand them; and my father has not read them."

The future was still an utter blank to Heine. On June 22, his sister Charlotte was married off to one Moritz Embden. The lordly Uncle Salomon, whose money had alone made the match possible, was present. He favored Heine with a smile and a few words accepting the dedicatory note in the new book of poems. But he would not at once commit himself to give any further aid, and so Harry had to follow him back to Hamburg. The young man made the journey with great reluctance, for Hamburg held too many sad memories. "The most painful sensations are excited in me," he told Varnhagen, "at the very sight of that city." For there he had loved—and lost. There he had suffered what always remained to him the most devastating experience of his life: his rejection at the hands of Amalie.

But he had to have money, and the millionaire had it to give; so he followed post-haste to Hamburg. He pre-

sented himself and asked for a loan to enable him to go
to Paris, possibly to follow a diplomatic career there.
But he did not beg for the money; rather he demanded
it, for he felt his philistine uncle was in duty bound
to provide for him. After all, was he not a poet? And
that antagonized the banker. He refused to do more
than promise the impertinent young man just enough to
pay for a "cure" at a health resort.

2

HEINE swallowed his pride and took what was offered.
He went off to Cuxhaven, a watering place on the North
Sea, and rested there six weeks. And again a new feeling came over him, a glorious excitement that made him
suddenly alive and almost happy. At Cuxhaven he saw
the ocean for the first time in his life, and its majestic
sweep moved him to the very depths of his being. Wondrous songs seemed to well up in him each time his eyes
caught sight of the vast expanse; magic rhythms beat in
his veins at the very sound of the breaking waves. He
felt a strange kinship with the sea, for it, too, seemed
never at rest.

> "My heart is like the ocean
> With storm and ebb and flow—
> And many a pearly treasure
> Burns in the depths below."

But it was not merely the sight of the great water that
brought to him his new emotion; far more it was the

memory of a girl. He had seen her at his sister's wedding, and again for a moment at the home of his uncle in Hamburg. For she was none other than Amalie's younger sister, Therese. When Heine had lived in Hamburg she had still been a mere child; but now, four years later, she was a grown maiden, small, shy, but already beautiful. She greatly resembled Amalie and this was what first attracted Heine to her.

> "The little one's like my darling;
>   And when she laughs I see
> Those self-same eyes whose sweetness
>   Has brought such woe to me."

He tried for a while to fight off all thought of her, for as he well knew:

> "He who, for the first time, loves
>   Even vainly, is a God.
> But the man who loves again—
>   And still vainly—is a fool."

So at first he made sport of his infatuation, describing it with mocking extravagance. He wished to protect himself, to fend off a second catastrophe. His heart was still sore from the first, and the lyrics he wrote now —for he wrote almost incessantly during those weeks— were often only of the sorrow Amalie had brought him. He still found it necessary to write savagely of the poor, silly girl who had preferred a banker to a poet.

But more and more he began to yield to his new passion. When he left Cuxhaven, healed somewhat by the

Fragment of Mss. of a poem by Heine.

long rest and quiet, he went directly to Hamburg, where he spent three exciting weeks at his uncle's country-house. They began rather unpleasantly, for Harry had overdrawn his allowance at Cuxhaven and thus precipi-tated a quarrel. Uncle Salomon was furious for he felt the young man was not merely a congenital fool, but an ingrate as well. He could not see why he should con-tinue throwing money away on such a wretch. Only on one condition, he declared, would he ever contribute another groschen, and it was that the young scapegrace drop all nonsense and get down to studying law. Harry would have to grow "serious" at once, and take his de-gree with the utmost dispatch—or look elsewhere for money. It was an ultimatum.

Harry capitulated. If his uncle would give him a further grant of one hundred louis d'or, he promised to return to dull Göttingen and take his degree. He would have preferred to spend the money going to Paris, but his uncle would not hear of it. So Heine had to agree to Göttingen. Perhaps he would have been more reluc-tant to bow to the banker's fiat had it not been for Therese. Heine was living at his uncle's house during the time the negotiations were going on, and he was see-ing his cousin daily. He knew by this time that he was deeply in love with her. But he also knew that unless he forgot his poetry—for a while, at any rate—and became a reputable *Doktor juris*, he would never be considered eligible by her father. He had no such fear concerning the girl, for he fondly imagined she was above being impressed by trumpery honors. Therese, though physically much like her elder sister Amalie, was spiritually of much finer stuff. At least, so the poet told himself. It was to her, in all probability, that he wrote what is today the most popular lyric in all the literature of the world, that beautiful poem, *Du bist wie eine Blume.*

"Thou seemest like a flower,
　　So fair and pure and bright;
A melancholy yearning
　　Steals o'er me at thy sight.

I fain would lay in blessing
　　My hands upon thy hair;
Imploring God to keep thee
　　So bright and pure and fair." *

Thus he thought of her, as a fragile, lovely, almost unearthly thing: a flower to be worshipped, an unsullied spirit to be adored. We know very little about Therese, for Heine veiled all his references to her and never so much as named her even in his letters to his closest friends. So well did he preserve his secret that not until about thirty years after his death was the fact of his love for Therese even discovered. As a consequence, all of Heine's early biographers fail to do more than merely mention her. Nevertheless we may be safe in deciding that in character and outlook Therese was a true product of her environment: a doll-like child reared amid the material splendor and spiritual poverty of Hamburg

* This translation is by Emma Lazarus.

bourgeois society. So long as her cousin betrayed his feelings only veiledly in verse, she did not even perceive that he loved her. And when at last he declared his passion openly, she refused to take him seriously. She merely "laughed long and drolly, and made a twinkling bow." She even refused to give him a "single, parting kiss."

But Heine was not dismayed. He comforted himself with the thought that in a little while, but a very little while now, he would be back with his degree—and then all would be different. He felt quite certain he needed only to establish himself in the eyes of the Hamburg Jews in order to win Hamburg's most desirable Jewess. Evidently he had learned nothing from his tragic experience with Therese's sister. Nor had his philosophic discipline under Hegel been enduringly effective. Heine's old weakness for wish-dreaming was still strong in him. No matter how many galling disappointments had come to him in the twenty-six years of his life, he still refused to surrender his fantasies. So, with a heart full of love and courage, he went off to prepare for his return to the university.

3

HE went to Lüneburg, and stayed there at the house of his parents almost four months. Most of the time he spent at his law books; but he could not abstain altogether from literature. Life in the little town was intolerable and he could find relief only in the writing of verse and letters. He wrote almost daily to Moser, Varnhagen, Immermann, and others, and usually at exhaustive length. He was dreadfully lonely. His own family was not sympathetic to him, for in their eyes he was a failure. Here he was, already twenty-six, and still incapable of supporting himself! It was, therefore, a gloomy atmosphere in which Heine spent those months. His father was kindly but dull. His sister, whom he loved dearly, did not in the least understand him; and her husband was secretly hostile. Embden seems to have been a quite mediocre person, conventional, cheaply ambitious, and totally antipathetic to all of Heine's thoughts and ways. As the poet expressed it in one of his letters: "The difference between Embden and me is that the screws in his head are too tight, and in mine are too loose! . . ." As for his own brothers: Gustav, the elder, was not to be trusted, and Max, the younger, was friendly but cowardly. Max showed a talent for verse, and wrote sporadically, but Heine discouraged him, saying, "One poet in the family is misfortune enough! . . ." Gustav needed no discouragement, for he dreamed of becoming a millionaire. Heine's more distant relations were almost all of them treacherously antagonistic. They spread gossip about him and did everything possible to injure his position with his uncle. He stood between them and the coffers of the banker, and their hostility to him arose out of the need to elbow him out of the way. And Heine was worried that they might succeed. Largely because of his own youthful boasting, he had managed to acquire a most unpleasant reputation as a rake. And his success as a poet was still far from sufficient to excuse such a reputation.

"Almansor" had been produced in Brunswick at the *Hoftheater*, but had not survived the first performance. Some ruffian had been admitted on the opening night, and he had set the whole audience hissing at the play. And the news of the fiasco had been brought post-haste to Hamburg by certain gossipping Jews from Brunswick.

"Ratcliff," the other tragedy, could not possibly find a producer after the scandalous failure of "Almansor." And the "Lyric Intermezzo" received more condemnation than praise. Heine had sent copies of his new volume to the greatest poets then living in Germany, to Goethe, Wilhelm Müller, Uhland, and Tieck; but no one of them so much as acknowledged receipt of the book. Only two or three of the minor poets wrote to congratulate him, and their words, though effusive enough, hardly made up for the silence of the others. In Hamburg, fortunately, the journals published highly favorable reviews of the volume, perhaps because it was dedicated to the powerful Salomon Heine. But elsewhere the reviews were preponderantly hostile. Most of the critics were disturbed because the poems did not conform to the sacrosanct tradition of the Romanticists. Many of the lyrics violated the stock conventions, and were realistic and sometimes even cynical. For instance, they told of a beautiful maiden who refused to listen to a poet's protestations of love not out of modesty, but

solely out of philistine disdain for protestations coming
from one who was not a banker. That shocked the little
critics. It was too realistic, too human, too earthly for
them. So they howled at the daring poet and called him
a blasphemer and a fool. Actually the "Lyric Intermezzo" contained a number of poems destined to become
in time among the most popular in literature: for instance: *Die Lotosblume, Ich grolle nicht, Ein Fichten-
baum steht einsam*, and *Vergiftet sind meine Lieder*.
Before many years were out, the foremost composers
in the world—Schumann, Schubert, Mendelssohn, Wag-
ner—were setting them to music, and people everywhere
were chanting them in every tongue. But the critics of
his own day could not foresee the verdict posterity would
render. To them the verses seemed only vulgar, shoddy,
meretricious.

And the cordon of trucklers who surrounded the millionaire in Hamburg were not slow to bring report of
what the critics said. Heine lived in daily dread that
the allowance of a hundred louis d'or for the next year
would be withdrawn, and he wrote frantically to his
Jewish friends in Berlin to use their influence with the
banker. Most of all he wrote to Moses Moser, a generous and sympathetic young man whom he had first
met through the Verein, and who had since become his
most loyal friend. Week after week Harry wrote long,
sad letters to him, complaining of his loneliness, of
the "pack of dogs" who were besmirching his name in
Hamburg, of his poverty, of his almost unmitigated ill-
fortune. Several times he also wrote to the Varnhagens.

Save for these, and two or three other people in Berlin, Heine felt himself to be completely without friends. Sethe, Jean Baptiste Rousseau, and all the other students with whom he had been intimate at Bonn, no longer had anything to do with him. In Düsseldorf and the rest of the Rhineland his name had become anathema because he was too much a Jew and seemed an enemy of Germanism. And in Hamburg he was despised because he was not enough of a Jew, and because he openly scorned the proud bankers who sustained the synagogues. In Lüneburg he was deserted, having neither companions, money, books, nor love. He had to borrow right and left to meet the petty expenses of existence there. Trifling sums he borrowed—a louis, half a louis—from Moser, his parents, or even chance acquaintances. He lost all pride, asking for books and favors like a professional beggar. And thus he dragged out three dreadful months.

4

AT last the new year opened, and the money promised by Uncle Salomon arrived. Immediately Heine packed his belongings and left for Göttingen. He arrived there on January 19, 1824, and was received most favorably. The professors, especially Dr. Sartorius, were not unconscious of his poetic achievements, and treated him almost as a younger colleague rather than a student. They forgot entirely the escapade which had led to Heine's rustication from the university three years earlier; they remembered only that he was the author of two volumes of striking verse. And the students, too, seemed to respect him.

But still he was far from happy. His headaches, now fiercer than ever before, made his waking hours a continual agony; and his law studies were intolerably boring. He tried to interest himself in the student life, and attended most of the duels either as a second or a spectator. "That amuses me," he wrote in one of his letters to Moser, "because I have nothing better to do." He could not endure the lectures, especially those of a Professor Meister, which were given in a street called "Pandect Lane"; and Heine made no secret of his feeling. He spread the report that every night there walked in "Pandect Lane" the ghost of a student who had been bored to death in the classroom. And there it would continue to walk, Heine declared, until Herr Professor Doktor Meister actually cracked a joke! . . .

Yet despite the dullness of his studies, Heine did devote himself to them as never before. He was determined to take his degree that year, for he could not endure the thought of having to be a mendicant at the door of his uncle any longer. As he wrote to Moser:

"The events of last summer have made a dreadful, a daemonic impression on me. I am not yet strong enough to bear humiliation. . . . [So] I now live altogether for jurisprudence, and if you think I shall not make a good lawyer . . . you must not express your opinion to other people, or I shall die of hunger."

But by the time Easter arrived he could no longer stand the grind in "that accursed hole, Göttingen," and he ran off to Berlin. Ostensibly he went only for a rest, but actually it was to see if there were any prospects of securing a professorship later at the university in Berlin. The closer he came to his final examinations, the more certain he grew that he was not made for the profession of law. He cared only for learning and literature, and he was terrified at the thought of having to spend all the rest of his life haggling over torts and petty thievings. So, in a characteristic fever of fantastic hopefulness he suddenly conceived the idea that he might be able to become a university professor. His reception on entering Berlin was, however, far from auspicious. When he came to register his presence with the local authorities, he was closely questioned as to the purpose of his visit, and was frankly told that the political views he had once expressed in his article on Poland had made him suspect to the Prussian Government. He was further told that he would not be allowed to stay in Berlin unless he promised to hold his tongue—and pen.

But once he reached the homes of his old friends, he quickly forgot the episode in the chambers of the *Staatsrat*. He spent happy hours in the company of the Varnhagens, and renewed all his old friendships in the Union for Jewish Culture and Learning. He ran about from one salon to another, seeking to enlist the support of every influential person he met. He was most respectful and polite; indeed, to the very end of his visit he managed to maintain his best behavior. But once he returned to Göttingen he became his old sarcastic self again. For he had failed in Berlin. After a fortnight of assiduous cadging and truckling, he had come away with not even a promise of a professorship.

He no longer attempted to interest himself in the student life at Göttingen. Instead he spent his leisure hours in the library studying medieval Jewish history. He had conceived the idea of writing a novel dealing with the life of the Jews in medieval Germany, and was carrying on his research in preparation for this work. It was to be a novel about a rabbi living in the little Rhine town of Bacherach, and of his sufferings at the hands of the bigoted Christians of that day. And, as Heine wrote to Moser, "with love unspeakable I carry it in my bosom." Indeed, it was only out of his love for the theme that he devoted himself to the romance. The Jewish nature of the work would, he realized, arouse intense hostility among the anti-Semites; but he was not deterred. He felt he could no longer repress the resentment that seethed in him, the turbulent resentment of a sensitive Jew buffeted by a Christian world. He found keen relief in plotting the "Rabbi of Bacherach." "It will be an immortal book," he solemnly assured Moser; "an eternal lamp in God's Cathedral, not a flickering light in the theatre."

But when he had completed his researches and began the actual writing of the book, he found the labor distressingly difficult. Early in 1824 he reported to Moser: "I have written about a third of my 'Rabbi,'

but my headaches have broken in upon it terribly. . . ."
One doubts whether the headaches alone were responsible for Heine's difficulties with the novel. More profoundly it may have been his temperament that was to
blame, his volatile, impatient, inconstant nature. From
childhood his whole sad life had conduced to make him
incapable of any sustained effort. He had so often
been torn in uncongenial directions, and then had been
forced to turn off into others almost as uncongenial,
that now he seemed totally incapable of holding fast
to any path. He could do well as long as he occupied
himself with lyrics, or sonnets, or short feuilleton articles. These he could begin and end in a day, sometimes
even in an hour. But a novel—that required weeks of
sustained and concentrated effort: and of this he was apparently incapable.

5

BUT the headaches were real even though Heine did
use them as an excuse for his failure to continue with
the novel. All of the Göttingen students who wrote of
the poet in their diaries or later memoirs, tell of the
sufferings which he endured in those days. For instance, an entry in the diary of Edward Wedekind dated
May, 1824, tells how Heine once begged him to put
away the watch on the table because he could not stand
its ticking. Or again, when asked by Wedekind if he
felt poetic inspiration continually, or only intermit-
tently, Heine answered: "Continually—when I feel
well."

There were those who claimed Heine's headaches were largely imaginary, and that he complained of them only to elicit sympathy, or else to show off his beautiful white hands as he stroked his throbbing temples. And it was undoubtedly true that under certain circumstances Heine could quite forget his pain. Wedekind reports that Heine, nervously exhausted, would often come into the room with the stereotyped phrase: "Let me alone, dear fellow, I'm ill"; and then would sink into the nearest chair and lose himself in gloomy silence. But then Knille, a fellow-student, would resort to the equally stereotyped: "Tell me, Heine, how was that? How did that pretty poem of yours go"—and invariably Heine would come to life. He would spring to his feet, lay his hand on Knille's shoulder, and, entirely forgetful of his pain, would ask warmly: "Which one do you mean, dear fellow? . . ."

But not all of Heine's fellow-students were as considerate as Knille, and therefore he was not often oblivious to the pain in his head. Most of his acquaintances found his company trying. This pale, emaciated, nervous little Jew seemed to like nothing better than to talk of his own poetry. When he or his work was not the subject of conversation, he was quite wretched. If he did not sulk, he made caustic remarks and poked fun at any victim he could find. At such moments his mouth would open wide, his little red-lidded eyes would almost disappear, and his whole face would suddenly become what his fellow-students described as "very Jewish." There was no real malice behind his witticisms. He was not a cruel fellow, but on the contrary quite sentimentally soft and generous. When in funds he would never refuse to help his friends; and he could be reduced almost to tears by the slightest tale of woe. Yet at the same time he could rarely resist any chance for making a quip, even if it had to be at his own expense. If others poked fun at him he took it with poor grace. He even leaped to the defense of any other student who was being persecuted by the rest. But when he himself was the persecutor, he enjoyed the sport inordinately.

He lived alone in lodgings that were usually very disordered, the bed unmade, and the tables, chairs, and floor always littered with books and papers. But he dressed carefully, almost like a dandy. Usually he appeared, according to Knille, "in a green cap, a brown overcoat with a double row of buttons fastened to his throat, and a little black silk scarf knotted loosely about his neck." And he was very particular about his food, often angering his friends by his habit of holding onto the meat platter until he could find a slice of roast that suited him. Not unnaturally, therefore, he was left to himself much of the time.

But though he had little social life to distract him, he was not able to get on with his novel. He worked at it desultorily for months, and then finally, leaving it unfinished, he went off on a walking tour. Clad in his brown overcoat, yellow trousers, and green cap, with a knapsack of green oil-cloth on his shoulders, he tramped off to the Harz Mountains. And there he wandered for weeks on end, exulting in the beauty of the countryside, writing poems, playing pranks on fellow travellers, laughing, groaning, singing, weeping—but finally returning to dull Göttingen and the inescapable Pandects. He did not then resume his novel, however. Instead he began to gather together the poems and witty paragraphs he had written during his wanderings, and around them he spun a web of narrative which was certainly the most striking document his pen had yet produced. There was a nimbleness about its wit, a grace in its style, and a chuckling impudence in its whole tone, such as had never before been seen in German prose.

Heine opened this essay, which he called the "Harz Journey" (*Harzreise*), with a derisive description of poor old Göttingen, "celebrated for its sausages and university."

"The town itself," he wrote, "is pretty, and presents its most agreeable aspect—when we have turned our back upon it. . . . Its inhabitants may be roughly classified as students, professors, philistines, and cattle; but these four classes are by no means strictly differentiated. . . . I must take the author of the 'Topography of Göttingen' to task for not emphatically contradicting the false report about the big feet of Göttingen women. For many years I have been occupied with a solemn refutation of the calumny. To confirm my views I have studied comparative anatomy, made extracts from the rarest volumes in the library, and have also stood in the Weenderstrasse for hours on end, studying the feet of the ladies as they walked by. And in the profoundly erudite thesis which will embody the results of these researches, I shall treat of: (1) feet in general; (2) feet in antiquity; (3) elephant's feet; (4) the feet of Göttingen women; ... (6) feet in connection with each other (here extending my observation, of course, to ankles, calves, knees, etc.), and (7) if I can obtain sheets of paper of sufficient size, I shall add some copperplate facsimiles of the feet of Göttingen women."

So he went on and on: ribald for a while, then suddenly poetic, then sentimental, or philosophic, vulgar, learned, dull (but dull only for a moment), brilliant, and then perhaps poetic once more.

"Clear morning air blew over the road, the birds sang merrily; and little by little my mind also became fresh and cheerful. Such a change was needed for one who too long had been imprisoned in the stall of legal lore. Roman casuists had so covered my soul with grey cobwebs . . . that I took a tender pair of lovers seated under a tree for an edition of the Corpus Juris with clasped hands. . . .

"Milkmaids passed by, and also donkey-drivers with their grey pupils. . . .

"Unfortunately, my coffee was spoiled by a youth who sat down to converse with me and boasted so outrageously and vainly that the milk soured. . . .

"Night was out hunting on her black steed, and the long mane fluttered on the wind. . . .

"He was a young merchant, and looked like an emetic powder in a long brown wrapper. . . .

"Pour forth, ye perfumes of my heart, and seek behind yon mountains the loved one of my dreams! Now she lies in slumber, while at her feet the angels kneel, and if she smiles in her slumber, 'tis a prayer the angels repeat. . . .

"Love! Immortality! Suddenly my heart became so hot that I thought the geographers had misplaced the equator. . . .

"The mountains stood still in their white nightrobes, the firs shook the sleep out of their drooping limbs, and the birds sang their morning prayers. . . .

"Goslar, with its pavements as rough as the hexameters of the Berlin poets. . . .

"God hath created man that he may praise the beauty and glory of the world—for every author, be he ever so great, desires that his work should be praised. . . .

"He looked like a monkey that has put on a red jacket and then says to itself: 'Clothes make the man.' . . ."

Thus he went on and on with a staccato brilliance, a tender beauty, and a savage, nervous intensity. No one before had ever dared even attempt such a thing in the German tongue; perhaps no one had even imagined it to be possible. German had until then been a sober, severe, at best classic, at worst clumsy, language. No one had ever dared to toy with it, crack it like a whip, toss it like a bubble, or hurl it like a thunderbolt—no one save this impudent young poet named Heine. And literary Germany could not make up its mind what to do with him. . . .

6

BUT one episode in his wanderings Heine did not even mention in his narrative. On his way back to Göttingen he so shaped his course that he was able to pass through Weimar, the home of the great Goethe. Heine had never forgotten the aged poet's failure to recognize his existence, and he now planned almost to force the other's attention. First he indited a most respectful letter:

"Your Excellency—I beg you to grant me the happiness of being in your presence for a few moments. I shall not trouble you much. I shall only kiss your hand and depart. My name is H. Heine; I am a Rhinelander. . . . I, too, am a poet, and three years ago I took the liberty of sending you my 'Poems,' and a year and a half ago my 'Tragedies,' together with a 'Lyrical Intermezzo.' I am ill, and three weeks ago I journeyed to the Harz Mountains for my health; and as I stood on the

Brocken I was seized by a desire to make a pilgrimage to Weimar to pay my respects to Goethe. In the literal sense of the word have I made a pilgrimage hither: that is, on foot and in rags. And now I await the granting of my prayer. . . ."

But when in a day or two Heine was admitted into the presence of the foremost poet of the age, he was sadly disappointed. To begin with, he was so overawed that he could only blurt out inanities.

"I had thought out on so many winter nights what sublime and profound things I should say to Goethe if ever I were able to see him. But when at length I did see him, I could only say that the plums on the road between Jena and Weimar tasted very good!"

Goethe tried to be friendly at first and smiled; but when the nervous youth boastfully asserted that he too was writing a Faust, the old man became frigid.

"Have you no other business in Weimar, Herr Heine?" he asked sharply.

"With one foot over the door-step, your Excellency, all my business in Weimar is ended," came the quick reply. And then Heine took his leave.

It was, all in all, an unpleasant episode, and the memory of it rankled in Heine long after he got back to Göttingen. As he afterwards rationalized the encounter, it seemed to him inevitable that it should have been unpleasant. He told himself he was temperamentally of a different caliber from Goethe.   As he wrote to Moser in a letter nine months later:

"At bottom Goethe and I are of opposite natures which cannot but be mutually repellent.   He is essentially a man on whom life sits easily, who looks on the enjoyment of life as the highest good. . . . I, on the contrary, am essentially an enthusiast; that is, I am so inspired by the ideal as to be ready to offer myself up for it. . . ."

It was a specious bit of rationalization.   The essential difference between the two was not that Goethe was a hedonist and Heine an altruist, but probably that the Christian had all along been at ease in his Zion, while the Jew had all his life sat by the waters of Babylon and wept.   Goethe was at home in Germany; he *belonged*—and Heine did not.   If this, however, occurred to Heine he did not confess it.   He still felt sensitive about his Jewishness and was reluctant to talk of it to the world.   He had tried to ease his heart of the burden in writing the "Rabbi of Bacherach"; but, as we already know, he had not been able to finish the work.   So now he tried to choke the whole matter down, and forget its existence.

But it would not be choked, and as the winter months passed it kept rising again and again until at last he had to deal with it openly.   The time was now approaching when he would be permitted to take his degree— and this meant he must at last be baptized   For it was the law then in Germany that none save professing

Christians could ever be admitted to the bar, or accorded almost any other governmental recognition. It is moving to see how bitterly Heine loathed the very thought of baptism, and how desperately he tried to put off its consummation. He recoiled from apostasy not out of any love for Judaism, but rather out of a care for his own self-respect. He was being coerced into Christendom, forced in by the sheer necessity of making a living. And this he resented. As he told Moses Moser: "None of my family is against it . . . but I consider it beneath my dignity and a stain on my honor to allow myself to be baptized for an appointment in Prussia!" He knew he could never possibly accept the theology of the Church, for, as he wittily put it years later: "No Jew can ever believe in the divinity of another Jew." The dogma of the Virgin Birth and the dilemma of the Trinity were to him things to laugh at, not to believe. And in addition, the "turn-the-other-cheekiness" of Christianity, the self-denying, non-resisting, good-for-evil ideal, was to him profoundly revolting. Already he thought of himself as a pagan, as an unashamed lover of the flesh; and asceticism made his gorge rise. So his baptism could not but be an act of blatant hypocrisy.

Nor was that all. Harry realized his baptism would be for him an act not only of hypocrisy but also of treachery. It implied treachery to his brethren in Israel, treachery to his friends in the *Verein für Kultur und Wissenschaft der Juden,* and to all those hapless, vermin-infested Jews he had seen and pitied in Poland. When, during his early days in Hamburg or at Bonn, he had thought of his eventual apostasy, such a consideration had not even occurred to him. In those days he had thought of himself only as a German, not at all as a Jew. But he had experienced much since then. He had learned to despise the cheap and obstreperous chauvinism which called itself Germanism. Already three years earlier he had been so embittered on the score that he had been able to write to his boyhood friend, Christian Sethe: "Everything that is German offends me." And during his months of affiliation with the Verein in Berlin he had learned to feel a measure of pride, or at least of responsibility, in being a Jew. The measure had been neither large nor enduring—but it had left its mark, nevertheless. And now that he had to renounce his Jewishness and proclaim himself at least in name a Christian, he felt outraged.

"I really don't know how to help myself," he complained to Moser. "In exasperation I may yet become a Catholic and hang myself. . . . Now I understand thoroughly the words of the Psalmist: 'Lord God, give me my daily bread that I may not blaspheme Thy name!' "

He put off the hateful act as long as was possible. In April, 1825, he presented the customary Latin petition for permission to submit himself as a candidate for the degree of *Doktor juris*, confessing therein with disarming frankness that he was not as well prepared for his examinations as he might have been had he not suffered from a chronic tendency to poetry and headaches. Only two months later did he finally offer himself for baptism, for by then he had already passed his examinations (with a third-grade mark), and the act could no longer be delayed.

On June 28 Heine suddenly appeared at the house of the Lutheran pastor in the neighboring village of Heiligenstadt. It was about ten in the morning, and Pastor Grimm was seated in his dark, low-ceilinged, miserable study, conversing with a colleague from a town not far away. Heine had told no one in Göttingen what he was about to do, and was unaccompanied when he entered the little room. He presented various documents to "legitimatize" himself, and then submitted himself to an hour of catechism during much of which it was he who asked the questions and the examiners who tried to answer. Finally, at about noon, the farce was ended. The second clergyman stood as godfather to the new convert, and Harry received the holy water and emerged as Christian Johann Heinrich! Dinner followed, a dismal meal at the board of the pastor. The convert looked obviously dejected, and spoke hardly a word. And as soon as the meal was ended he asked permission to leave. With nervous haste he shook hands with the host and his godfather, and turned to the door. But when he reached it he hesitated a moment, and, with tears suddenly starting in his eyes, he looked around at the two clergymen and in a choked voice bade them goodbye a second time. Then he disappeared.

7

LESS than a month later he presented himself for his degree. In his dissertation, delivered in the university auditorium, he made so flagrant an error in his Latin that the whole audience was moved to laughter. But he passed nevertheless, and not without a certain distinction, for in the final charge the chief examiner took occasion to refer most flatteringly to Heine's poetic talents, even comparing him to Goethe, who also had been—so the learned gentleman slyly pointed out—a greater poet than jurist. . . . And then at last Heine was formally declared a Doctor of Jurisprudence. After five long years of broken study, at the price of stifled resentment, humiliation, debt, and baptism, at last Harry (now Heinrich) Heine was—respectable. . . .

THE EXILE IN GERMANY

CHAPTER
FIVE

*"I will send you something quite un-
usual for Christmas—a promise that I
shall not shoot myself. . . ."*

V

August, 1825. Heinrich Heine was a *Doktor juris* at last: a respectable person with a diploma, a baptismal certificate, and—by virtue of those two documents—a profession. But he was still poor—penniless indeed. And ill. Once more it was imperative that he go off to a watering place, to some quiet retreat where he could breathe the salt air into his narrow lungs and brace his shoulders against the wind. So once more there was need to come begging to Uncle Salomon. But this was the last time—positively! For did he not have his degree now, and would he not soon be earning money?

The help was forthcoming; Salomon Heine may have felt this was indeed the last time—almost the last, anyway—that he would be called upon, so he produced another fifty louis d'or; and off the young man went to Norderney. The resort was not fashionable, and was frequented mainly by poor aristocrats. Heine soon made many friends, especially among the ladies. He became quite a favorite with a certain elderly Princess Solm, and also with a far from elderly person whom we know only as "the beautiful woman from Celle." He even became intimate with several of the young Hanoverian officers summering there, and took a hand at gambling with them. He found Norderney society delightful—for a while. Before a fortnight had elapsed, however, the delight had palled. The officers he found amiable enough, thoroughgoing gentlemen— but stupid. It was impossible for him to enjoy their trivial conversation and he could hardly share in their amusements. He lost a good deal of his money at cards very soon after his arrival, and from then on he had to keep discreetly distant from the gaming tables. And he did not enjoy gull-shooting, which was, next to gambling, the chief amusement of the visitors. As he wrote in his account of this holiday:

"A feeling for sport is in the blood. If a man's ancestors have from time immemorial shot roebuck, he, too, will find pleasure in that legitimate occupation. But my forebears were never hunters, but rather among the hunted, and if I were to let fly at the descendants of their old colleagues, my blood would cry out against it."

So gradually he withdrew from the genteel summerboarders and began to spend most of his time among the native fisher folk. He loved to lie in the little boats, and, while swaying on the sea, dream of glories to come —of marriage to Therese (he still hoped for that!), of wealth, position, and, above all, leisure for poetry. The thought of practising law he carefully avoided. He

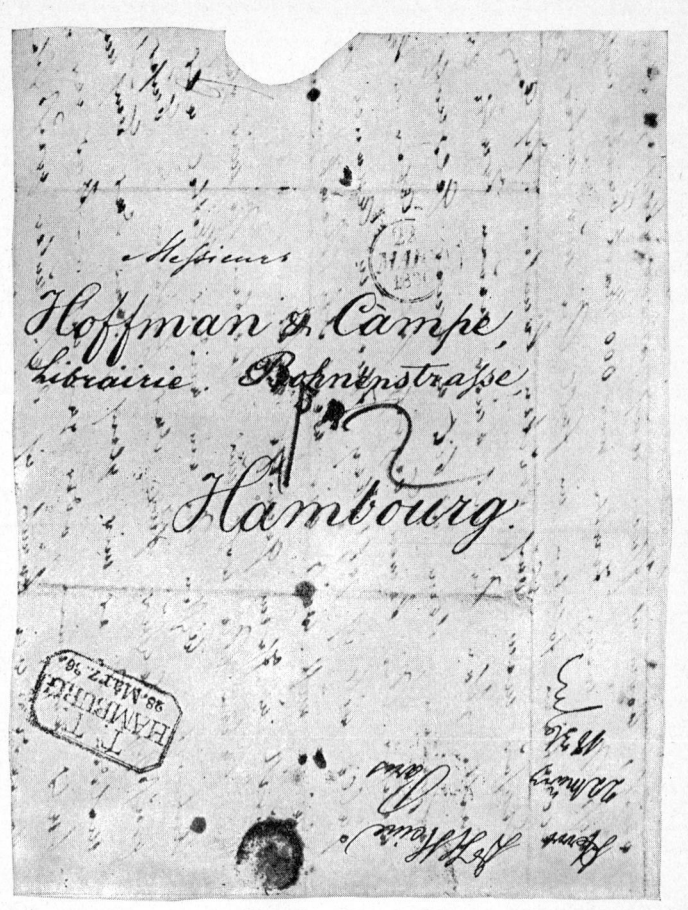

Facsimile of an envelope addressed by Heine to his publisher.

trembled at the prospect of being shut up in dusty solicitor's chambers, drawing up briefs and figuring petty accounts. He wanted to remain a poet, a troubadour of love and a crusader for liberty. Songs kept rising in his breast, and every day he thought of new beauties he must recount. And ever and again his arms grew taut and the blood pounded in his veins at the thought of the world-ills he must destroy. For hours on end he would walk alone on the deserted beach, singing lyrics to the heaving sea or shouting defiance in the knife-like wind. His head no longer ached, and his whole body grew strong and hale. As the weeks passed he became actually happy and almost content.

But then his money gave out. He managed to borrow a few louis d'or from Christian Sethe, who chanced to be at Norderney that season, and the loan tided him over for an additional fortnight or so. But when this money, too, was gone, Heine had to leave. Instead, however, of going directly to Hamburg to begin his career as a lawyer, he went to little Lüneberg, where his parents lived. Even at this late hour he still wanted to avoid the hated profession of law. He cherished the hope that, given sufficient time, he might yet be able to get a professorship at Berlin or some other university. But, though he wrote desperately to Varnhagen and what other influential friends he had, no such post was offered him. After several weeks of idle waiting, he finally surrendered and took the stage to Hamburg.

Just what happened after he arrived there we do not know. Apparently he still could not reconcile himself to the idea of setting up as an advocate, and in miserable irresolution he loafed about the town and continued to wait. He waited, possibly, for Therese's hand, for he still loved her and hoped to make her his wife. He felt that even according to Hamburg standards he was not unworthy of her now, for he was no longer merely a poet but actually a certificated solicitor. He had an academic degree and was—potentially, at least —a respectable professional man.

Therese was well cognizant of Heine's love for her, and probably she was far from displeased by his poems addressed to "Evelina" but obviously intended for herself. In a light way she may even have encouraged his passion. But she was not serious, and showed no promise of ever satisfying the appetite which she yet delighted to sharpen. But this the lover would not realize, and he persisted in picturing himself as the eventual husband of Therese—and son-in-law of the millionaire Salomon. . . .

But as the weeks dragged by and his suit came to no issue, despair began at last to come over him. He could not receive a professorship and he would not become a lawyer. He was penniless and he had no prospects. No one could understand his mad unwillingness to settle down as an advocate. His mother grieved, his uncle fumed, and his other relations frowned disapprovingly. Patently he was a hopeless ne'er-do-well. Not merely was he a spendthrift, a rake, and a gambler; an impudent ingrate and an irreverent rogue: he was lazy as well. Here he was, almost thirty years old, and still unwilling to do anything but scribble silly verses, or indite indecent quips. The good temple Jews of Hamburg despised him because he was no longer a Jew; and the zealous Christians loathed him because he was not really a Christian. As he wrote to Moser:

> "I am very sorry I had myself baptized. I do not see that things have gone any better with me since. On the contrary, I have had nothing but misfortune. Is it not absurd? As soon as I am baptized I am decried as a Jew. . . . Now I am detested by Christian and Jew alike! . . ."

2

LIFE became intolerable for Heine. He could not forgive himself that he had ever submitted to the indignity of baptism. He saw now that it had been an egregious error, for, as he later declared:

> "You can't change your religion. You can only renounce the one from which you are estranged, for another to which you will never belong. I am baptized—but I am not converted! . . ."

He felt he had made a mess of his whole life. His faith in himself and his genius began to crumble, and the dark sea of doubt which all along had been held back, now of a sudden swept down on him. And it almost destroyed him. For a time he seems actually to have contemplated suicide, for in December he wrote to Moses Moser:

"As I am not in funds and do not wish to buy you an ordinary toy, I will send you something quite unusual for Christmas—a promise that I shall not shoot myself. If you knew what is going on inside me at present, you would see that the promise is indeed a great gift and you would not laugh, as you do now, but would look as grave as I do at this very moment! . . ."

He lived largely in isolation. His companions were for the most part unstimulating mediocrities: a bad dramatist, a parlor-entertainer, a sugar-broker, and a Hebrew teacher. He was openly snubbed by the elect of the city, both Jews and Christians, and was freely insulted by his rich relations. As he declared to a friend, the humiliations he had to suffer were endurable only because he alone knew of them. "Call it what you will," he said of his existence at the time, "but not living."

He could find little solace in writing, for he felt sterile. He was restless, nervous, worried; even when he could manage to make himself take up his pen and prepare to write, words would not come to him. He thought for a while of finishing the novel, the "Rabbi of Bacherach"; but after a feeble start or two he gave it up. The most he could do was to write a ballad which he called "Almansor," in which he revealed how vehemently he now loathed the Christianity he had been forced to profess. For the rest, he could only revise and polish old lyrics. At Norderney that summer he had written a whole sheaf of sea poems—"Every summer I emerge from my chrysalis and a new butterfly flutters forth"—and it occurred to him he might make some money by publishing them in book-form. But he realized they were not enough in number to fill even a thin volume, and he therefore thought of printing them together with a group of other poems and with that droll account of his journey through the Harz Mountains which he had written a year earlier. He cherished no high enthusiasm for the idea. As he wrote to Varnhagen:

"My fame will not be served much by the publication of the volume. . . . But what am I to do? I have to publish something, and I think that even if the book is not of general interest and is not a great work, yet nothing in it can be called really bad."

Because he was publishing the volume for money, not fame, Heine was not as generous with it as he had been with his two earlier works. He put a price on it, and when Dümmler, the publisher of his "Tragedies," thought the price too high, Heine forthwith began looking about for a better customer. Such a customer he found in Julius Campe, of the firm of Hoffmann and Campe, a Hamburg publisher who specialized in the works of the younger and more daring of the German authors. This man Campe was destined to become, next to Salomon Heine, the most important male character in the whole drama of Heinrich's life. He was a short, stocky young German, shrewd, energetic, and not over-scrupulous. He possessed little culture, and no particular taste; but he did have a marked flair for the trade-value of books, and had an uncanny way of ferreting out literary successes. To be sure, many of these were successes *de scandal* rather than *d'estime,* for Campe had a penchant for books that other and more sober publishers considered too radical to print. The young Hamburger was by nature an adventurer. He loved to pit his wits against those of the government censors, and much of his business was conducted with stealth, chicanery, and sometimes open fraud. Often he had his books printed in Wandsbeck which was then Danish territory, in order to escape the censors; and usually he had actually to turn smuggler before he could get his books into Prussia and other of the German states. He had developed a most elaborate technique for the distribution of his forbidden volumes, and with the aid of the radical young booksellers scattered throughout Germany and Austria, he managed to elude the proscriptions of even the most reactionary state governments. Later his machinations became so flagrant that at one time a blanket ban was put upon *all* of his publications; and the ban was successfully enforced for several months. He was never free from surveillance, and his mail was often intercepted by the police. He had to maintain a whole system of counter-espionage, and lived daily in an atmosphere charged with danger and excitement.

But not out of high idealism did Julius Campe thus

devote himself to the publishing of radical literature. Rather it was out of a knowledge that such publishing could be made highly profitable. Campe was primarily a business man—moreover, a shrewd, sharp, successful business man. He was always more than a match for the authors with whom he dealt. He made a fortune out of Heine's works alone—but Heine himself would have starved to death had he depended solely on his royalties for a livelihood. Campe, who had few scruples in his dealings with the censors, had almost as few in his dealings with his authors. He made their reputations, but starved their bodies. He paid poorly, defrauded blandly, lied heatedly, and yet ever managed to play the injured one in any altercation. He was suave, cruel, crooked, and clever. But also he was an extraordinarily successful publisher.

3

IT was May before Heine's book finally appeared. "Travel Pictures" (*Reisebilder*) it was entitled, and it made an immediate impression. Five hundred copies were sold in Hamburg alone within the first month or two; and everywhere else in Germany it attracted attention. In large part this was due to the prose "Harz Journey" which it contained: that brilliant, impudent, irreverent narrative from which quotation has already been made here. Other writers—Brentano, Tieck, and Eichendorf, for example—had also satirized the accepted faith of junker Germany; but they had at least done it with an honoring fury and rancor. Heine, however, simply laughed uproariously. Apparently, he counted the ideas of the reactionaries merely funny. He refused to lose his temper over them. And thus he assailed them most devastatingly. He literally laughed them out of court.

The satiric strain ran also through many of the poems in the book. This Jew dared to laugh not only at the flatulent patriotism in the breast of the Germans, but also at the sentimental love which once had been in himself. He had a trick—it really seemed no more than that—of lifting the readers to the highest heavens of sentiment, and then of suddenly letting them drop into the lowest pits of realism. In poem after poem he caressed his readers until they melted with romantic love, and then suddenly froze them with a jet of icy cynicism. It was flagrantly against all the canons of decent Romanticist taste. To many good critics it seemed no less than unforgivable blasphemy. And the worst of it was that Heine did it consummately. None could deny the rascal was a master lyricist. There was a music in his simple diction, a beauty in his rhythm, a deftness in his rhymes, that made certain of his verses superlatively great. For instance:

"He's a king, this happy herd-boy,
    And his throne's the grassy down;
And the sun above his forehead
    Is his great and golden crown.

At his feet the sheep are lying,
Flattering courtiers, soft and sly;
And his cavaliers are cattle,
Stamping arrogantly by.

.   .   .   .

Like a minister, his watch-dog,
Governs with an open ear—
And his loud suspicious barking
Makes the very echoes fear.

Sleepily the young king mutters:
'Ah, to rule is hard and mean;
How I wish that I were home now
With my cozy little queen!' "

Not all of the poems were as delightful as that. Many were obviously inferior, and rang sourly, like carillon bells cast too hurriedly. But those which rang true were so magnificent that to improve on them seemed impossible. Indeed, though it was not realized at the time, with certain of the verses to be found in the "Travel Pictures," Heinrich Heine showed himself the greatest lyric poet that had ever lived in Germany, and —if we are to agree with Georg Brandes—the greatest that had ever lived on earth!

4

THE "Travel Pictures" shocked many readers and horrified many critics; but it did bring Heine a renown he never before had enjoyed. Even his rich relations in Hamburg were impressed by the fame which began to attach itself to the name of the poet, and they began to look to him almost with respect. And some of them may have been pleased with the unequivocal tribute to Therese which the book contained, for, although her name never once appeared in it, at least the immediate family knew it was to her that the poet referred when he sang of "Evelina."

The sudden change in the attitude of his relatives had its immediate effect on Heine. His gloom vanished, and life became all at once pleasant and promising. Success agreed with him: it reduced his conceit and gave him in its place a measure of self-confidence. In certain passages of the "Travel Pictures" he had laid about him with considerable freedom, avenging himself on more than one old enemy. In Hamburg itself there were several individuals to whom he had paid his merciless respects in the book. One he had described as a "Jewish *mauschel*," and another as "that Hamburg trader in cotton goods who still goes about unhanged." And the knowledge that he could thus poke fun in public at whomever else incurred his displeasure, brought Heine immense elation. It gave him a feeling of power, of importance. He was no longer a defenseless dreamer, an ineffectual poet whom one could treat with contempt. He was still thin, stoop-shouldered, and sickly; but it behooved one to beware of him now, to walk softly in his presence, and speak respectfully. For he had learned how to use Harlequin's whip. . . .

He actually began to like Hamburg now.   He was invited out into society, and was to be seen in the houses of the very élite of the local Jewry.   "A regular Christian I have become," he chuckled to Moser, "for I feast in the homes of rich Jews!"

Even the climate of the place seemed for once to agree with him.

> "Do not imagine I shall be leaving here soon—
> I am quite happy here.   This is the classic ground
> of my love.   Everything seems invested with magic;
> sleeping life has awakened in my breast; spring is
> come again in my heart. . . ."

Evidently his guttering hopes of winning Therese had flamed up anew.   He saw no reason now why either she or her father should consider him ineligible, and he thought it was but a matter of days before his dearest dream would be realized.

But his elation was short-lived.   He had overestimated the prestige which his new book had won him, and soon he suffered a most annoying humiliation.   Walking along the Burstah one day, Heine was suddenly attacked by a Jew who claimed he had been insulted in the "Travel Pictures."   Heine did not even know the man, and at once suspected the assault had been plotted by others.   He brought the fellow to court, but somehow, though the attack had been made in broad daylight, there was no one to testify against his assailant.   He had to drop the charge and nurse his injury in silence while the philistines of the town chuckled with glee.

Heine had also overestimated the favor which the "Travel Pictures" had won him in his uncle's household, and he soon discovered he was still counted a ne'er-do-well there. Once more the hope of winning Therese was shattered—this time forever. His headaches returned with a vengeance, and he felt he could stand Hamburg no longer. The city had again become hateful, intolerable. So he fled to Norderney.

Heine's bitterest pain arose from his loss of Therese. He could not forget her no matter how assiduously he now made love to every other girl he met. Years later he wrote that the only cure for women is more women; but the therapy was slow to work in this instance. At Cuxhaven, on his way to Norderney, he dallied full nine days merely in order to spend pleasant hours in the company of "the beautiful and lovely Jeannette Jacobson, whose married name is Goldschmidt." But when he reached Norderney he still had not forgotten Therese. He gambled recklessly, lost, won, and then lost again. He tramped furiously along the beach, or lolled about for hours in a fishing-smack; he flirted with one woman—"We said never a word—only one deep look, what time the moon made music—and as she passed I took her hand and felt her press mine stealthily" —and he made love to another; he debated for hours with a witty diplomat, took sea-baths regularly, quarreled with Hanoverian officers, listened to the fishermen tell wild yarns of the sea; he dreamed, worried, read, and wrote verses. But he was not happy. "I have thoughts of papier-maché," he wrote, "and feelings of cheese."

Still smarting from his humiliations in Hamburg, he was far less successful in Norderney society this season than the one previous. He suspected everybody around him of veiled hostility, and took umbrage at the slightest jest or shrug. His identity had been discovered; but Heine imagined he was being shunned by the noble summer-boarders not only because he had written the satirical "Travel Pictures," but even more because he was known now to be a Jew. In a fury he wrote to Moser:

"I long to say farewell to this German Fatherland of mine. The ineradicable Jew in me hounds me from the place."

In September he returned to the house of his parents in Lüneburg. The baths and clear air at Norderney had somewhat relieved his headaches; but he was still far from well. Yet, despite that, he felt "full of poetry." He settled down in the house of his parents and began to write with enormous industry. He had composed a number of poems while at Norderney, and he was now fashioning a brilliant prose frame for them. He was minded to publish a second volume of the "Travel Pictures"—"an extraordinary book which should make a great stir." It was to be far more daring in its satire than the first. "I am going to ply the scourge and shall ruin the book forever with the leaders of public opinion. But something of the sort is necessary." He felt in a mood of utter recklessness, and was ready to make public not merely his own radical views, but also to avow those of his friends. He actually wrote to several such friends to give him any ideas they might not care to publish under their own names. Quite frankly he told them:

"If you have any particular grudge, if you wish to see any matter expressed, or any of our friends lashed, then tell me of it, or better still, do you yourself write in my style the patches which I am to sew into my book, and you can rely implicitly on my discretion. I dare write anything now."

The reason for this recklessness he revealed to very few people. He planned to flee Germany! He was sick of the country, utterly tired of it. He felt he had never been accorded in it the honor he deserved, or the position his talents merited. He had failed to win a wife, and had been denied a professorship; the leading poets in the land had not deigned even to recognize him; the government frowned on his prose and the critics fumed at his poetry; he was despised by the Jews and rejected by the Christians; and his own relatives considered him a failure. Why then should he remain in Germany? Why cling to the Fatherland when it spurned him away? . . . It was not merely a petty irritation because of personal injuries that so embittered Heine against Germany; even more it was high resentment against the evil in the whole scheme of things there. Ever since his second term at Bonn there had been growing in him a profound loathing for the established order. No doubt his personal grievances against the order had aggravated that loathing. Certainly his own sufferings had helped to make him see how grievous were the sufferings of all the rest of the poor in the land. His *Judenschmertz* may even have been the very core of his *Weltschmertz*. But it could have been no more than the core. Heine's hatred of clerical, tory, junker Germany was not the puling soreness of a frustrated mediocrity. He was a man of superlative intelligence, and had he only cared to be "sensible" and "practical," he might quite easily have become one of the rich and accepted. No, his hatred of the established order was in essence the rich, strong, healthy resentment of a poetic soul bogged in a philistine world.

5

OUT of such a resentment was the second volume of the "Travel Pictures" created. The book seemed altogether inchoate—by turn lyrical, caustic, sentimental, blasphemous, gentle, impudent. But it was brilliant through and through. It was, as Wolff points out, a satire in the Latin sense of the term: that is, a work in which the author feels free to set down whatever he pleases, whether it be germane or no. If the book had any affinities at all, they were with the writings of Ariosto, for, like those writings, it chuckled from beginning to end with hidden malice. Immermann had contributed a few rhymed epigrams attacking a certain poet

named Platen; but save for that the whole work was
from the pen of Heine. It sang sadly of unrequited love,
laughed ironically at the clerics, rang ecstatically with
praise of Napoleon, and roared boisterously at the stupidity of the philistines. For its day it was quite recklessly radical. Here, for instance, is the way Heine
permitted himself to talk about the Church and the
aristocracy:

"If there be poison in me, it is only a counter-
poison for those snakes which lurk so menacingly
amid the shelter of old cathedrals and castles. . . ."

And this is the way he dared make sport of the government censors: he made the whole twelfth chapter of
the book consist of the following:

"Chapter XII

The German censors of the press . . . .
. . . .
. . . .
. . . .
. . . . blockheads . . . .
. . . .
. . . .
. . . . !"

The moment the book appeared it aroused a storm
of furious protest. Campe by a stratagem had managed
to slip the book under the noses of the Hamburg censors, and, advertised by its official suppression in Prus-

sia, Austria, Hanover, and other of the Germanic states, it sold wildly. The book really could have dispensed with such advertizing. To quote Moses Moser: "The government did not need to proscribe it; it would have been read anyway." The book was reviewed in most of the important journals, for despite its attacks on all that was sacrosanct in the land, despite its thrusts at the university, the church, and the government, despite even its praise of Napoleon, it was obviously too brilliant a book to be left unnoticed.

But Heine did not wait to see how the volume would be received. The day it was published he fled to England. He feared he might be arrested if he remained in Germany, and he had no great desire to play the martyr's part. As he himself said:

> "It is not anxiety that drives me away but the law of prudence, which counsels every man not to run any risk where there is naught to gain."

So with a few louis d'or from Campe, and an impressive letter of credit given to him by his uncle, he took the boat for London.

He approached England with inordinate expectations. For years he had thought of it as a land of freedom, progress, and intelligence—the very cradle of all he desired to see regnant in his own Fatherland. But he was immediately disappointed. London, with all its urge and noise, its "colossal uniformity, machine-like movement, its shrillness even of joy," terrified him. "A stone forest of houses, and in between the surging stream of living human faces, with all their wild passions, with all their horrible flurry of love and hunger and hate"— that was all he could see. "Send a philosopher to London," he cried; "but, on pain of your life, not a poet!"

He was not happy in England, though he did remain there over three months. His spirit was bewildered by the tempo of its life, and his body was racked by its wretched climate. His headaches became unendurable, and for a while deafness shut him up "as in a leaden coffin." He had no access to society, or to the literary world. His only associations were with the musician, Moscheles, one or two rich Jewish bankers to whom his uncle had given him letters of introduction, and the lodging-house keepers, gamblers, and street-walkers to whom he was recommended by his gold. He could not make more than chance and brief acquaintances because he spoke English with difficulty. "The devil take those people and their language!" he cried. "They snatch a dozen words of one syllable into their mouths, chew them, gnaw them, spit them out again—and call it talking!" Besides, he could not stomach the intense conservatism of the English; he was revolted by the common reverence for the Established Church and the Ruling Class. At Westminster Abbey his delight in seeing the honor done to England's poets was more than balanced by his regret that the collection of dead kings there "was not complete." Indeed, the more he studied the English, the better he thought of his own countrymen, the Germans.

"An Englishman," he observed, "loves Freedom as he loves his lawful wedded wife: he regards her as a possession, and though he may not treat her with especial tenderness, yet he knows how to defend her if need be. A Frenchman loves Freedom as he does his beloved bride: he will commit a thousand follies for her sake. But a German loves Freedom as he does his old grandmother. Yet one can never tell how things may turn out in the end. The grumpy Englishman, in an ill temper with his wife, is capable of some day putting a rope around her neck. The fickle Frenchman may become unfaithful to his adored one, and be seen fluttering about in the Palais Royal in pursuit of another. But the German will never quite abandon his old grandmother. He will always keep a nook by the chimney-corner for her, where she can tell fairy tales to the listening children. . . ."

Despite his disappointment, however, Heine was not miserable all of his time in London. His uncle had given him a letter of credit on the Rothschild banking house for four hundred pounds sterling, and though the poet had been expressly commanded *not* to cash it, but to use it merely to create an impression, he did cash it the moment he arrived. He had several small debts to pay off—one for five louis incurred at Norderney a year earlier, another for two louis incurred while a student in Göttingen, a third for one louis due actually since his Berlin days!—and these he wanted to settle while he had the chance. And because he knew that so vast a sum as four hundred pounds sterling would not soon again fall into his hands, he prudently sent a portion of it to Varnhagen to hold for him against a rainy day to come. With what was left he set out to study English life. For the most part, however, it was only the lower side of English life that he could investigate. His sharp, acquisitive mind managed to pick up much information touching the nation's politics, economics, and culture; but his sensual nature drove him to learn more of the nation's vice. "If I am able to leave England alive," he boasted in a letter to Moser, "it will not be the fault of the women. They do their best. . . ."

6

By July, however, he could stand London no longer. He was physically exhausted, and was beginning to run low in funds. He therefore went to Ramsgate, which then was a very elegant seaside resort. There he rested a while, carried on a flirtation or two, dreamed a little, and regained sufficient strength to be able to undertake the journey back to his homeland. In a sudden gust of courage, however, he did not go directly back to Hamburg. Having heard that certain Hanoverian officers he had known at Norderney had threatened to make short shrift of him if he ever dared to show his impudent face at the resort again, he forthwith presented himself there. He felt he owed it to his self-respect, for now he was rather ashamed of the cowardice he had shown in fleeing from Hamburg in the spring. But nothing violent occurred at Norderney. He was simply cut dead by society and left to find companionship among the natives. Even these seemed unfriendly toward him, perhaps because of the hostility of the summer-guests. So in a little while he moved to the island of Wangeroog, a dreary place which he could not stand for more than a fortnight. Finally, hounded by boredom, he returned to Hamburg.

But in Hamburg Uncle Salomon awaited him, and trouble began immediately. The millionaire was furious. He had not yet forgotten his nephew's rascality in cashing that "formal" letter of credit for four hundred pounds, and when the young man blandly presented himself at the counting-house, the banker could hardly contain himself. "You empty-headed idler," he shouted cholerically. "You are good for nothing except to squander money and—and write books!" Whereupon Heinrich, who all along had sat listening with an air of insolent mockery, quietly retorted: "But, my dear Uncle, did you really expect not to have to pay for the honor of bearing my name?"

That was the last straw. Salomon exploded, and Heine was almost driven from his presence. It seemed that the final break had come, and further help from the Maecenas was not to be looked for. But Heine did not let himself grieve. He felt he had suffered his uncle's churlishness long enough, and was glad he had at last been able to assert himself. Besides, he was in an extraordinarily independent position at the moment. He had given up all hope of ever winning Therese's hand, and he did not intend to set up as a lawyer in Hamburg. He was determined now to remain a writer, and, with the fame he had already gained, with his publishing connections, and, most of all, with the eight hundred thaler reserve he had cached with Varnhagen, he felt confident as to the future. He would be able to get along now. The devil take his stingy uncle! Heinrich Heine, already the most brilliant young writer in all Germany, would hardly be left to starve!

But the heady mood of confidence soon passed. He began to realize he must decide once and for all just what was to be the line of his writing. It could not be poetry, for somehow that seemed hardly large or firm enough a mold to contain the outpourings of his soul. He began to think poetry was no more than a "holy plaything," a fragile vase fit only to hold the gentle sighs of love-sick youth. No, he was a man now, and he felt it incumbent upon him to reveal himself as something more than a mere poet. He had to be a great political writer now, a "crusader for the Holy Ghost of Freedom." Almost from necessity he had to be that, for circumstances were driving him out of the sylvan glades of lyric poesy into the battle-grounds of polemic prose. The success of the "Travel Pictures" had thrust him out into the forefront of the radicals. Whether he liked it or no, he was now looked to as the David of the hosts of Liberalism. And, like David, he was expected to leave his lyre behind, and go forth with sling in hand to slay the Goliath of Reaction. He

was not altogether happy that this was so, for at heart
he was still a poet, a lover of beauty rather than reform,
an artist rather than missionary.   But the exigencies of
the hour were too strong for him.   He felt the time had
passed for idle minstrelsy, for rhymes and sweet-sound-
ing metaphors.   He had to forget the nightingale and
give ear to the eagle; he had to throw off the poet's velvet cape and buckle on steel armor.

But he could not desert the past without at least a
gracious gesture of farewell.   It occurred to him that
he ought to gather up the best of his songs and publish
them in one final definitive volume.   At present they
were scattered about like waifs, many of them lost in
old newspapers and almanacs, and the rest crushed between satiric essays or dolorous tragedies.   He felt he
ought to find a pleasant resting place for them, a home,
or at least a grave.   And therefore he now settled down
in Hamburg and began arranging a "Book of Songs."
He knew it would bring him little money, but he felt he
must produce it nevertheless.

He stayed in cheap lodgings somewhere in the town,
and rarely went out among people—chiefly because he
was not invited.   Rosa Maria Assing tells us in her diary:
"In our circle almost everyone is against Heine, and I
am alone in the joy and delight I take in his work."   His
only friends were a few bohemian characters, and even
with these he could not be thoroughly companionable,
for he was too sickly to take part in their carousals.
He was still tormented by headaches, and had to be
constantly careful not to strain his nerves.   August

Lewald, a young journalist whom he had met earlier
in the year, and who was perhaps his closest friend at
this time, reports:

> "Heine often slept at my place, and not only did
> the clock have to be removed from his bedroom,
> but even the one in the next room had to be stopped.
> Had that not been done, the ticking and the striking
> of the hours would have so affected him that the
> next morning he would have had the most dreadful
> headache."

Largely alone therefore, and altogether in misery,
Heine dragged out the days in Hamburg while his new
book went through the press.

The "Book of Songs" (*Buch der Lieder*) appeared in
October, 1827, from the press of Hoffmann and Campe.
Heine received but fifty louis d'or for his entire rights
in it, and probably counted himself fortunate. For at
first the book was not at all successful. It took ten years
to sell the first edition of five thousand copies, and almost
as long to sell the second. Only when a new generation
arose did the book attain real popularity, for with its
originality, its brave flaunting of the Romanticist tradition, with its realism and cynicism and wit and simple
beauty, it was too much for its own day. But when
that day passed, the book began to grow in favor as no
other lyric collection in the language. Great composers
set music to its words, and in one country after another
—even in Japan!—it was translated and read. Not
even Goethe's verses were as widely sung. Indeed, at

the present day the "Book of Songs" by Heinrich Heine is far and away the most popular collection of lyric poems in all the literature of the world!

7

BUT the young scapegrace who created that collection and got fifty louis d'or for it, could hardly live off its incalculable future success.   There he was in "that damned Hamburg," more notorious than famous, surrounded by more enemies than friends, poor and without position or prospects.   Obviously he had to bestir himself and discover some means of making a livelihood.   Further help from his uncle was not to be looked for, and adequate support from his publisher was likewise out of reason.   He had to find a job, some regular employment—and immediately.

It was not long before such employment was offered him.   Baron Cotta, a noted publisher with marked liberal tendencies, wanted Heine to become the associate editor of a new political journal in Munich.   The position was to be well paid and would not involve any arduous duties.   Really it was Heine's name more than his editorial services that Cotta desired for the projected *Politischen Annalen.*   The publisher had already engaged a trained journalist, a Dr. Lindner, to attend to the actual work involved in the bringing out of the journal; from Heine he asked little more than the prestige of his name and a regular contribution to each issue of the "Annals."   For these Cotta was ready to pay two thousand gold marks a year—a stupendously large sum considering the time and the circumstances. What was more, he was ready to give Heine free scope in his work and promised to print whatever he wrote—if the state censor sanctioned it.

Yet, in spite of the almost unbelievable attractiveness of the offer, Heine did not at once accept it. He was afraid of it, afraid just because it was so attractive. Intuitively he realized it was dangerous, for to accept the offer meant to declare himself a political essayist. It meant he would have to devote himself to propaganda, to leading in effect as well as in name the battle for liberalism in Germany. And this he was suddenly reluctant to do. He realized he was hardly equipped for the task. Actually he knew almost nothing about political economy, and, what was worse, he was but little interested in it. The whole subject seemed to him essentially trivial and boring. His radicalism did not grow out of scientific conviction but poetic passion. His desire to change the order of things was emotional, not intellectual. All he knew was that the world was not as it should be: that it was ugly and dark and close with the vapors of prejudice. He knew this because all his experiences in life had taught it to him. And therefore he had become one of the rebels. He had cried out for a revolution in the order of society because it was not an order into which a poet could fit. It was stolidly philistine, shunning beauty, distrusting light, and crushing all that was novel and daring. Besides, it was Christian. Consequently, not only the artist in him rebelled against the order, but also the ineradicable Jew. Merely to be a poet in Germany was trying enough; but to be a Jew in addition—that was beyond bearing.

It was inevitable, therefore, that Heine should hate the established order, and seek to change it. But just how to change it, and to what, he had never stopped to ask himself. He was, after all, a poet, not a political scientist. He had neither the will nor the capacity to work out a detailed and reasoned program for the future. All he could do was cry out for certain brave, generous, but essentially quite indefinite ideals like "Liberty," "Freedom," the "Divine Rights of Humanity." This limitation did not render him unworthy of a hearing— so long as he remained a poet. If he confined his revo- lutionary outbursts to verse, if he claimed for himself merely the rôle of prophet, then he was still within his rights. But to write in polemic prose, to set up as editor of an erudite political journal—that demanded in him more than just prophetic passion.

It may have been Heine's realization of this that held him from immediately accepting the associate editorship of the "Political Annals." But in the end he surren- dered. He was too poor, and too hungry for prestige, to be able to refuse the offer. He would not blind him- self, however, to the ironic absurdity of the whole affair.

"I am now the editor of the 'Political Annals,'" he wrote to Varnhagen, "and I am convinced that when donkeys foregather and wish to insult each other, they call one another men. . . . In the new

Bedlam in London I talked to a mad politician, who told me in confidence that God was a Russian spy. The fellow shall be the associate editor of my 'Political Annals'!"

———◆———

CHAPTER
SIX

"They do not know that all I ask in the world is a quiet room. . . ."

VI

It took the poet almost a month to travel from Hamburg to Munich. He protracted the journey from choice, making it almost a triumphal tour. First he went to Lüneburg to spend a few days with his parents. Probably they were the happiest days they had ever had together, for Heinrich was now no longer a ne'er-do-well rhymester, but actually an editor with an assured and impressively large salary. Those two broken old people who had been so eagerly ambitious for their son must have been proud of him at that moment. . . .

From Lüneburg he went to Göttingen, to strut a little before his former professors, and then to Cassel, to make the acquaintance of the historian, Jakob Grimm, and his brother, the artist, Ludwig. He was most hospitably received by these two famous men, and he seems to have impressed them favorably. Ludwig Grimm painted his portrait while he was there: a profile study which makes Heine look rather unconvincingly Byronic. Apparently they knew little of their visitor's history, for in a letter to their brother, Ferdinand, in Berlin, they later asked:

"Is it true that he is a Jew, or was one?" To which enquiry Ferdinand replied:

"Yes, Heine is still a real Jew, and as genial and witty as a Jew can be; but personally he is not very pleasant. His works, however, deserve reading. There is some excellent material in 'Ratcliff,' and in 'Almansor' the Christian religion is very finely ridiculed. Irony is especially his element."

From Cassel Heine moved on to Heidelberg, where his brother Max was studying medicine; but there his stay was spoiled by the police. At a little excursion into Wurttemberg which Max had arranged in honor of his famous brother, an official suddenly appeared, and, walking up to the poet, asked whether he had the honor of addressing the author of the "Travel Pictures." Heine was most pleasantly excited, for he naturally imagined the gentleman in the frock coat was about to compliment him on the book. But Heine's delight was short-lived, for instead of offering him compliments, the man gruffly declared him a prisoner in the name of the law, and forthwith escorted him across the border!

But Heine soon forgot this humiliating experience in the warmth of his reception at his next stopping-place, Frankfurt. There he made the acquaintance at last of Ludwig Börne, who now was no longer a mere theatrical critic, but the foremost political writer in Germany, and a veteran in the war for liberalism. Only twelve years had elapsed since the day when Heine, no more than a schoolboy at the time, had seen the great writer but had not dared go up to him. Yet now he already seemed Börne's equal. The two men had much in common, for both were Jews by birth and Christians by formal baptism. Both had suffered at the hands of the Jew-baiters, and both were full of rebellious passion. But there the likeness ended. Börne was not an artist, but essentially a missionary, a world-saver. Art for its own sake was a blasphemy to him; it had to be for the sake of the masses, or not at all. His radicalism, therefore, was not a mere poetic enthusiasm, but a very solemn, sober, dreadfully earnest conviction. Unlike Heine, he could not possibly poke fun at the stupid reactionaries, or laugh at them satirically. Born and reared in the horror of the Frankfurt ghetto, steeped all his life in the gall of Jewish sorrow, Börne was too embittered a person to be capable of laughter. He could not be a cynic; he was a fanatic. The white hot passion for justice which flamed up in Heine only sporadically, burned and burned in Börne continually.

In later years, when the contrast between the temperaments of the two men led to open conflict, Heine claimed it was because he himself was by nature a Hellene, and a spiritual descendant of Aristophanes, the Greek, while the other was a Nazarene, a descendant of Jesus, the Jew. But this was an overstatement. Heine had considerable of the Nazarene spirit himself. He, too, could be so moved at moments that the cynic laughter died on his bloodless lips and a roar of fury escaped him. He, too, could show himself on occasion a thorough Jew. But not often, nor for a long time. Always the scoffing imp retook possession of his being, and the thunderous frown gave way again to the sardonic smile. But not so with Börne: he was the stern Hebrew prophet perennially.

The profound difference between them was, however, not obvious to the two men when they met for this, the first time. On the contrary, they imagined themselves to be profoundly akin in spirit as well as outlook. Börne received the young poet with vast warmth and kindliness:

"He would not let me go," Heine wrote several years later. "With droll kindness he won from me a promise to give him three days of my life . . . and I had to go about the town with him and call on all sorts of friends, both men and women. . . . The three days passed in almost idyllic peacefulness. Up to the last moment of my stay at Frankfurt, Börne went about with me, watching me to see if he could show me some further affectionate consideration. . . . 'Beware of coming into collision with the parsons in Munich,' were the last words he whispered in my ear when I left. And as I rode away in the coupé of the stage-coach he stood watching me long and sadly, like an old sailor who has retired on shore and is filled with pity when he sees a youngster going to sea for the first time. . . ."

Thus ended Heine's visit to Frankfurt. He moved on thence to Stuttgart, to visit there another noted writer, Wolfgang Menzel. The newly-appointed editor of the "Political Annals" was eager to make as many personal contacts as possible with the outstanding liberals of the day, and Menzel, who had just published a most courageous attack on Goethe, was obviously one of these. The meeting was a gratifying one, and when Heine departed from Stuttgart in a day or two, he felt he had made one more faithful friend.

2

AND then at last the journey came to an end. Late in November Heine arrived in Munich to take up his duties as an editor. He was hardly thrilled by the city.

"Things here look as I had expected—very bad indeed. The people are afraid of its not pleasing me, and they do not know that all I ask in the world is a quiet room. I shall keep myself to myself and write much."

And he carried out his intention. He let Lindner, his associate editor, do all the work involved in the publication of the "Political Annals," and for his own part contributed only a regular article, and, just to manifest his interest, an occasional gratuitous complaint. His only concern as editor was that those who wrote for the journal should be well paid, and that their contributions should not be censored. With all other details he refused to interfere, for he felt he had other and more important work to do. "Do not be afraid," he assured Campe: "the third volume of the 'Travel Pictures' will not suffer, and my best hours shall be given to it."

What he wrote for the "Political Annals," and for the other Cotta publications, was patently hack-stuff. Even then it was far superior to most of the other material in the papers, for at its worst it was brilliantly phrased. But it lacked that forthrightness which had won for Heine his high position in liberal circles; it was discreet, mild, and often ambiguous. Heine showed excessive caution in expressing political opinions, qualifying his words so that they could not offend any save the most bigoted reactionaries. Obviously he was playing a part. He was trying to live down his reputation for radicalism and win the favor of the Bavarian Court. For he was not minded to remain an editor for long; he wanted to be a professor at the state university. A post of that sort, he imagined, would give him leisure to devote himself to his first love, poetry. It would assure him a steady income and yet not require him to fritter away his time and energies on pot-boiling journalism. Therefore he did all in his power to ingratiate himself with the King and his councillors. He took Baron Cotta into his confidence, and asked him to see to it that the King received copies of his earlier writings. "Please do not forget," he begged the publisher, "to take the three books with you when you go to the King. I should also be very glad if you would hint to him that their author is much gentler and better than he was when he wrote them.

I think the King is wise enough to judge the sword only by its sharpness, and not by the good or ill use to which it has been put." He did not consort much with the liberals in the city, but cultivated instead the society of the aristocrats. He was more than a little attracted to certain of the court ladies, and put himself out to win their favor.

When he cared, Heine could be delightfully ingratiating. Like most individuals who are not well-integrated socially, Heine possessed a multiplicity of personalities. To some people he could be the most genial and generous of good fellows, while to others he seemed only a bitter-tongued, conceited prig. Here in Munich, for instance, one person who met him—it happened to be none other than Robert Schumann, then a young student of music—was most favorably impressed by the poet. As he wrote:

"From what I had been told . . . I pictured a gloomy, misanthropic man who felt himself too exalted above mankind and life to wish to associate with anyone. But how different he was. . . . He approached me in a most cordial way . . . pressed my hand in friendship, and took me about Munich for hours. . . . About his mouth lay a bitter, ironic smile—but it was a smile only for the pettiness of life, and a scorn only for petty people. . . ."

Others were similarly impressed, for Heine's demeanor always reflected his circumstances, and in

Munich his circumstances were comparatively excellent. He made fast friends with a certain Baron Tjutschew, and paid especially assiduous court to an aristocratic lady, Gräfin Bothmer. And he shamelessly overpraised the verses of a certain influential statesman, Eduard von Schenk, who fancied himself a poet. Only in public, however, did Heine overpraise those lispings; in private he laughed at them hilariously.

Heine stooped even lower in his effort to advance his interests. He became friendly with a shady character named Wit von Dörring, a hireling of the Duke of Brunswick, the "Diamond Duke," who was perhaps the vilest ruler in all Germany at the time. Heine knew full well that von Dörring was an *agent provocateur*, and a spy —indeed, thoroughly "a bad case."

"Had I the power," Heine wrote to a friend, "I would have him hanged. But he has a personal amiability which often makes me forget his character. He always affords me vast entertainment, and I have been prompted to support him at times just because the rest of the world attacked him."

But the scoundrel's personal amiability was not the only reason why Heine befriended him. Von Dörring seems to have promised a Brunswick decoration to the editor in return for the privilege of having an article in praise of the "Diamond Duke" published in the "Political Annals." And the editor—he, Heinrich Heine, the scourge of aristocracy, the "Tribune of the People"— actually agreed to the bargain! To be able to appear among the aristocrats of Bavaria with a decoration of his own would add immensely to his prestige—and Heine realized he had to have prestige in order to get his coveted professorship. Not a "climber's" yearning for a trumpery honor drove Heine to conspire with von Dörring, but a poet's hunger for a chance to work in peace. So agonizing had the hunger become in the man that to allay it he was ready to stoop to anything—even to the betrayal of his trust as editor of Germany's foremost liberal journal. . . . And, to add the climacteric touch to the sordid episode, after betraying his trust, Heine did not even receive the decoration!

But he was not discouraged. Though von Dörring had failed him, other agents would not. So for weeks on end he fawned and intrigued, tugging pathetically at every wire he could lay hold of. And finally his objective seemed attained. By July the papers appointing him to a professorship had already been drawn up, and only awaited the royal signature. The King, Ludwig I, a man of culture and some liberalism, seemed quite favorably disposed toward the appointment. Everything was in order, and it seemed now only a question of days before all of Heine's difficulties would be ended. Indeed, so confident was he, that he threw up his job as editor of the "Political Annals" and went off for a rest. He was in very bad health by this time. The Munich climate had proved most deleterious, and he had suffered all the time he was in the city. Not merely had he had his old headaches, but in addition his lungs had begun to trouble him. Once he had even had a hemorrhage.

Fears of imminent death began to obsess him. In December, 1827, he wrote to Campe: "I am afraid of the fate of German writers—namely, early death. For seriously, I am very ill." And to another friend he declared: "This terrible weather here is ruining me. I haven't had a single hour of health."

Nor was it only the climate that affected Heine adversely. As he confessed in one letter:

"I am having delightful relations with women— but these hardly benefit my health."

By the following April he was in such a bad state that he wrote post-haste to Varnhagen for the eight hundred thaler he had cached with him in Berlin. Heine felt he dared remain no longer in the "blooming beer-Athens," and wanted to escape to Italy. But he had to postpone his departure until the middle of July, for not until then did his campaign for the professorship seem definitely successful. Once his mind was relieved on that score, however, he delayed not another moment. "Write to me 'poste-restante' in Florence," he begged his friend at court, Eduard von Schenk: "there let me read the happy lines."

3

THUS did he set out for Italy, almost blithe of spirit because his future seemed assured. He travelled slowly, stopping in the Tyrol, in Verona, Milan, Leghorn, and, for a long time, at Lucca. It was altogether an entrancing experience for him, for Italy with all its color and music, with all its glorious old ruins and even more glorious young women, was as a flood of nectar to his parched poetic soul. He had difficulties because of his ignorance of Italian; but these were not insuperable. As he wrote to von Schenk:

"Often I am not altogether without conversation. The stones here speak, and I understand their silent language. They seem to feel deeply what I am thinking. A broken column of the time of the Romans, a crumbling Lombard tower, or a weather-beaten Gothic pillar, understands me right well. . . . [And] there is, of course, one language which can be understood from Lapland to Japan . . . and this language flourishes especially in Italy. What use are words where such eyes cast their eloquent glances deep into the heart of a poor Tedesco? . . ."

All during the tour he wrote desultorily, chiefly of the scenery and of the people he met. At Lucca, where he rested several weeks, he took the baths, climbed the hills, flirted with the ladies, and wrote a great deal. He was in the highest spirits. As he wrote later:

"That was the most glorious time of my life: a time when, drunk with confidence and good fortune in love, I ran about on the peaks of the Apennines rejoicing; and I dreamed of great wild deeds whereby my fame would spread over the whole earth, even to the farthest isles!"

Even the news of Therese's marriage could not destroy his good humor. "I rejoiced in a measure over Therese's marriage," he was able to write to her father. "Next to myself I would have granted her to no one so willingly as to Dr. Halle." The whole of that particular letter was written in such a half-jocular vein. "Farewell," it ended, "my dear, good, magnanimous, stingy, noble, eternally beloved uncle!" Had Heine not felt so strong and independent at the moment he might have modified his tone a little in writing to the millionaire; but under the circumstances the poet saw no need for caution. He felt certain that the news of his appointment was already awaiting him in Florence. Why then should he fear to talk up bravely? . . .

But when at last he did reach Florence, lo, the expected letter was not there! Heine was not dismayed, however. He immediately leaped to the comforting conclusion that von Schenk had not known where to send the letter; and forthwith Heine wrote him anew. It was a most ingratiating letter, for it informed the statesman that Heine's new book was to be dedicated to him.

"Yes, dear Schenk, you shall have to give your honest name to this book: it is dedicated to you. But do not be afraid: it shall first be given to you to read, and it will contain many pleasant things, and most of it will be mild. I must give some public testimony of my feeling for you. You have deserved it of me: you are one of the few who were interested in assuring my position, and, as truly as

God helps me, I hope the King of Bavaria will some day thank you for it."

So he wrote; and then he sat down in Florence and waited. Two weeks passed; three, four, five! But still no answer. Heine could not understand what had happened. He was certain the appointment had been signed by the King—positive! Yet he could not make out why von Schenk failed to inform him of it. He tried to tell himself that von Schenk had merely delayed writing; that he had been indolent, as became even a bad poet, and had forgotten to send on the good news. So he wrote once more to von Schenk, and also to Cotta, to Baron von Tjutschew, and probably to other of his influential friends in Munich. "I *must* have the news as quickly as possible," he wrote to them frenziedly.

But still no news came. He could hardly sleep at night, so nervously eager was he for the morrow and for the chance that it might bring what he awaited. Again and again he rushed off hopefully to the post-office, only to be told each time that nothing had yet arrived for him. Another week passed, and Heine could stand the suspense no longer. His headaches returned, and a score of worries suddenly beset him. Most of all he began inexplicably to be concerned about his father. When Heine had last seen him, the old man had been in excellent health; and in the meantime there had been no report of a change. Yet for some unknown reason the son began to fear for him. He had a premonition that disaster threatened his father, and in a panic he at once packed up and started back toward Germany. Strangely enough, in Venice the poet found a letter from home confirming his sudden fears. His father, it declared, was desperately ill; he had had a stroke. So Heine, more frightened now than ever, pushed on all the faster toward his home. But when he arrived in Würzburg he learned it was already too late. Word had come there from Hamburg that his father was dead!

4

THE news almost destroyed him. Heine, for all that he had rarely manifested it, had loved his father intensely. He had known all of the man's weaknesses and foibles, had been keenly aware of his indolence and incapability in the world of affairs; but that had only heightened Heine's fondness for him. For just those defects had made the old man indulgent to the poet. The mother had always been too ambitious, too hungry for success, to be sympathetic with Heine's lack of practical sense. From his childhood she had tried to prod and push and drag him along over the one path which to her seemed golden. But his father, dear, vain, gentle, good-for-nothing that he was, had let him alone. He had, as far as we know, never plagued the boy for his unwillingness to do what the world deemed proper, had never nagged him for his indolence and wilfulness and passion for dreaming. And therefore even twenty-five years later the poet still lamented his loss.

"Of all men on this earth," he wrote, "my father was the most beloved to me. I never thought that I must one day lose him and even now I can hardly believe he is indeed lost to me. It is so hard to convince ourselves of the death of those whom we have greatly loved. . . . There has never been a night when my father has not been in my thoughts, and when I awake in the morning I often seem to hear the ringing sound of his voice like the echo of a dream. . . . Yes, yes, they talk of meeting again in transfiguration! What good would that do? I know him in his old brown overcoat and I shall see him again in it. He used to sit at the head of the table with salt-cellar and pepper-pot in front of him, one on the left, the other on the right; and if the salt-cellar were on the right and the pepper-pot on the left he would carefully change them around. . . ."

But the loss of his father was not the only blow. When Heine reached Hamburg, whither he had travelled post-haste to be with his widowed mother, he knew he had lost all chance of obtaining the professorship. At the last moment the King, either out of parsimony or fear of the clericals, had refused to sign the appointment. So now Heine was left stranded once more. He was ashamed to return to Munich and take up again his editorial position. He felt that the whole city must be laughing at him because, despite all his humiliating efforts, he had failed to receive the appointment. Nor

could he remain in Hamburg. Things in that hateful
city were now even worse than they had ever been before.
His mother was penniless and dependent entirely upon
Uncle Salomon's charity. She had even had to come to
the millionaire for money wherewith to give her dead
husband a burial. His brother Max was still a student,
and Gustav, who had tried his hand at one business after
another, had just gone bankrupt. His sister Lottie was
wretchedly mated to a stupid, gossipy, narrow-minded
man whom Heine could not endure. And Therese was a
married woman. . . . Heine had always hated Hamburg, and now that unhappy circumstance had dragged
him back, he refused to stay more than a week or two.
He went off to Berlin, hoping that among his old friends
there he would emerge from the gloom which darkened
his soul. But it was in vain. No matter how much he
tried, he could not shake off his dejection. He was continually ill-tempered and rancorous, and made no effort
to be pleasant to the people he met. In a letter written
by Fanny Hensel in the spring of 1829, we read:

> "Heine was here, and I do not like him at all.
> He is affected. If he would let himself go he would
> be the pleasantest naughty fellow that ever kicked
> over the traces. . . . But instead he is affected.
> He always talks about himself, and at the same
> time watches people to see if they are looking at
> him."

Even his most loyal friend, Rahel von Varnhagen, had
to chide him for his unpleasant manner, and so short

was his temper that he took offense at her words and for a long time refused to come to her house. He met many new young writers and artists, but could become intimate with no one of them. Full of fury at the world and pity for himself, he sulked in his own quarters most of the time—and wrote. But it was not poetry he essayed now. The hate in his heart was too vast for him to be able to find relief in so refined and delicate a medium as verse. He had to write in prose; in sharp, harsh, lacerating prose. "Poetry," he now declared, "has always been to me a consecrated instrument, a divine plaything, as it were. If ye would honor me, lay a sword rather than a wreath upon my coffin—for I was ever a fearless soldier in the war for the liberation of humanity!"

Heine was at work now on the third volume of his "Travel Pictures," and in his present mood the book could not but be savage. It began as a narrative of his trip through Northern Italy, but as it gradually took shape beneath his angry, jabbing pen, it became rather a diatribe. Fiercely he labored away at it all the winter of 1829 in Berlin, and all the following spring and summer at Potsdam. For the most part he kept away from people, especially at Potsdam. "I live here like Robinson Crusoe on my island," he wrote. "The boot-black is my man Friday." He could not endure the sight of people.

"For company I had only the statues in the gardens of Sansouci. I kept from all contact with the outer world, and if anyone so much as brushed against me in the street I felt an uneasy sensation. I had a profound horror of such encounters, a horror perhaps like that which the spirits of the dead feel when in their wandering by night they meet a living man."

By June he had completed a sketch entitled "A Journey from Munich to Genoa," and at once sent the manuscript to Cotta for publication in one of his periodicals. At the moment Heine was desperately in need of money, but he assured the publisher that unless the essay could be printed without expurgation, he would not sell it at any price. Cotta promised to respect the author's wishes and immediately sent him a remittance. But the essay was mutilated nevertheless. Cotta's editors hacked at it until it was made to mean either the opposite of what Heine had intended, or else nothing at all. When Heine saw what had been done to his work, he swore with rage. He vowed to himself that when that essay appeared in book form he would make it even more bluntly radical than in the original draft. For by now he was so ill and wretched and infuriated as to be utterly reckless. He felt that no matter what literary offenses he might commit, he could never be more bitterly persecuted than he was already.

5

HE remained in Potsdam until July when his new book was finished, and then he ran away to the coast.

He went to the island of Helgoland and found relief there from the headaches which had been plaguing him, and from the gloom which had been in him for months. "I am very well here and very cheerful," he wrote to Moser; "the sea is my affinitive element,. and the very sight of it works a cure for me." But he kept very much to himself. His only association for a while was with a Mr. Vogt, a melancholy person who finally shot himself there in Helgoland. After that, as Heine later confessed, he went with nobody save "one or two little English women, some sea-gulls, the clouds, and Tacitus."

He remained at Helgoland until the end of September, and then the imminent publication of his new book dragged him to Hamburg. He was afraid that unless he was there to watch the printing of the work, Campe might take advantage of his absence and make changes in the text. And this Heine would not have. He realized the book was written with rash daring and blasphemy, and was certain to arouse the bitterest antagonism; but he did not care. He was determined to vent his spleen without restraint, to be mordacious and savage to his heart's content. So he sat there in Hamburg and like a hawk he watched to see that no slightest deletion or change was made. And when at last, in December, the book appeared, he was elated. Word for word it was just as he had written it.

But Heine's elation did not last long. He quickly discovered that he had made a mistake, that this time he had gone too far. He had been in this book so venomous and obscene that even those who had until then upheld him, were forced to recoil. As for those who had all along disliked him—they literally raged. They called it the most vulgar, the most immoral, the most dangerous, the most seditious, the most atheistic, the most offensive book ever published by a German author. They were largely correct, too—though in fairness they might have added it was also perhaps the wittiest and the most entertaining book that had yet appeared. The volume was read, and discussed everywhere, and even in Paris, Vienna, and St. Petersburg echoes were to be heard of the scandal it caused in Germany.

What aroused the bitterest antagonism was the section entitled the "Baths of Lucca." The first part of the volume, the "Italian Sketches," though bristling with sallies and caustic witticisms, was saved by its superlative beauty. In this part the poet in Heine was still not entirely submerged, and certain bits of scenic description in it were ineluctably beautiful. Even its recurrent satirical slashes were not unforgivable, for they were obviously prompted by a broad and generous enthusiasm for humanity and its rights. For instance:

". . . renegades from freedom declare . . . that millions of men are born to be beasts of burden for a few thousand privileged nobles; but they will never convince us until they prove . . . that the former are born with saddles on their backs, and the latter with spurs on their heels. . . ."

"The sun of freedom will warm the world with a more thrilling joy than that which comes from

cold aristocratic stars. There will spring up a new
race, begotten in the embraces of free choice, and
not in the bed of compulsion or under the control
of clerical tax-gatherers; and with free birth there
will arise in mankind free thoughts and free feelings whereof we poor born slaves have no conception. . . ."

"The great instrument which ambitious and ava-
ricious princes were once wont to employ so effec-
tively, namely, Nationalism, with all its vanity and
hatred, is now rusty and worn-out. . . ."

"But what is the great question of the age? It
is Emancipation! Not merely the emancipation of
the Irish, the Greeks, the Frankfurt Jews, the West-
Indian Negroes, and other oppressed races, but the
emancipation of the whole world . . . which now
tears itself loose from the leading-strings of the
privileged class, the aristocracy."

But in the "Baths of Lucca," the middle section of
the book, there was little courageous heresy and no pity.
From beginning to end this was a spiteful and merciless
satire. Originally this section had been planned as a
long novel, but Heine, never able to accomplish a sustained piece of writing, had allowed it to fritter away
into a mere fragment of brilliant burlesque. Its main
characters were two Jews: one a loud, vulgar, baptized
millionaire from Hamburg who called himself the Mar-
quis Christophero de Gumpelino, and the other, his

impudent, rascally servant, Hirsch-Hyacinth. Both were apparently caricatures of individuals living in Hamburg, and in their person and through their words Heine set out to lampoon all he disliked in the people to which they and he himself belonged. He spoke of this people as "that very ancient world-family into which the blessed Lord Himself once married without fear of mésalliance." Of their noses he declared: "It may be they are a sort of uniform whereby Jehovah recognizes his old body-guards even when they have deserted." Of religion in general, Heine here declared: "A common man must have something stupid to make him happy." But Judaism, he made Hirsch-Hyacinth declare, is not a religion at all. "The mischief take the old Jewish religion! I don't wish it to my worst enemy! It brings nothing but abuse and disgrace. I tell you, it isn't a religion but a misfortune! . . ."

Thus Heine carried on through full ten chapters, twitting and laughing at his fellow-Israelites with almost no restraint. Only his fellow-Israelites, however, were angered by those ten chapters. The good Hamburg Jews were incensed, especially those rich baptized Hamburgers who suspected Gumpelino might be a caricature of themselves. But the eleventh chapter of the section infuriated also the Christians. Herein Heine sank to a personal vindictiveness which seemed inexcusable even to his most loyal followers. The victim was Count Platen, a poet of some talent who had been lampooned in the epigrams contributed by Immermann to the second volume of the "Travel Pictures." These epigrams

had evoked an angry retort from Platen in the form of
a play entitled "The Romantic Oedipus" (*Der romantische Oedipus*).   Evidently the poet had found out that
Immermann and not Heine had written the epigrams, for
he directed almost all the vituperation in his play at the
former.   But he did manage to aim a blow or two also
at Heine.   He did it chiefly by recalling Heine's Jewish
birth.   "The Pindar of the little tribe of Benjamin,"
Platen called him: "the majestic Petrarch of the Feast
of Booths," the "baptized Heine, the Pride of the Syna-
gogue," whose "kisses smell of garlic. . . ."

One cannot wonder that Heine lost his temper.
Platen had found out his sorest spot and had mercilessly rubbed in the salt.   The Christian nobleman had
attacked Heine not as a poet but as a Jew; and that
Heine could not forgive.   He had not sought to avenge
himself immediately, however.   He had waited until
Immermann had had a chance to strike back at Platen;
and only when Heine saw how clumsy was the counter-
assault, did he himself gird his loins.   But once he went
out to battle, he did not know when to stop.   He enjoyed
his own brilliant vindictiveness far too much to be able
to hold it within the bounds permitted even by the lax
canons of the day.   Campe, the publisher, begged Heine
to moderate his blows; but the author was adamant.   He
regarded the matter not as a "tourney in jest but a war
to the death"; and heatedly he declared: "I should be
a fool or a rogue, were I to give quarter."

The attack did not lack blunt aspersions on Platen's
talent as a poet, and quite frankly it declared, for in-

stance, that Platen would be immortal—*so long as he
lived*. But the assault achieved its greatest and least
honorable effectiveness not with open witticisms, but
with insinuations and nasty hints. Gossip had it that
Platen was a sexual pervert, and Heine managed again
and again to drag that bit of scandal into his essay with
the craftiest indirection. For instance: "as for winning
the willing love of Genius, it is beyond his [Platen's]
power; he must perseveringly run after this youth—as
after others—and his utmost ability is to catch the outward form." Or again: "The want of natural tones in
the poems of the Count is due to the fact that he lives
in an age when he dares not so much as name his real
feelings: the current morality is so directly opposed to
his love, that it forbids him even to give voice to his
sorrow." Or again: "Platen did not spare even Houwald, that kind soul, soft-hearted as a maiden. Ah,
perhaps it is just because of Houwald's gentle woman-
ishness that Platen hates him! . . ."

There were other such insinuating asides in the chapter, all of them sly and indirect and indefensibly vulgar. But Heine felt quite justified in daring to put them
into print. Since Platen had assailed him on personal
grounds, why should he, Heine, scruple to reply in
kind? Since Platen had based his attack chiefly on the
personal fact that Heine was not completely a Christian, why should not Heine base his counter-attack on
the even more personal fact that Platen was not completely a man? He fully realized, as he once wrote
in another connection, that as a Christian it was his

duty to love his enemies; but satirically he urged in his
defense that he was "only a young beginner in Christian love."   Actually he felt it was not so much his own
lack of Christian love that was to blame for the eleventh
chapter of the "Baths of Lucca," but the lack of it in
those around him.   Christian Germany was largely to
blame for the chapter, the Christian Germany that had
fretted and harried and badgered the Jewish Heine until
he had gone half-mad with hate.

Once the "Baths of Lucca" appeared, the aristocrats
and the clericals were in an uproar.   They bellowed
with impotent fury that the son of a Rhineland merchant, and of a Jew, should dare attack so viciously—
and, alas, so brilliantly!—one of noble estate.   Not
merely the junkers, however, but also the liberals were
revolted.   Heine was denounced on every side, and
hardly a critic in the country cared to raise his voice in
the poet's behalf.   Even tried old friends like Moses
Moser vehemently expressed their displeasure with the
book, and only Varnhagen felt its publication was jus-
tifiable.   Therefore it was to Varnhagen that Heine
almost tearfully unburdened himself.   In February,
1830, six or seven weeks after the publication of the
book, Heine wrote to this one friend:

"No one knows better than I that I have done
myself untold injury with the Platen chapter . . .
[and] that I have offended the better class of the
public.   But I feel also that with all my talents I
could not have done better, and that I *had* to make

an example of him. . . . When the clericals in Munich first attacked me and first flung the Jew in my face, I laughed—I thought it mere stupidity. But when I scented a systematic attack, when I saw how the absurd bogey was gradually growing into a menacing vampire, when I perceived the aim of Platen's satire, when I heard through the booksellers that similar productions steeped in the same poison were being passed around secretly in MSS. —then I girded my loins and struck as quickly as possible, and as lustily. Robert Gans, Michel Beer, and others, have always borne in Christian fashion, and have maintained a prudent silence when attacked as I have been. But I am different, and it is well. It is well when the wicked find an honest man who will fight recklessly and mercilessly to justify himself and those around him."

Thus did Heine write while all around him sounded the croakings and thunderings of hostility. He refused to beg forgiveness. He would not be cowed and admit he had erred. As he wrote to Immermann: "For three months I pondered over what I wanted to do, and then I did only what the most rigid necessity demanded."

6

THOSE were harrowing weeks for the poet. The dismal winter climate of Hamburg set his head racking with pain. He was not on the best terms with Salomon

Heine, his uncle; and he had begun to have difficulties with Julius Campe, his publisher. The Jews distrusted him because he had created Gumpelino, and the Christians hated him because he had almost destroyed Count Platen. He was surrounded by enemies, and had very few friends. At times he was greatly concerned about his personal safety, and always he worried because he was poor. Little wonder, therefore, if he could write on one occasion:

"Today, in order to remove myself in thought as far as possible from here, I wrote to my brother Max, who is a physician in Turkey—lucky fellow, he has only the plague to fight!"

When Heine had returned to Hamburg the previous September, it had been only in order to see the new volume of the "Travel Pictures" through the press. But now that his task was accomplished, he did not know where to go. He knew no place that would receive him, for the book had brought his name into disrepute everywhere. In January he asked Varnhagen whether it would be wise for him to return to Berlin; but apparently he was advised against it. So he remained on in Hamburg. He never actually settled down there, but always seemed on the point of flight.

Ludolf Wienbarg, one of his few friends in Hamburg, has left us an excellent picture of Heine's quarters at this time:

"I called on him early one morning and I was reminded of Goethe's bird of passage . . . an open trunk, linen strewn about, two or three volumes from a loan library, a couple of elegant canes . . . and [in the midst of all that] the little man himself . . . a red silk kerchief about his hair . . . one end of his gay mephistophelian dressing gown tossed over his shoulder like a Faust cape. . . . Although he had been breathing Hamburg air for several months, and was settled with a decent, middle-class family, he seemed to bear the mark of the traveller who got out of the stage just the day before and has spent a wretched night at the inn. . . ."

So did Heine live during those dragging, evil months of 1830. He kept very much to himself, shunning the salons of the city, and even walking the streets "with his arms crossed as though to fend off any casual contact." Occasionally he spent an afternoon or an evening in the company of a few bohemian acquaintances in the town: August Lewald and Ludolph Wienbarg, the writers; Baron von Maltitz, a radical journalist who had been expelled from Berlin; Peter Lyser, a deaf painter; Albert Methfessel, a second-rate musician; Professor Zimmermann, a sarcastic high-school teacher, and one or two others. But most of the time he went about alone. He wrote very little, for he was physically too ill and mentally too distraught to be able to concentrate. Instead he took to frequenting notorious beer-halls in the lower end of the town, seeking to forget his troubles in the shoddy revelry that obtained there. He still re-

frained from drinking; but he would not refrain from
the companion vices cultivated in such surroundings.
Desperately he tried to find solace in the low company
of the dance-halls. Night after night he went down to
Peter Ahrens' "balls," or to the public-house called *Zum
König von England*. Late in February he had another
hemorrhage of the lungs, and he was terrified by the
thought that he might be becoming a consumptive. He
fled from Hamburg, taking refuge in the woodland village of Wandsbeck not far away. And here he tried to
nurse himself back to health. He lived quite alone. As
he wrote to Varnhagen on April 5:

> "I've been speaking to none here save Thiers and
> the good God, reading the 'History of the Revolu-
> tion' of the one author, and the Bible of the other."

And slowly he recovered both in body and spirit.
His chief concern was the lack of funds; but even that
did not trouble him greatly, for he had begun to work
once more.

> "I have left the fleshpots and the she-fleshpots,
> the delights of theatres and balls, the good and bad
> society of Hamburg, with indifference and a light
> heart, and have brought myself to solitary study.
> . . . Great projects are whirling in my brain, and
> I hope that many of them will appear in public
> this year."

Three months in all he remained in seclusion in
Wandsbeck, and then he moved on to Helgoland to take

the sea-baths. There, in his "affinitive element," his
happiness was almost complete, and his whole being
was full of song. The Muse returned to him, taking
him to her bosom. He lost all interest in politics.

"I haven't brought a single book about the affairs of the day with me. My whole library consists of Paul Warnefried's 'History of the Lom-
bards,' the Bible, Homer, and some trash about
witches."

His old love, poetry, returned to him with a passion
he had not experienced in years. And dearly, desperately, he wished he might never be torn from it again.

"I am weary of political bickering, and long for
peace, at least for a condition of affairs in which I
can give myself freely to my own natural inclinations, to my dreamy way of living, to my imaginings and brooding thoughts. What irony of fate
that I, who am so fain to sleep on the pillow of
. . . silent contemplation, should be marked out to
whip my fellow-Germans out of their torpor. . . .
I, who most dearly love to occupy myself with
watching the flight of clouds, with devising the
magic of metrics, with listening to the secrets of
the elemental spirits, with losing myself in the
wonder-world of old tales. . . . *I* had to edit the
'Political Annals' . . . and had to pull the nose
of the poor, honest German Michel to rouse him
from his giant sleep!"

But, as Heine well knew, there was no escape. He was already enlisted in the army of liberalism, and there could be no discharge for him until its battle was won. Even were he actually able to draw a nightcap over his ears and join the "poor, honest German Michel" in slumber, he would never be able to find a place to rest his head. For, as he wrote, "every moment a policeman would come and shake me to find out if I were really asleep. . . ."

But though he knew full well how inexorable was his fate, he was full of bitter resentment nevertheless. "I am tired," he cried angrily; "I must have rest. Oh! if only I knew where to lay my head! . . ."

Thus did he complain from Helgoland because the harsh exigencies of life would not let him be a poet.

7

AND then of a sudden all his resentment left him. In a trice his whole spirit changed again, and politics, which a moment before had seemed but a pestiferous nuisance, now became again the dearest concern in life. It was all because a newspaper had reached him from the mainland, a journal bringing him the belated tidings that at last, at long last, the revolution had come. Not in Germany, of course; no, in France. But this made little difference at the moment. What alone seemed to matter was that the revolution *had* come.

"Lafayette, the tricolor, the Marseillaise!" Heine suddenly burst forth in ecstasy:

"Ah, gone is my yearning for rest. I know now what I will, what I shall, what I must do. . . . I am the Son of the Revolution and I again take up the charmed weapons upon which my mother has breathed her magic words of blessing. . . . Flowers! Flowers! I will crown my head with flowers for the fight unto death. And my lyre, give me my lyre that I may sing a battle-song. . . . Words like flaming stars that shoot from the heavens to burn palaces and illumine hovels . . . words like bright javelins, that go whizzing up to the seventh heaven and smite the pious hypocrites who have crept into the Holy of Holies. . . . I am all joy and song, all sword and flame!"

Thus did Heinrich Heine shout for joy when the news of the July Revolution of 1830 first came to his ears.

Almost immediately he set out for Hamburg. Wild rumors had reached him that the town had joined in the revolution, that the Marseillaise was to be heard in all its alley-ways, that the tricolor was flaunted everywhere there, on the mast-heads of the ships, in the docks, and on the bosoms of the fat ladies in the theatres. So, exultant, full of joy and mad hopefulness, he rushed back as fast as packet-boat and stage could carry him.

But when at last he reached the end of his journey, alas, no sign of revolt was to be seen. Stodgy old Hamburg had apparently not even heard that in Paris a new order had come into being. The "Three Days of July," which had overturned all France, had not im-

parted so much as a tremor to Germany. Not until
about a fortnight after his return did Heine see any
evidence of unrest in Hamburg, and then—irony of all
ironies!—it showed itself only in a series of riots
against the Jews. Mobs emerged from the slums of the
town, and yelling "Hep! Hep!" raucously, they took
to smashing windows in the Jewish quarter, and to beating and stoning every Jew they could lay hold of. Two
days the *Judenkrawall*, the Jew Riot, lasted before the
police could restore peace. And this was the only mani-
festation of the "holy revolution" in Hamburg! . . .

The sorry event must have sobered Heine with horrid
suddenness. It must have revealed to him, as it did to
other radical leaders, how foolish had been his hopes.
Utterly dejected by the failure of the revolution to
spread in their own land, Börne and many of his colleagues were already packing their bags and fleeing to
Paris. But Heine, for some reason, would not join the
hegira. For years he had yearned to go to Paris; but
now that he had a most valid excuse for the move, he
refused to take advantage of it. It may have been because the French capital was now not so alluring to him
as formerly. He had all along wanted to go to Paris
because he had thought that there, established in some
diplomatic sinecure, he might be able to devote himself to his poetry. But he knew that if he went to
Paris now, poetic interests would have no chance. He
would find himself in the midst of a fierce political
struggle, and willy-nilly he would have to take part in
it. Inevitably he would have to give himself up once

more to journalism, and the poet in him would be utterly crushed. Besides, he would be a foreigner in France, an alien compelled to speak in a language not his own. Germany, for all that it had never accepted him, was still his Fatherland; and German could not but remain his mother-tongue. It was well enough in a moment of excitement to grow ecstatic about a French revolution; but once the passion of the moment was passed, Heine knew he was before all else a German poet.

8

BUT even in Germany, far from the rioting and the sound of the Marseillaise, he could hardly be a poet unless he had leisure. And to acquire leisure he had to have an income. But in November he had quarrelled again with his Uncle Salomon, and now this source of income was closed. There was nothing left for him, therefore, but to go hunting for a position again.

"I must have an assured position," he wrote Varnhagen pleadingly, "for without it I can accomplish nothing. If I don't find one soon in Germany, I'll simply *have* to go to Paris."

He imagined he might even now obtain a professorship at Berlin or Vienna, and when Varnhagen finally dispelled this naïve idea, the poet actually tried to have himself appointed a City Councillor in Hamburg! He went so far as to ask Varnhagen and others to write letters to the Hamburg papers suggesting his name for the office! And when that absurd chance also was lost, Heine still did not give up all hope.

But then circumstances conspired to put a sudden end to the poet's delay. During all the autumn of 1830 he had not been idle in Hamburg. Day after day he had sat in his little room and had worked away at a new book, a supplement to his "Travel Pictures." In this book he had tried to give expression to his hopes for a new freedom in Germany. He had written without restraint, feeling that now he had less reason than ever to be circumspect. As he confided in a letter to Varnhagen:

"The book is deliberately one-sided. I know very well that the Revolution embraces every social interest, and that the aristocracy and the Church are not its only enemies. But I have purposely represented them as the only allied enemies, so as to consolidate the struggle."

The book was published by Campe in January of 1831, and almost immediately it was pounced upon by the police. It was officially proscribed in April and all copies on the shelves of the booksellers were confiscated. According to the chief of the Bureau of Censors (a man of seventy-eight years of age!) the volume was "blasphemous, indecent, subversive against the state, replete with *lèse majesté*," and in every other way unfit for circulation. And actually it was indeed far from a temperate document. To quote only one passage:

"Perhaps you are correct, and I am only a Don Quixote; and the reading of all manner of strange books has turned my head, even as that of La Mancha was turned. . . . [But] he desired to restore decaying chivalry, while I on the contrary, would utterly destroy all that is left over from those days. . . . My colleague regarded windmills as giants; I, however, see in the giants of the day only noisy windmills. . . . He took beggars' pot-houses for castles, ass-drivers for cavaliers, stable-girls for court ladies; but I take our castles for mere lodging-houses for blackguards, our knights for ass-drivers, and our court ladies for common wenches. And just as he mistook a puppet show for the deeds of a State, so do I regard our State-deeds as mere puppet-comedies. Yet just as bravely as the bold knight of La Mancha do I let drive into the wooden trash. . . ."

In such a tone much of the book was written, and it so incensed the state officials that even Campe, an old hand at conflict with the censors, was worried. Heine himself quite lost his nerve. For a long time he had feared something might happen. Since July the police had become more vigilant than ever, and were halting at nothing in their efforts to keep the revolution from spreading over into Germany. There was talk of arrest for all political insurgents, and threats of direst punishment for those who would not hold their peace. So far no person had yet been actually arrested for radicalism, but Heine could not feel certain that it might not happen in another day or two. Certainly if any radicals were arrested in Germany, he would be first among them—if he remained within reach. So, nervously, he began to think of flight. He did not leave at once, however, for apparently he had no money with which to get away. Not until he had swallowed his pride and had gone begging once more to Uncle Salomon, was he able to make his departure. He got the millionaire to give him some money at once, and with it a promise of an annual allowance of four thousand francs. And then he shook the dust of Hamburg from his feet.

It was late in April, 1831, when Heine left the hateful old town on the Elbe. His heart was not light. He realized he was going off into exile and that in exile the poet in him would have little chance to thrive. "A German poet," he lamented, "must live on German soil." But it was of no use to cry now—*he had to go*.

He halted for a week in Frankfurt, where he was fêted by the liberals as one of the martyrs for their cause. Then, on the first of May, he crossed the frontier into the land of his exile. And two days later he was in Paris.

THE EXILE IN FRANCE

CHAPTER
ONE

". . . when one fish in the sea asks an-other how he feels, the reply is, 'Like Heine in Paris!' . . ."

I

Ah, the sweet Parisian scent of politeness! How it refreshes my soul after all the tobacco smoke, sauerkraut smell, and rudeness it swallowed in Germany!" So cried Heine the moment he arrived. All the pangs of leave-taking from the Fatherland—and they had not been slight—were forgotten in the ecstasy of his first sight of the "Holy Soil of the Boulevards." Paris seemed veritably the New Jerusalem to the exiled poet, for he found there a freedom, a gayety, and a politeness such as he never had known before. Most of all it was the politeness of the Parisians that charmed him.

"Everybody was polite here. The men seemed all *so* courteous, and the lovely ladies all *so* amiable! If any man jostled me without at once begging my pardon, then I could have wagered he was a countryman of mine. If ever a pretty woman looked sourly, then I knew she had been eating sauerkraut, or could read Klopstock in the original. . . ."

It is not surprising that Heine should have been so profoundly impressed by the politeness of the French. His thirty-four years of life in Germany had hardly accustomed him to politeness. On the contrary, what with his Jewish birth, his caustic temperament, and his radical inclinations, he had known little save prejudice and insult all his days in the Fatherland.

But in France it was otherwise. Here he did not feel that every hand was against him; that he was persona non grata. His radicalism did not mark him off as an undesirable in this, Europe's wellspring of radicalism. Nor did his Jewishness brand him here, for France knew none of that savage anti-Semitism which was the curse of the German states. And therefore Heine was suddenly reft of much of his old sensitiveness. He could walk on the boulevards with an air of ease, of jauntiness, for he was confident that his slightly aquiline nose drew no hostile glances from the passersby. And life as a result became joyous, and all his world took on grace and comeliness.

"France looks like a garden where one picks the most beautiful flowers to bind them into a bouquet—and that bouquet is called Paris!"

Everything about the city seemed invested with a rare loveliness.

"I find everything so amusing, the sky is so blue, the air is so sweet, so generous; the beams of the sun dance hither and thither, touching with flaming kisses the cheeks of the fair Lutetia."

He felt almost at home here, at ease at last in what seemed to him a Zion. "If anyone asks you how I am," he wrote to a friend in Frankfurt, "tell him, 'Like a fish in water'"; or rather, tell people that when one fish in the sea asks another how he feels, the reply is, 'Like Heine in Paris!' . . ."

He made acquaintances rapidly. There were then living in the city a large number of German emigrés— about eighty thousand, it is reported—most of them artisans, clerks, and small shopkeepers. But there was also a cultured group enlarged from time to time by visiting artists and scholars, and Heine was received into it most cordially. Nor was it long before he was given entrance also into the French literary and artistic circles. Although none of his works had yet appeared in French, his reputation as a poet and a wit was already known in Paris. He became acquainted with Gautier, Dumas, George Sand, de Musset, Béranger, and other of the greatest writers of the day, and with Rossini, Berlioz, Liszt, and Chopin, among the great musicians. Moreover, a letter of introduction to the local Rothschild brought him into contact with the leading financiers, and through them with the noteworthy diplomats and statesmen. To be sure, those contacts were only slight, as we know from the fact that Heine's name is rarely if ever mentioned in the French memoirs, diaries, and letters of the period. But in Heine's own mind, and in his correspondence with his friends in Germany, he imagined himself altogether an intimate of the great ones of France. As he declared in one of his letters: "I am watching the history of the world with my eyes, and I consort familiarly with its mightiest heroes." Actually, however, he was rarely invited to the homes of those "mightiest heroes" during his first months in Paris, and his only association with them was at the more or less public functions.

2

BUT at least one interesting group of Frenchmen did receive him with great warmth the very day he arrived in Paris. These were the Saint-Simonians, the devotees of a new religio-political cult that had only recently sprung up in Paris. The movement was named after Claude-Henri de Rouvroy, Comte de Saint-Simon, a strange turbulent character who had been its founder. This man had sought to create a new religion for the world, one that might bring ease to man in the reigning turmoil. In essence his religion was a generous humanitarianism: it preached the equality of all men in a world ruled by artists and educated by scientists.

The religion had become widely known only after the death of Saint-Simon. It had first become publicly articulate during the July Revolution of 1830, and within a year thereafter its fame had spread throughout Europe. It won converts all over France, especially among the intellectuals who had discarded Christianity and who hungered for a new faith. And, significantly, not a few of the converts were Jews. That was but natural, for many Jews, particularly of the wealthier and more emancipated class, were spiritually homeless. They had drifted beyond recall from Judaism, and yet had not been able to find a haven in Christianity. Therefore to them this new religion came as a veritable godsend. Just as in our day a number of Jews clutch at every new cult that lifts its head—at Christian Science, Theosophy, Bahaism, Ethical Culture, and the like—so then they clutched at Saint-Simonism. Those Jews simply could not live without believing; but save for this new faith, they could find nothing in which to believe. Judaism seemed to them spiritless—a mere farrago of rites and observances lacking all passion and meaning. And Christianity seemed to them either beneath acceptance—or beyond it. How blessedly convenient, therefore, was this new cult of Saint-Simonism! With its services presided over by priests who were artists, it satisfied the yearning for mystery; with its preachments in favor of the oppressed and the persecuted, it satisfied the hunger for righteousness; and with its doctrine of the "rehabilitation of the flesh," it sanctified the appetite for pleasure. No wonder, then, that this cult proved attractive to the Jeshurun that had waxed fat by the Seine.

Heine had heard of Saint-Simonism while still in Hamburg, and it had immediately fired his imagination. One can well understand why. This religion was just what the poet had been seeking for years. It seemed to hold out to him all that he most desperately needed in life: a mighty faith that polarized all his efforts and dignified all his life. For Saint-Simonism was spiritual, aesthetic, and ethical; and yet not superstitious, tawdry, or puritanical. It preached freedom for all men; it declared that artists and scientists, not kings or princes, were the true aristocrats of the race; it declared for internationalism and world-peace; it scorned asceticism and exalted the pagan love of the flesh; above all it believed in the holiness of beauty. What more could Heine demand? Here was his new evangel; and he was not long in recognizing it. Indeed, one of the factors which most drew him to Paris in 1831 was the knowledge that there the new movement had its headquarters. This seems certain from a statement he made in a letter to Varnhagen on April 1 of that year.

"I dream every night that I am packing my box and going to Paris in order to . . . devote myself completely to the blessed emotions of my new religion, and perhaps to be consecrated as its priest."

And he did not dream in vain. He had not been in Paris twenty-four hours before he was already present at a Saint-Simonist meeting.

3

THE devotees of the cult made no secret of their pleasure at Heine's interest. They knew of his position in German literature and saw immediately that no better man could possibly be found to spread their doctrine on the other side of the Rhine. They said as much in print in their journal, declaring "a magnificent mission is reserved for Monsieur Heine."

But the poet seemed in no great haste to undertake any such mission, perhaps because he already saw that this new religion was not all he had imagined it to be. Its leader was a strange character named Prosper Enfantin, a fascinating personality, brilliant, prophetic, but perhaps just a little mad. And many of his followers seemed young men and women with decided hysterical tendencies. There was a vast amount of enthusiasm among them, but not much rational action. And Heine, who in certain directions was capable of exercising the shrewdest insight, must have seen this almost as soon as he came into direct contact with the movement.

Or he may have been reluctant to throw himself immediately into the work of the Saint-Simonians for another and quite different reason. Perhaps it was because he had not yet had his fill of the innumerable pleasures Paris held out for him. Here he was, thirty-four, eager, fairly attractive, and with pockets still not empty of money. There was therefore a great, great deal for him yet to enjoy in Paris before he settled down to work. There were still museums to visit, concerts to attend, and balls to go to. Above all, there were the boulevards to walk and the pretty women to eye. In Paris all the women, from the grandest ladies at the opera to the cheapest flower-girls on the streets, seemed pretty to Heine. At first he did not admire their figures so much, for he was used to the tall, broad-boned women of Germany, and by comparison the French girls all seemed slight and frail. But from the beginning he was held by the charm of the Parisiennes.

"I am their greatest admirer and I admire them for their faults even more than for their virtues. I know nothing more apt than the legend that Parisian women came into the world with every possible fault, but that a good fairy took pity on them, casting a spell on all their faults so that they became new attractions. That good fairy is Charm. . . ."

At first Heine, being a stranger, was far better acquainted with the girls on the boulevards than with the grand ladies in the salons. His favorite haunt was the Passage des Panoramas, a place one usually avoided in the evening if accompanied by a lady. There he was to be seen almost daily, sauntering up and down with his hands in his pockets, his head thrown back, and his short-sighted eyes staring eagerly through gold-rimmed glasses at the cocottes that minced their way there.

To us it may seem a paradox that a poet who was so sensitive to beauty, who could write with such exquisite delicacy about nightingales and flowers, could at the same time find joy in the company of those shoddy street girls. Perhaps the paradox can best be explained on the ground that Heine was emotionally not yet quite mature. He seems not yet to have outgrown the intense sexual instability of adolescence, for he ran from woman to woman with much the avidity and questing hopefulness one might expect in a mere boy. And, as far as

women were concerned, Heine was indeed no more than
a boy. He had not yet attained that poise, that confidence in his dealings with them which is the hall-mark
of maturity. This may have been because he had not
yet been able to live down the memory of his rejections
at the hands of Amalie and Therese. Or, more probably it may have been because from childhood he had
labored under an obsession of inferiority. Even as
a boy, it will be remembered, he was terrified in the
presence of the pretty daughter of the Düsseldorf judge,
and could feel at ease only in the company of a girl
of the people like Red Sefchen. And he was no more
courageous now, even though he was already thirty-
four and famous. He was still secretly awed by women
of the upper class. In the dark, privacy of his unconscious mind he still could not quiet the fear that
they counted him beneath them.

And only because he had to crush this subconscious
fear, did he resort to the cocottes of the Passage des
Panoramas. For those girls gave him confidence. The
ease with which they succumbed to him made him feel
strong and masterful—a veritable Don Juan. Of course,
had he dared pause to consider what sort of girls they
were, he would not have been so elated by his success
among them. But the poet in him restrained him from
ever growing realistic about them. Protectingly it
blinded him to their cheapness and venality, and made
him see them all as princesses graced with beauty and
pride. He was quite sincere when he wrote a few years
later:

"Even in my crazy youth I never knew a woman without being inflamed by her beauty, the physical revelation of God, or by the great passion which is just as divine because it frees us from all petty selfish feelings and demands the sacrifice of the vain possessions of life, even of life itself. . . ."

Heine was never a mere rake, never a mere satyrical rounder consorting with prostitutes to satisfy sheer lust. Had he been that, he could never have written of them as he did. He would have gratified his desire and then left; but instead he remained to write lyrics. This is the clearest proof that Heine, despite his four and thirty years, was no more than a boy among women. No grown man would ever have written lyrics to those Angéliques, Hortenses, Dianes, Seraphines, Maries, and Catherines, who infested the Paris boulevards. But Heinrich Heine did. During his first months in Paris he wrote very·many lyrics, and almost without exception they were inspired by street-girls. Yet none of these verses was lewd or vulgar. On the contrary, many of them were almost sentimentally chaste!

4

BUT after three months of boulevard life, Heine had to go off for a rest. His headaches had returned, and he needed the sea-air once more. In August, therefore, he moved to Boulogne. Evidently he was already none too flush in funds, for the room he occupied there was so small that when a friend called, Heine humorously suggested that he himself would leave the room so the other might be able to enter! The poet remained at Boulogne two months, writing desultorily, and trying to live as quietly as possible. Late in September he returned to Paris.

One of the first persons he met after his return was Ludwig Börne, whom he had not seen since his brief visit in Frankfurt, four years earlier. The reunion was fraught with great significance, for it marked the beginning of an association destined to disturb the lives of both the men from then on. At first the relations between them seemed to be altogether pleasant. Heine, in the book he later wrote on Börne, described the first meeting as follows:

"The little flesh I had formerly noticed on his body had altogether disappeared, perhaps melted by the rays of the July sun which, alas, had also penetrated to his brain. Sparks flashed from his eyes. He sat, or rather he lived, in a great dressing-gown of bright silk like a tortoise in its shell, and when he thrust out his skinny little head I had an uncanny feeling. But pity gained in me. . . . There was a certain quavering sickliness in his voice, and on his cheeks was the hectic flush of consumption. The sharp distrust in his every feature and movement was perhaps a result of the hardness of hearing from which he had long suffered, and which had steadily increased until conversation with him was quite difficult.

" 'Welcome to Paris,' he cried; 'this is good! I am sure that all the good men, those who have the best intentions, will soon be here. This is the convention of the patriots of all Europe!' "

So did Heine describe the meeting. But Börne's account of it, given in a letter written the next day to his friend, Frau Wohl, hardly tallies with Heine's. Börne wrote:

"Yesterday morning a young man came in, rushed up to me happily, laughed, and gave me both hands—it was Heine. He had been back from Boulogne a week, and immediately blurted out: 'I was ill and fell in love with an English woman,' etc., etc. . . . I don't like this Heine . . . he has no soul. . . ."

Börne did not, however, at once reveal to the younger man how he felt. For weeks he continued to meet Heine frequently, yet he gave no outward sign of his displeasure with the poet. The two of them would often dine with a group of other artists, among them Meyerbeer, Lewald, and Liszt, at Pestel's, Périgords, the Palais Royal, or some other restaurant; and there they would enter into lengthy discussions of the political questions of the day. It was in the course of these discussions that the profound differences between Börne and Heine first began to reveal themselves. Börne, as we have already seen, was by nature a puri-

tan and a fanatic, while Heine was inclined to be a
Pagan and a cynic. And this temperamental difference
gave them two entirely different attitudes toward the
whole problem of political change. At heart Heine
was not at all a republican. Much as he hated the
aristocrats, he distrusted the mob even more. As August Clemens once commented shrewdly:

"Heine with his fine pale face, his delicate
hands, his aristocratic manner, was always a republican only in words; at heart he was the most exclusive aristocrat."

Börne dressed very plainly, and regularly kept company with the radical German artisans who gathered
in smoke-filled halls in the poorer sections of Paris
and vehemently harangued about political events in
their Fatherland. But Heine kept aloof from all such
gatherings; he felt he did not belong in them. He did
not like to fraternize with the sweaty workers, and refused to address them as his "comrades." He liked to
dress quite elegantly, usually in black, which was then
extremely distingué. He always wore kid gloves, and
often he was to be seen holding a rose delicately between
the fingers of his left hand. The only reformers with
whom he cared at all to associate were the salon-radi-
cals who belonged to the Saint-Simonian movement;
and even with these he associated but little. He still
preferred to take life lightly, wandering from café to
café with his familiar smile habitually curling his lip
and an epigram always ready on his tongue. It was not

long before his genius as a wit was known in most of the fashionable salons, and in time his epigrams came to be quoted throughout Paris. People began to recognize his short, frail figure and flowing blonde locks, and pointed him out to each other. Philibert Audebrand, a young French writer, tells how one day, when he was walking with Dr. Heller, a member of the Academy of Medicine, past Frascati's restaurant, the latter stopped suddenly and whispered: "One moment—I want to show you the wittiest man in Europe!" And then he pointed out Heinrich Heine.

The poet well deserved his reputation. Not since the time of Voltaire had Paris seen a man who could point so truly or strike so destructively with the rapier of wit. Already there were a number of men in the capital who bore the scars of epigrams dealt them by Heine; and as the years passed, the number of the wounded rapidly increased. The philologist, Léon Halévy, brother of the celebrated composer, could never get over it that Heine once said of him: "He is as boring as if his brother had composed him." Nor could the Danish dramatist, Oehlenschläger, ever forget how once, after he had spent a whole evening reading one of his own tragedies aloud in his best German, Heine's only comment was: "I never would have dreamed I could understand Danish so well!" Of Moritz Hartmann, the poet, Heine had said: "He is a very handsome fellow, and all the ladies are in love with him—with the exception of the Muses!" And of some other illustrious contemporary Heine had once said: "It is too funny! He acts as

though he considered himself a Jupiter hurling light-
nings—and he can hardly strike a match with his
flashes!"

It was rarely with malice that the young German uttered such mordant witticisms, for he would aim them
at his closest friends, or at himself, as readily as at his
enemies. That was why many of his more sensitive
friends stood in continual terror of him, and some allowed themselves to be virtually blackmailed to prevent
his becoming humorous at their expense. Meyerbeer,
for instance, "proceeded as warily with Heine as a dog
with a lion," according to Börne's report. And if we
are to believe Franz Grillparzer, the great Rothschild
himself was afraid of Heine whenever he invited the
poet to dine at his home. Probably that was why Heine
was never unreservedly popular in Parisian society:
people liked to quote him but they dreaded to have him
present in person. This brilliant, sarcastic little German cared nothing for politeness. No matter who suffered, he could not forego the slightest chance to be
brilliantly epigrammatic.

Most of his leisure hours were therefore spent on the
boulevards and quays. In the memoirs of Philarète
Chasles, we find a reference to Heine which reveals the
manner in which the poet may have spent a good deal
of his time.

"Opposite the Pavillon Marsan," says Chasles,
"I saw a little blonde man leaning on the rampart of
the quay and holding his dripping hat in his hand

while he watched the passers-by in the storm. The cloud parted; a ray of sunlight fell on his flowing hair, and illumined his highly distinctive face . . . he kept on raptly observing the people. . . . But were not all extraordinary men observers of people in the market-places and on the street?"

Heine did not, however, always wander about alone on the streets. There is ample testimony to the fact that he still paid assiduous court to the Phrynes of the boulevards, squandering on them not alone his time but also his money and his strength. Probably he did not consort with them nearly so frequently as he himself tried to make people believe. His worst weakness was for boasting. He proclaimed his gallantry even in verse. For example:

"It makes a man feel happy,
    It drains him to the dregs,
When he has three fair sweethearts
    And just one pair of legs.

I visit the first in the morning;
    I seek the second at night;
The third does not wait but comes to me
    At noon in a blaze of light.

Farewell, my three fair sweethearts,
    Two legs are all I've got;
I'll go and make love to Nature
    In some more quiet spot."

But Heine boasted of his libertinism in conversation far more than in verse. This was one of Börne's chief complaints against him. Börne's mettle can be judged from the fact that for more than twenty years he lived on terms of the most intimate friendship with a young widow, Frau Wohl, and yet never became her lover. She lived in Frankfurt, and when Börne fled to Paris he wrote to her almost daily. In those letters he spoke of Heine frequently, and always in dispraise. On one occasion, for instance, he declares:

"Heine has no soul. Nothing is sacred to him— he loves only the beautiful element in truth. . . . He is said to be immoral in a very low way. . . a German told me that Heine said to him he could actually be bought over by Metternich, but only if offered all the girls of Paris (I say girls, but he used a much more vulgar expression). Heine is a kind of sensualist I have never met with in books or in real life, and that I cannot explain psychologically. One often finds ordinary sensuality, but seldom does a young man speak so openly of his low dissipations, as though they were something beautiful."

In another letter, Börne writes:

"Heine is worthy of pity, but I think he should be held to account for his health, which he ruins daily by his dissipation. . . . He has brought upon himself a condition which will entirely destroy his nerves, so that this clever person may in the end become stupid, yes, mad—if he is not fortunate enough to die early. He is so exhausted—and this is the expression he himself uses—that at nine o'clock at night he cannot carry on the slightest conversation and has to go to bed."

In still another letter, Börne declares that Heine

"looked torn, played out, colorless, like a woman's old frayed silk skirt, gloomy, downcast, melancholy. When he left me in the street I watched him for a while and he seemed to me like a withered leaf that the wind sweeps along until finally, grown heavy with filth, it remains on the ground and becomes in the end filth itself."

One cannot trust Börne in these reflections on Heine. The patriot was by inborn nature a man who took life and his work sternly and soberly. He was, therefore, totally incapable of understanding an incorrigible *enfant terrible* like Heine. He took the young man seriously, and actually believed all his Rabelaisian tales. He could not realize that had Heine really been a rake and a profligate, he would never have gone to such pains to boast of it. Börne's was a direct and simple mind; he saw what he was shown, and, seeing it, he either approved or disapproved. In the case of Heine he disapproved most severely. Years later Heine declared that this disapproval was due to sheer envy on the part of Börne; but that was only partly just. Undoubtedly there was a measure of envy in Börne; but more than that there was chagrin. Börne, being a missionary by ineradicable instinct, was positively chagrined that Heine should be so lax in his radicalism. For Heine did not merely keep aloof from the revolutionary activities among the working-men in Paris; he failed now to carry on any radical propaganda even through his press letters to Germany. Heine had arranged with his old friend, Baron Cotta, to write regular letters from Paris for the *Allgemeine Zeitung* in Augsburg; but at least during the first year his reports were confined almost entirely to matters of art. These articles, later collected in a series entitled "The Salon," exercised considerable influence in Germany—but only on the cultural, not the political developments. Heine was the first to send the news across the Rhine of the new departures in painting and music which just then were emerging in France; and the younger German artists learned to look to him almost as to an oracle. Actually Heine had very little equipment as a critic of the arts. Line, color, tone, phrasing, harmony—these things meant little or nothing to him. He was interested only in the possible meaning, the message, the moral point, in every canvas or score he looked at. Essentially he had the preacher's, not the aesthete's interest in art. Ferdinand Hiller, the composer, wrote in one of his letters:

"Heine understood nothing about music theoretically or practically; and yet, because of his imaginative and penetrating mind, he divined more

in music than many so-called musical people. . . .
I don't believe it ever occurred to him to have me
play for him. Music did not interest him greatly,
although he wrote some clever and truthful as well
as very humorous things about it."

Nevertheless Heine's reports were taken quite seriously in Germany, perhaps more because of their
style than their contents. Heine had indubitable genius
as a journalist. No matter how little he knew about
a subject, he yet could write on it brilliantly and even
convincingly. It was because he always sought to be
lucid and simple in his language, and because he wrote
with the most painstaking care. It is illuminating to
examine the manuscripts of his articles, and to see how
scratched and erased and interlined they are. Heine
wrote with fierce labor and pain, draughting and re-
draughting his reports until he knew them almost by
heart before he dispatched them. The musician just
quoted, Ferdinand Hiller, declares in another of his
letters:

"One day I found him [Heine] working at his
desk, and I glanced inquisitively at the papers before him. There was scarcely a line that had not
been crossed out and another substituted. He saw
my astonishment and said ironically: 'And then they
talk of inspiration, exaltation, and the like! I
work like a goldsmith when he finishes a chain—
link by link, one after another, one within another.'"

5

BUT the time came when Heine ceased to talk exclusively of art and music in his reports to the *Allgemeine Zeitung*. It was inevitable under the circumstances that sooner or later he should be drawn back into the discussion of politics, for in Paris he was, as he himself declared, "drowned in the vortex of events." But in his political writings now he studiously endeavored to appear moderate, and at times he purposely lapsed into ambiguity and evasiveness. This was chiefly because he feared the shears of the German censors. Heine wrote his articles with tremendous care for their literary quality, and he dreaded to have them mutilated by the stupid government officials. He was willing, therefore, to make any reasonable compromise in order that his letters might appear precisely as he wrote them. For even in these hack reports Heine was an artist first and a propagandist second. Therefore, he begged Cotta:

"Please see to it that very little is changed in my articles, for they are already censored when they come out of my head."

But this moderation in Heine's writings infuriated Börne and the other German radicals living in Paris. They began to suspect the poet of treachery, and they even spread the rumor that he was in the pay of the reactionaries. By the end of the winter Heine found

himself surrounded by more enemies than he had ever
had in all his life before. First there were the agents
of Prussia and Austria watching him at every turn.
Regular reports were sent to Berlin and Vienna telling
of all his activities, and often these reports came from
men whom Heine thought to be his best friends. But
far more irritating and menacing than the government
spies were the fanatical radicals in Börne's camp.
These so plagued Heine that in May, 1832, he was
moved to cry out to Varnhagen:

> "I need your sympathy now just as much as at
> the beginning of my career, for I am just as much
> alone in the world as then. The only difference is
> that now I have more enemies—which is, of course,
> a consolation, but hardly sufficient a one."

An open break had come in the relations between
Heine and Börne by this time. To the credit of the
poet be it said that after the break he anxiously endeavored to avoid the older man. But the latter would
not be avoided. With that nagging quality which is
perhaps characteristic of the world-saving zealot, he
persistently followed Heine from place to place, and
continually tried to involve him in argument. Heine
was, of course, more than a match for the older man
in repartee; but neverthelss he disliked to meet him.
Word-battles with a fanatic like Börne only irritated
Heine, for they usually forced him to take up positions which he could not whole-heartedly defend. They
tended to edge him into the camp of the aristocrats, and

that infuriated him, for he was, after all, still an enemy of the aristocracy. So he preferred to keep away from the radical leader.

It was a wretched situation for Heine. Dearly he wished he might be left alone to dream his dreams and sing his songs undisturbed by the intrigues of the police and the revolutionists. But it was not to be. Here in Paris, in the very maelstrom of the revolution, he could not possibly keep himself out of the furious swirl. He had known before he ever came to Paris that this would happen; but *la force des choses* had been too strong for him. As he wrote to Varnhagen:

> "I foresaw all this six months ago, and would fain have retired into poetry at that time and left to others the rough and tumble of battle—but it could not be. . . ."

It was the general opinion among the Börne radicals that Heine's reluctance to take part in their war was due entirely to cowardice. They could not attribute his attitude to anything else because most of them were at bottom rather small-souled, narrow-minded individuals. They were typical radicals, and therefore— like typical conservatives or typical reactionaries—they were mentally and spiritually of ungenerous calibre. They had their grievances against the established order, and they knew that Heine shared them. Therefore they expected him to join in the bloody struggle to satisfy them. They could not imagine he might have what he considered a higher and greater task to fulfill. Not

even Börne, their leader, had sufficient breadth of imagination for that.   Only the greatest of the next generation of radicals, men like Karl Marx and Friedrich
Engels and Ferdinand Lassalle, were capable of understanding Heine.   These three came to know him well
in later years, and they all learned to admire and love
the incorrigible non-conformist.   They realized that he
was, as Marx once put it, "that queer fowl, a poet,"
and was not to be measured by ordinary rules.   They
saw in Heine that most tragi-comic of all created things:
a spirit so torn from every mooring that it impinged
everywhere, yet belonged nowhere.   But the Börne group
had no such understanding of the man.

6

IT must be admitted that Heine on several occasions
did flee from danger; but in each case it may well have
been not out of essential cowardice so much as discretion.   Heine may well have been a little mad; but he
was no fool.   That he was quite capable of courageous
action he proved the year after he came to Paris.
In March, 1832, at the height of the annual carnival, a
dreadful epidemic of cholera broke out in the capital.
Spring had just come to the city, and while the sun shone
gaily all over, the people died by the scores and hundreds.   As Heine wrote: "The trees grow green and the
people grow blue."   In one day two thousand men and
women fell mortal victims of the scourge, and panic
swept through the whole city.   All those who could possibly afford to flee the place, did so.

"Most of the foreigners, especially my fellow-countrymen, left at once. Obedient parents had received orders from their children to come home as quickly as possible. God-fearing sons fulfilled at once the tender prayers of their dear parents who wished them to return home; 'Honor thy father and thy mother that thy days may be long upon the earth!' In others there awoke an infinite longing for the dear Fatherland . . . for the land of devout love and faithful women and pleasant songs —and a more healthy air. It is said that more than one hundred and twenty thousand passes were issued at the Town Hall. . . ."

But Heine himself would not leave. He remained on in Paris despite all the horror and danger solely because his cousin, Karl Heine, a brother of Amalie and Therese, lay there stricken with the plague. We have this not on Heine's own word, which might be questioned, but on the word of a most trustworthy witness, August Lewald.

"Heine is capable of any sacrifice for his friends," Lewald declared. "When the cholera was raging everywhere in Paris . . . and all his friends fled and begged him to flee with them, he remained behind to nurse a sick cousin. He told me he considered it a sacred duty to preserve this son of his Uncle Salomon, who already had had to mourn the loss of several children who died abroad."

What is most striking in this connection is that Heine in his own writings imputed no such heroism to his conduct. To Varnhagen he declared he had not left Paris during the scourge because he had been too lazy to run away. And to Cotta he wrote that he had remained behind because he had thought it his duty to be on the scene in the event that there should be anything important to report for the *Allgemeine Zeitung*.

Both reasons were patently flimsy. Apparently Heine, who was forever boasting of intentions which he had never really entertained, or of feats which he had never even remotely accomplished, was overcome with modesty when he actually did have something upon which to preen himself. It is impossible to believe that Heine could have remained in Paris merely out of laziness or a sense of duty to the *Allgemeine Zeitung*. One needs only to read Heine's descriptions of the epidemic to realize it must have been an inordinately profound obligation that alone could have kept him in the stricken city.

"It was very disturbing to hear too clearly the sound of Death sharpening his scythe. . . . It was a fearful time, far more horrible than that earlier time when executions took place so quickly and so secretly. A masked hangman with an invisible guillotine drove about Paris. 'One after another we are put into the sack,' groaned my servant every morning, as he told me of the number of the dead or of the death of a friend. The phrase 'put into

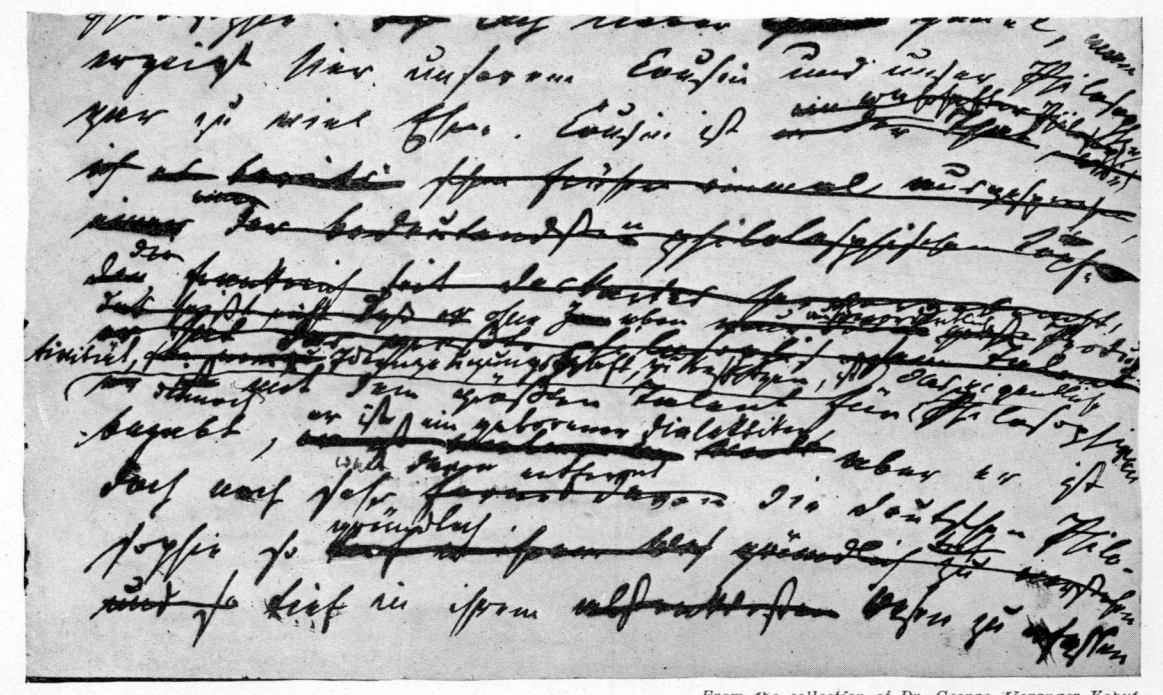

A fragment of original Mss. of the "French Affairs."

the sack' was no figure of speech. Coffins soon
gave out and the majority of the dead were buried in sacks. . . . They were piled high one on
the other in the halls of the public buildings, hundreds of white sacks each containing a corpse.
. . . The only voices one could hear . . . were
those of the guards counting the sacks to the grave-
diggers with gruesome indifference, and in muffled
tones recounting them as they loaded the carts.
Sometimes they complained harshly because they
had been given a sack too few! . . . I remember
two little boys who stood by me with sad faces,
and how one of them asked me if I could tell him
in which sack his father was! . . ."

But at last the epidemic came to an end and Paris
again became the capital of joy. Karl Heine recovered and returned to Hamburg, and Heinrich was left
once more to his own devices. But now he was considerably sobered. He had had his fling, and now he was
ready for work. One cannot doubt that had his money
held out he might have still protracted the bout of
pleasure-seeking which the epidemic had interrupted.
But as he confessed in a letter to a friend: "I need six
times as much money to live in Paris as ever I needed
in Germany"—and, therefore, "I have to be more industrious than ever before."

THE EXILE IN FRANCE

———————◆———————

CHAPTER
TWO

*"I do not belong to the atheists who deny
—I affirm. . . . The beginning and end
of all things is in God!"* . . .

II

HEINE lived at this time on the second floor of a large house in one of the poorer sections of Paris. He was attracted to the place because it was inexpensive, quiet, and because the windows of his room looked out on a grass-covered court. Heine loved clamor and excitement—when he was out for pleasure. But when at work he needed absolute stillness. He was, as has already been noted, peculiarly sensitive to sounds, and the least disturbance so jangled his nerves that it was quite impossible for him to do his writing. In this dwelling, however, he had the stillness he required for work. His only companion was an ugly Moor who brought him his tea and brioche in the morning, and made the bed when he arose. The place was too far from the centre of the town for visitors to happen by, and therefore the poet was able to work uninterruptedly for hours on end.

Unhappily, however, he was not able to work at that which was his chief passion—poetry. In the first place, he was too pressed for money to dare indulge himself in verse; and in the second place, he could not get himself into the proper mood. "The whirlpool in which I am swimming," he wrote to one of his friends, "is too furious for me to be able to work in poetry."

There was nothing left for him, therefore, but to occupy himself with journalism. He refused, however, to let his journalism be mere hack-work. On the contrary, he sought to invest it with an authoritativeness and literary quality that might make his slightest report a document destined for immortality. He read widely and diligently in the literatures of Germany and France, and he tried to keep himself closely informed on all that occurred in the political and cultural life of both lands. For by this time Heine had already decided that he had a distinct mission to fulfill: the mission which had been suggested to him by the Saint-Simonians when first he arrived in Paris. He regarded himself now as the logical person to serve as intermediary between Germany and France. This, it seemed to him, was far more important a task than running about with Börne and shouting in Paris for revolutions in Berlin. Heine had come to the conclusion that the highest obstacle in the way of revolution was the hostility between nations. He felt certain that once this hostility was ended, the downtrodden in each land would at last be free to turn on their real enemies; and then the overthrow of the aristocrats would be inevitable.

"We shall no longer need, out of mutual distrust, to feed standing armies of many hundreds of thousands of murderers; we will use their swords and horses for ploughing, and thus shall we obtain peace, prosperity, and freedom."

It was to help end this "mutual distrust" that Heine wrote as he did for the *Allgemeine Zeitung.* "My life is consecrated to this duty," he declared. "It is my office." He wanted to make the land of his birth and the land of his residence know each other and learn to trust each other. Jew that he was, he took unto himself his people's almost predestined position—that of the middleman. Just as his ancestors had been the entrepreneurs between Saracen and Christian, so now Heine assumed the rôle of entrepreneur between Frenchman and German. And he played his rôle with an earnestness and a passion deserving perhaps of greater recognition than has yet been awarded him. He was, as is now quite generally admitted, the first of the great modern internationalists, and for this reason, perhaps more than any other, his life was, as Nietzsche declared, veritably a "European event." One is tempted to suggest that had there been enough others to aid Heine in his internationalist activities, the sorriest tragedy of all history, that mad upheaval of hate and murder which was the World War, might never have occurred. . . .

2

But Heine was alone in his work, and moreover he was sorely hampered. To begin with, he had to contend daily with ill-health. His headaches were still with him, and in addition he had begun to be troubled by strange nervous disorders. In August he was compelled to go off once more to the sea, and at Dieppe he had to take salt-water baths for more than two months. Yet when he returned to Paris in October he was still far from well. "I wear light coats and gay vests," he wrote to Ferdinand Hiller; "my cheeks are red—but *two fingers of my left hand are paralyzed!*"

But even more hampering than ill-health was the illiberality of the government. There was no freedom of press in the Confederacy, and though Heine exercised all sorts of ingenuity in the way he phrased his ideas, he could not elude the censors. They saw through his careful ambiguities, and cut his articles to shreds. And Cotta was powerless to help him. Indeed, after a few months the publisher was practically ordered to discontinue printing Heine's reports altogether. The all-powerful Metternich let it be known that he looked with extreme disfavor on those articles from Paris, and after June 9, 1832, they ceased to appear. Heine was not at once informed of the ban, and innocently continued to send in his reports to the *Allgemeine Zeitung*. Only after some weeks did he learn what had happened, and then, in furious indignation he gathered together all his articles, restored them to their original, uncensored form, and had them published in a book. He prefaced the collection with a vitriolic essay which, to quote Strodtmann, "cut the poet off forever from returning to his Fatherland."

In this preface Heine flatly stated that to his mind the peace of Europe was most endangered by the King

of Prussia and his aristocratic and clerical cohorts.
Savagely he mocked and gibed the German people for
tolerating the tyranny that made cannon-fodder of them
all, and despairingly he called on his compatriots to
gird their loins and demand the constitution which the
King, Friedrich Wilhelm III, had promised.

"The King of Prussia is a very religious man; he
holds strongly to religion; he is a good Christian,
firmly attached to the evangelical confession of
faith; indeed, he has even written a liturgy and believes in holy symbols. But, ah, I wish he believed
instead in Jupiter, the Father of the Gods, who pun-
ishes perjury—perhaps then the King would give
us that promised constitution."

Heine was even more reckless when he spoke of the
Prussian aristocracy:

"A handful of common nobles who have learned
nothing beyond horse-trading, card sharping, drinking feats, and similar stupid rascally accomplish-
ments. . . . Such are the men who think they can
fool an entire race, and, moreover, the race which
invented gunpowder and printing and the Critique of Pure Reason. . . . They are indeed like
thieves who pick one another's pockets while they
are being led to the gallows. . . ."

But when, late in the autumn of 1832, this preface,
together with the collection of letters, appeared from
the press of Hoffmann and Campe, Heine was morti-

fied. The preface had been so mutilated that it had
been made to mean quite the opposite of what he had
intended. Instead of an open attack on the reactionaries, the butchered preface was almost a defense of
them. Fortunately the censors had made so bungling
and ragged a job of it, that no reader could fail to see
that the preface had been tampered with. But Heine
was incensed nevertheless. As he wrote to Baron
Cotta: "This will reflect upon my honor in Germany
and endanger my person in France."

Heine knew only too well what Börne and his fellow-
radicals would say now. They would not give him the
benefit of a single doubt, but would see in the emascu-
lated preface the completest proof of the poet's defection from the cause of liberty. They would accuse him
of having written every word of the wretched document
as it stood. There was nothing for him to do, therefore, but immediately to have the thing reprinted in its
original form. He wrote at once to Campe ordering
him to do this. Heine asked that a special pamphlet
be printed containing the preface, and with it a lengthy
explanatory essay which he had hurriedly indited.

"I was not a little astonished," this essay read,
"when I observed that the original preface was regarded as too harsh. Great God! What will it
be like if I give way to my feelings and speak out
from my heart in full freedom?"

The essay then proceeded to make clear what Heine
thought of the German reactionaries who had, with the

aid of their censors, attempted to escape the shafts of
his polemic. He called them poltroons and cowards,
and stooped to the vilest of personal abuse in his effort
to describe their baseness. At the very height of his
invective he pulled himself short and tried to act as
though he were really but little disturbed by his
enemies.

"I give them this title of 'enemies' out of politeness, for in reality most of them are only my
slanderers. They are little people whose hate does
not rise so high as my calves. They gnaw with
broken, blunted teeth at my boots, barking themselves weary down below there. . . ."

And having thus paid his compliments to the reactionaries, he then turned to deal with the radicals. He
confessed it vexed him more than a little that he should
be abused by those whom he considered members of the
"Heavenly Party," and who ought to be his friends.
So far as he could make it out their displeasure with
him was aroused chiefly by his perplexing ability to
avoid the cruder forms of martyrdom. He could write
polemics without end against the German Government,
and yet go scot free; but when they attempted to imi-
tate him, invariably they got into a mess.

"It happened to them as it did to the monkey
who had seen a man shave himself. When the latter left the room, the ape came, took the razor and
brush from the drawer, soaped himself, and then

cut his own throat. I do not know to what extent
these German Jacobins cut their throats, but I see
they are bleeding badly. Now they are scolding
me. 'Look!' they say: 'We have honorably soaped
ourselves and bled for the good cause; but Heine
did not act honorably in his shaving; he was want-
ing in true earnestness in using the razor; he never
once cut himself. He calmly washes away the soap,
whistling while doing so, and laughs at the bloody
wounds of the throat-cutters who had honorable
intentions.' "

But then Heine added grimly:

"Be satisfied; this time I have really cut myself."

At the last moment, however, Heine lost his nerve.
Even after he had announced with such sardonic satisfaction that he had really cut himself, he tried to escape with a mere grazing. In a panic he wrote to Campe
while the pamphlet was still in the press, ordering him
to destroy every copy that had yet been printed. But
though the command was obeyed, the pamphlet did become public nevertheless. Either through the carelessness of Campe, as Heine claimed, or with the secret
connivance of Heine himself, copies of the document
made their appearance a few months later in Poland,
and soon thereafter in France. And then the hue and
cry became more menacing than ever.

3

HEINE was now in really serious jeopardy. In the spring of 1833 he wrote to Heinrich Laube, a young liberal writer living in Germany:

"I have the government . . . the deceitful Catholic Carlists, and the Prussian spies on my neck. . . . I would send you a copy of the 'French Affairs' as printed here with the unmutilated preface, were I not afraid you might be compromised. Be careful. A person is not safe even here. Last Saturday a lot of Germans were arrested here and I am afraid I, too, may be arrested at any moment. . . . I am writing these lines in bed at the home of a beautiful friend. She would not let me go to my home for fear I might be arrested. . . . Perhaps my next letter will be dated from London. I am impressing all this on you to urge you to be careful and discreet."

Those were exciting days for Heine, but also ominous ones. He suspected—and not without reason—that the Prussian government was using its influence to have him expelled from France, and daily he feared he might be turned out of the country. What he would do in that eventuality, he did not care to think. A return to the Fatherland would be out of the question, for he was considered there the leader of the whole Young Germany movement. He knew he would be arrested the moment he set foot on the other side of the Rhine. There was, therefore, only England left for him, and he could not stand even the thought of having to drag out the rest of his days amidst its fog and unutterable ugliness.

And aside from his incessant fear of deportation, Heine had other troubles. He was short of money. Notwithstanding the allowance he received from his uncle, and the money he made by his writing, he still did not have enough to meet his expenses. In addition he was ill. On April 21, 1833, we find him writing to his brother Max:

> "Give me your advice as a doctor what to do for my headaches. I have suffered from them these last two months more than ever. It is perhaps the result of excessive mental strain. Not that I have been working much of late, for the trouble I have had as a result of political events has prevented me from working. My position is brilliant only externally; I am almost crushed . . . by necessity, vexation, distraction, and torment."

"*Almost* crushed," he wrote; but the adverb was extravagant. Actually he was at this period more determined and surer of himself than he had ever been before. Those devitalizing spiritual conflicts which had been raging in him since first he began to write, seemed now to be resolving themselves. Heine somehow was at last attaining that integration of the spirit which all along had been his most grievous want. He was beginning to find himself. Probably that was why he could write to Varnhagen:

"I am still suffering with this paralyzed hand, but I am still active. I won't let the sword fall from my hand until I die. . . . I had to choose between laying down my weapons altogether, and fighting all my life. I chose the latter, but the choice was not lightly made. I was forced to take up arms in the beginning by the scorn of strangers, by the arrogant pride of birth. Already in my cradle was the line of march laid down for all my life."

But evidently he did not consider that his "line of march" led necessarily to the barricades, for he continued with the words:

"I have no intention of seizing the moment in the fashion of the demagogues, for I do not believe in the possibility of an immediate effect upon the German people. Indeed, I am retiring from politics and am busying myself at present chiefly with art, religion, and philosophy."

At the suggestion of Victor Bohain, the editor of *Europe Littéraire*, Heine had begun to write a series of articles on German literature for that journal. There were eight articles in all, and they appeared between March 1 and May 24, 1833. They appeared, of course, in French, but Heine's original version was in German, and, for fear of piracy, he was careful to have the original version published simultaneously with the French. He called the little book "Contributions to a History of Recent Polite Literature in Germany" (*Zur Geschichte der neueren schönen Literatur in Deutschland*), and though the attention it attracted in both France and Germany was limited, it did not fail to leave its impress upon the intellectual life of the time. When, two years later, the author expanded the work and published it under the title, "The Romantic School" (*Die Romantische Schule*), it took its place as one of the most important of all of Heine's products.

Heine's avowed purpose in writing this book had been to correct a number of misapprehensions created in France by Madame de Staël's famous study, *De l' Allemagne*. His deeper intention, however, had been not merely to explain contemporary German culture to the French, but also to explain it to itself. Heine hoped "The Romantic School" might give to the insurgent writers of what had come to be called Young Germany, a philosophy and a definite trend. He wanted to show them whence they had come and whither they were going. The first premise of the book was the contention that art and literature in any age reflect the contemporary social and religious attitudes. To prove this contention Heine outlined the whole history of German culture beginning with the early middle ages, and going down to his own day. From this he proceeded to a searching analysis of the Romanticist movement into which he had been born. He showed how this movement had been an expression of the religious revival in Germany at the end of the eighteenth century, which in turn had been a result of the wretched political and social conditions then regnant.

> " 'Poverty teaches prayer,' says the proverb; and truly dire need was never greater in Germany. That was why the people were especially inclined then to resort to prayer, piety, and Christianity."

By Christianity Heine meant specifically Catholicism, toward which most of the Romanticist poets had been drawn, and which even he, in his youth, had almost accepted. Heine hated it now almost fanatically, for he saw in it the gravest hindrance to the attainment of all he counted desirable in life. Already years earlier he had noted how it strangled all thought, and in bitterness he had declared: "If thy tongue offend thee, tear it out; if thine eye offend thee, pluck it out; if thy hand offend thee, cut it off; and if thy brain offend thee— turn Catholic!" . . . Now, however, he felt that Catholicism strangled not only intellectual but also political liberty.

> ". . . that religion by teaching the repudiation of all earthly goods and by encouraging dog-like humility and angelic patience, has become the staunchest support of despotism."

Even worse, Catholicism strangled also personal liberty. Heine maintained that, with its emphasis on the spirit and its denial of the flesh, Catholicism devitalized life and dehumanized art. He was ready to admit that in an earlier time this tendency on the part of the Church had been immensely valuable in Europe. Its glorification of asceticism was a wholesome thing after the excesses of carnality which were reported to have marked the last days of the Roman Empire.

"The flesh had become so arrogant in this Roman world that it needed Christian discipline to chasten it."

But that day was past, and Catholicism had long outlived its one usefulness. There was no need to attempt to tame Europe any more. Indeed Europe was, Heine believed, too tame already. Now it was the spirit that was arrogant, and the flesh that needed a chance. So Heine maintained the days of Catholicism were numbered. The people were rebelling against its narcotic promises. They were no longer content to go without the barest necessities in this world in order to inherit incredible luxuries in some other world. Nor were they ready any longer to crucify their flesh in order to glorify their spirits. And therefore, said Heine:

". . . we may well believe that the Christian Catholic view of the world has reached its end. Every age is a sphinx which casts itself into the abyss the moment man has solved its riddle."

And with the passing of the Catholic attitude there necessarily had to follow the passing of Romanticist literature. This "consumptive" type of art, straining desperately to sustain itself on the "milk of the she-ass of the Viceregent of Christ," was doomed beyond all hope. A new art, realistic, vigorous, carnal, was already beginning to take its place. This was the art of Young Germany, and Heine hailed its emergence with hosannas. It was a harbinger of the new day—the day of freedom, of honor, of manliness—indeed, the Day of God!

4

SUCH in brief was Heine's thesis in "The Romantic School." It was not entirely original with him, as we shall see in a moment; but it was so presented as to seem original. The brilliance of its language, and the verve and raciness in its whole manner, gave to the essay an epochal quality. It made articulate in Germany what had for years been but vague, and set the goal for a movement which until then had been largely unorientated. Heine with his extraordinary insight had been able to discover the vital spark glowing beneath all the smoke of post-Romanticist writing, and, with his genius for direct expression, had been able to indicate that spark unmistakably.

But in making this discovery Heine had been guided not only by his own insight but even more profoundly by Saint-Simonism. The influence of the movement is to be seen in the very terminology Heine used. He himself confessed as much in his preface to the first edition of the book:

"In some expressions as to the existence of God I have used the same words as those which have been made familiar by the apostolic zeal of the Saint-Simonians; and as these phrases set forth my meaning quite lucidly and distinctly, I have retained them [not alone in the French, but also] in the German version."

A few years earlier Heine would have refused to use the term God except in mockery. Then he had been a dogmatic atheist, and the very utterance of the name of the deity had made his lip curl in scorn. But under the influence of Saint-Simonism his whole attitude toward the divine had been vastly modified. He made this obvious in the conclusion of his preface to "The Romantic School":

"Neither the ill-will of my foes nor the artful folly of my friends shall ever restrain me from expressing myself forthrightly as to that weightiest of all human questions: the Being of God. . . .

"I do not belong to the atheists who deny—I affirm. . . .

"The beginning and end of all things is in God!"

Those were amazing affirmations, and their only explanation is to be found in the hold which Saint-Simonism had taken on Heine. Before 1831, when the poet first heard of "the new evangel," he had been one of the most emphatic of the deniers. He had been that, however, not so much because he believed the deniers to be absolutely right, as out of resentment because the affirmers seemed relatively wrong. Actually, Heine had never been a thoroughly convinced atheist, as is proved by the unnecessarily loud way in which he proclaimed himself one. In reality he had all along cherished a rooted hunger for religion, and only his exasperation that he could not satisfy the hunger had provoked him into ribald irreligion. From boyhood he had ached for a feeling of spiritual security. He had sought it first in sentimental Catholicism, then in intellectual Judaism, then in official Protestantism; but in each instance he had failed. And repeated failure to find a faith had left him distraught and unhappy. For a time he had tried to make a religion out of his love of Liberty, and in the attempt he produced many of the finest passages in the "Travel Pictures." But soon this enthusiasm, too, proved inadequate, and he was left still a torn and furious soul.

The evidences of Heine's spiritual distress before 1831 are patent in all his work. First there is his corroding pessimism, his continual dwelling on death and the grave. Next there is his frequent indulgence in maudlin sentimentality—an almost unfailing symptom of spiritual instability. Sentimentalism is the device resorted to by one who has no really valid principles to which to cling, and who therefore must give a fictitious validity to whatever thin and flimsy beliefs he can lay hold of. It is the imputation of false values to things: the attribution of gravity and meaning to notions which in actuality do not and cannot possess such qualities. Sentimentalism is in the emotional morass what rationalization is in the intellectual: a desperate attempt to save oneself by believing that the reeds in one's clutch are really stout ropes. . . .

The third indication of Heine's spiritual conflict before 1831 is his weakness for dreaming. Had he possessed a healthy mind he would not have felt the need to flee at every crisis to his eerie fantasy-world. He would have been able to meet the harshest exigencies without a tremor, and would at least have *tried* to vanquish them in the realm of reality. But, as it was, Heine turned tail at the least sign of trouble, and he did not dare halt and show fight until he was safe in the realm of his imagination. He lacked the courage which can come only of spiritual conviction. His arms were weak because his mind was divided; his hands were nerveless because his soul was in turmoil.

But the most striking indication of all is Heine's wit. Sigmund Freud in his "Wit and its Relation to the Unconscious," points out the parallel that exists between the technique of wit and the technique of dreams. He makes frequent mention of Heine in that volume, and offers him as an outstanding example of an individual who used wit as a mechanism to relieve an internal spiritual conflict. Heine's willingness to mock his tenderest emotions reveals an acute consciousness of how open to mockery his emotions really were. More than that, it reveals a panicky fear that others might also be conscious of it, and might be laughing not only at those emotions but also at him who cherished them. That was why Heine so frequently concluded his most ecstatic poems with a line of devastating cynicism. He feared

his reader might be suspicious of the sighs and tears
whereof he so glibly sang, and therefore he hastily
leaped up and laughed at them himself even before the
reader could do so.

The same may be said of Heine's other forms of wit.
They were all in one respect or another mechanisms for
defense; motivating them all there was a deep, a ran-
kling lack of poise. Heine laughed not out of joy, but
desperation. His was typical "gallows-humor"—the
audacious humor of the man who will not let his enemies
triumph over him even when they have the noose around
his neck. It did not reveal strength in him so much as
bravado, not confidence so much as devastating doubt.
Most of the time Heine seems to have laughed only to
hold back the tears; he twisted his lips into a sardonic
smile only to keep from weeping. Every sensitive Jew
of great spirit has had to do that since the time Abraham
tried to laugh off a lie before Pharaoh. . . .

But his birth alone is not enough to explain the excess
with which Heine resorted to wit. Obviously there was
in this man an added source of disquiet: one that lay not
in his social so much as his spiritual psychology. Heine
was not merely at odds with the world, but even more
at odds with himself. In his breast there raged a per-
petual conflict between two hostile and apparently irrec-
oncilable natures. In later days he named these the
Hellenic and the Nazarene, or the Pagan and the Jewish.
All through his youth he seems to have been tugged
hither and thither by these two impulses. One moment
he was all sensualist, and the next he was all spiritualist;

now he could sing only of the holiness of beauty, and now only of the beauty of holiness. This explains the violent contrasts to be found in such a work as his "Travel Pictures." Did we know as little about the authorship of this work as we do, for instance, of the authorship of Ecclesiastes, we should necessarily have to conclude—as do the Semitic scholars concerning the Biblical book—that more than one hand had written it. And in a spiritual sense more than one hand *had* written the "Travel Pictures." Heine had not been in any sense an integrated individual when he produced that monument of satire and sentiment. Spiritually he had been at least two individuals: Aristophanes—and Jeremiah.

Such a dichotomy was, of course, by no means unique in Heine. In greater or less degree it has existed in all thinking men, especially in ages of stress and change. If it was so marked in Heine, it was simply because he was more than a thinking man: he was a poet. As he himself declared, the poet's heart is the center of the world, and when the world is rent in twain, ineluctably he must share the fate.

But though Heine knew the fate was ineluctable, he nevertheless sought to escape it. He could not endure the incessant conflict raging in him day after day. It made him incapable of any sustained effort, and led him into too many flagrant inconsistencies. His profoundest desire, therefore, was for an end to the war in his soul. This end could not be brought about, however, by the triumph of either one of his natures. Each was too mighty, and too deeply rooted in him, to be utterly banished by the other. His only hope, therefore, lay in the possibility of harmonizing them both. And it was because finally Heine thought he had accomplished this end, that he was able, in 1833, to write so unified a work as "The Romantic School."

Indubitably Saint-Simonism helped make the accomplishment possible. From the beginning there were certain phases of the movement with which Heine had only moderate sympathy. Its utopian program for industrial and economic reform, for instance, and its advocacy of feminism, were both causes which the poet found outside the range of his closest interests. And the whole practise of the cult—for Saint-Simonism had indeed developed into a cult—was so absurd and eccentric that Heine could not dream of subscribing himself one of its devotees. But the religious basis of the movement had attracted and influenced him tremendously. Saint-Simonism seemed to end the vicious conflict which had made Heine's spiritual life so agonizing. Unlike paganism, which was imagined to deny the spirit, and Judaism and Christianity, which were imagined to deny the flesh, this new religion denied neither. Instead it proclaimed the divinity of both, accepting the Nazarene evaluation of the spirit, but at the same time demanding a "rehabilitation of the flesh." Just how these two principles were to be brought into harmonious partnership, Heine did not pause to inquire (nor the Saint-Simonians to make clear). It was enough for him that here was a philosophy which declared the feat not impossible. He

demanded no more at the moment, so desperately sick
was he of the battle in his soul.

5

BUT it requires some study to discover the influence
of Saint-Simonist philosophy in the "Romantic School."
The influence is there, definitely there—but it is not
ubiquitous. When we come to Heine's next work, however, the presence of Saint-Simonist thinking is to be
seen on every page. This work, which he wrote the following year, and which appeared first in the *Revue des
Deux Mondes*, was entitled "On Religion and Philosophy
in Germany." It was a companion work to "The Romantic School," doing for the history of German
thought what the earlier volume had done for the history of German literature. But it far excelled "The
Romantic School," for it was more closely reasoned,
more coherently developed, and even more mordantly
phrased. Indeed, it is recognized today as the most
important prose work Heine ever accomplished. And
from beginning to end it showed the influence of Saint-
Simonism.

The main thesis in the book was the struggle for
supremacy in German thought between those old foes,
spiritualism and sensualism. First sensualism had
reigned unchallenged, and the wild immoral gods of old
Germany had set a gay though dangerous pattern for
man. But then came Christianity, and all seemed
changed. The old gods in the heavens were made devils

and banished to hell, and sensualism gave way to spiritualism. But the change was more apparent than real. The flesh continued to assert itself despite the prohibitions enacted by the holy men, and the ensuing struggle had no chance of abating until Protestantism unshackled German thought and made philosophy possible. And, through philosophy, the war was at last being ended.

Kant had destroyed deism in Germany, so Heine claimed, and now the way was clear for the coming of a doctrine which was broader than deism and could harbor both the contending hosts. This doctrine, Heine believed, was pantheism—the high faith taught by Spinoza (and in a different form by the Saint-Simonians) which could see divinity in matter no less than in mind. Such a doctrine did not, like Christianity, brand the flesh as evil, for it contended that God dwelt in the things of the flesh no less than in those of the spirit. God was in *all* things: in stones, plants, beasts, and—most gloriously of all—in men. Not in a single man dwelling in Rome, or in a tiny congregation of men lurking in some monastery, but in the whole of the human race. Every man was a part of the God, and the whole of mankind was the incarnation of God. Such, Heine declared, was the new evangel of insurgent Germany.

The *new* evangel? No, the old—the pristine faith of Germany. For pantheism was not a new creation or an importation from some other land. It was but the original faith of the ancient Teutons which the Christian monks had perverted into pandemonism. And now it was coming back quietly, almost imperceptibly, for it had not yet made its way beyond the citadel of the philosophers. But soon it would reach the masses, and then it would be manifest in the deeds of the many. And what a revolution would then occur! Heine was almost as frenziedly imaginative as the writers of the Apocalypses when he spoke of the "Great Day to Come."

"Then will come crashing the wild madness of the old champions, the insane Berserker rage whereof the Norse poets told. The Cross is brittle and the day must soon come when it will pitifully break. And then the old stone gods will rise from their long-forgotten ruins and rub the dust of a thousand years from their eyes. Thor, leaping to life with his giant hammer, will crush the Gothic cathedrals! . . . It is coming. . . . German thunder is indeed German, and it is in no hurry; but come it will, and when ye hear it crash as naught ever crashed before in the whole history of the world, then know that German thunder has at last hit the mark. At the sound the eagles will fall dead from on high and the lions in the remotest deserts of Africa will draw in their tails and creep into their royal caves. A drama will be enacted in Germany by the side of which the French Revolution will seem like an innocent idyll. Just now all is tolerably still. Even though here and there a few individuals are restive, let it not be imagined that the great actors have yet appeared. These restive persons are but the little dogs that run about

in the empty amphitheater and bark and bite at one
another before the hour arrives when the great
array of gladiators must appear.   And only when
that hour comes will the real battle begin. . . ."

Thus did Heine prophesy in the last chapter of this
work, and the very intensity of his language reveals the
aching eagerness with which he looked forward to the
Armageddon.   For that final battle meant the end of the
war in his own heart, as well as in the heart of the world.
It meant the coming at last of peace to his soul, the
attainment at last of salvation.

It is, therefore, a changed Heine we see in this "History of German Religion and Philosophy."   He is no
longer a tormented young man whose mind must forever
turn in its own path or else fly off at tangents because it
knows not where to go.   Now he seems to have found
his goal at last, he is able to pursue a thought right
through to its conclusion.   The old evidences of inner
conflict are largely gone now from his writing.   He is no
longer pessimistic or sentimental; he indulges in fewer
fantasies; and his humor is seldom rancorous.   He still
has his wit, but he employs it now to illumine ideas
rather than to sear individuals.   For instance:

"Fichte requires the mind to observe itself while
in action.   Thought must listen to itself while it is
thinking, even while it is getting warmer and
warmer until at last it is actually 'done.'   That re-
minds us of the ape which sits by the fireplace and
cooks its own tail on the principle that the true

science of cookery consists not only of objective cooking, but also of being subjectively conscious of being cooked."

That is still rich and brilliant humor, but it is not sour or spiteful.

It is a happier Heine, a spiritually healthier man, that we find in both "The Romantic School" and the "History of German Religion and Philosophy." And for this Saint-Simonism is to be praised. Heine made but few specific references to the movement in either of the two books; but he acknowledged his indebtedness to it nevertheless. In 1835, when the two works were published in one volume under the title "On Germany," he dedicated the book to Prosper Enfantin, the leader of the Saint-Simonians. In reply he received a rather solemn epistle couched in grandiloquent language which, while chiding him for his occasional blasphemous pleasantries, yet congratulated him on his achievement and named him the "first Church Father of the Germans." That letter pleased Heine not a little. He may have smiled wryly at Enfantin's chiding, but he was proud to be nominated the Saint-Simonian apostle to the Germans by one who was the Paul of the whole movement. Nor did Heine take the nomination lightly. He had grown to be a serious man, a believer, by this time. He was in earnest now, terribly in earnest—for he had a religion at last.

THE EXILE IN FRANCE

CHAPTER
THREE

"Have you read the 'Song of Songs' of
King Solomon? Well, read it again and
you will find in it all that I could tell
you. . . ."

III

I<small>T</small> was in 1834, when Heine was thirty-seven years of age, that he first fully sensed the joy of salvation through acceptance of the Saint-Simonian religion. But more than this happened to him in 1834. He acquired then not merely a religion but also a mistress. Crescentia Eugénie Mirat was her name, and Heine found her selling shoes in the tiny shop conducted by her aunt. She was a pretty dark-haired girl of about nineteen, and had only a few years before come down from her native village in the Seine et Marne province. According to her claim, she was the illegitimate child of a nobleman, but had been deserted and left to eke out a living in her aunt's shop. Heine had known many such girls during the three years he had lived in Paris, and he could have been under no illusion at first as to the sincerity or endurance of her affections. Yet he acted toward this girl as he had toward none other. Apparently she possessed attractions for him which were more than merely physical, for even after the excitement of conquest was over, he still continued to seek out her company.

Mathilde—he never called her Crescentia because, as he jokingly put it, the name was too hard on his throat— was physically of the type Heine had always preferred. She was more Belgian than French, and therefore not slight in figure but rather tall and well-built. Her coloring was dark and her features good; but many people who saw her did not think her especially beautiful. It could not have been her physical charms that held Heine, so much as her gayety of spirit and naïveté. She seemed like a helpless child to him, and her ignorance and pouting wilfulness, far from alienating him, seemed to make her the most desirable creature he had come across in years. Obviously he could enjoy no intellectual or spiritual comradeship with her, for she was totally unable to understand what he wrote. But that made her only the more attractive to the poet.

Like many another great intelligence, Heine could never fall in love with a blue-stocking. He somehow distrusted the type, perhaps because he suspected it was attracted more to his fame than to himself. He could have no such suspicion in connection with this pretty grisette, Mathilde. Even months after she became intimate with him she still did not know he was a poet; and never to her dying day did she learn, save from hearsay, how great a writer he was. To her he was merely a presentable and generous lover, a kind though sometimes cranky man who, despite his funny accent, seemed rather elegant and was altogether most *sympathique*. And this delighted Heine. He told himself that here at last was a person who loved him for himself, not for his intellect or his art. Few, very few, people had ever cared for him in that way. Most of them had seemed to despise him as a person, and had admired him only because of his work. But with Mathilde it was quite otherwise. She did not know he was a Jew and did not care that he was a poet; all she knew and cared was that he was her funny Henri.

Perhaps that was why Heine became so deeply involved with her. The passion began to tell even on his work, for he found less and less time for writing. Six months after he first met Mathilde he confessed in a letter to August Lewald:

> "I have been up to my neck in love, and have not yet extricated myself. Since October nothing has seemed of the least importance that is not connected with this affair. I neglect everything, see no one, and at best a sigh escapes me when I think of my friends. . . . Have you read the 'Song of Songs' of King Solomon? Well, read it again and you will find in it all that I could tell you."

But Heine labored under no illusions. Though not in many years had he met a girl who so attracted him as did Mathilde, he could not believe he would be attracted forever, or even for very long. Indeed, in that same letter to Lewald he wrote: "Wait: soon enough there will be a change in me, and then, rest assured, I'll write for your play-actors."

2

But the infatuation did not pass so soon as Heine
expected. Indeed, not until the following summer was
he able to tear himself away from the grisette. He fled
then to the castle of a friend, Princess Belgiojoso, and
there he tried to forget the little shop girl in Paris.

Before a week had passed he thought he had succeeded. On July 2 he assured Campe:

"Now, thanks to my indestructible force of
mind, my passion is conquered, my roused senses
are tamed, and I am living a cheerful carefree existence at the castle of a beautiful woman near St.
Germain, in the delightful society of cultured persons and personalities."

Princess Belgiojoso was one of the most famous
women in Europe at that time. Possessing intelligence,
wealth, position, and charm, she was able to draw to her
salon the foremost men of the day: Chopin, Liszt, Rossini, Lafayette, Thiers, Alfred de Musset, Victor Cousin,
Dumas, Gautier, Hugo, and many others. She had met
Heine first at General Lafayette's home, and she had at
once been drawn to him. But it was his genius and his
radicalism that had attracted her, not his character. As
a consequence Heine, though he was not unconscious of
her charms, could not bring himself to fall in love with
her. As he confessed in a letter to one of his friends:

"She is the most beautiful, most noble, and most
witty of women, but I am not in love with her. I

am condemned to love only the lowest and the most foolish. . . . Imagine what a torture that is for a man of so much pride and intellect!"

But though not in love with the Princess, Heine did find her company pleasant. He remained at her castle several weeks, and only the feeling that he had to get back to his writing induced him to leave. He did not return immediately to Paris, however, for he knew work would be impossible there. He thought he was cured of his love for Mathilde, but he was by no means so sure of it that he dared expose himself to danger. So instead he went to Boulogne, "that lovely little coast town which is my best work-room." There he planned to write what he told Campe would be a "rare, delightful book —one far better than any of my earlier works."

But he found it difficult to carry out his intention. The mood which had been induced in him by the pleasant company at Princess Belgiojoso's was dissipated quickly at Boulogne. He became morose and irascible and he found it difficult to write. Obviously his passion for Mathilde was tormenting him. His whole body cried out for her, and his spirit could not sing loudly enough to drown out the torturing sound. Yet he knew it would be ruinous for him to return to her, for then work would be altogether impossible. So in agony he remained on at Boulogne. . . . How he conducted himself toward the people around him is indicated by an anecdote that was told of him in the town. One day in the reading-room two English women were chattering loudly while

Heine was trying to read. He stood it as long as his jangled nerves would allow, and then caustically he remarked: "If my reading disturbs your conversation, of course I shall be glad to leave." . . .

A somewhat different and yet not contradictory picture is given us by Lucy Austin, Lady Duff-Gordon.

". . . as a child of eleven or twelve at Boulogne . . . I sat next to Heine at a table d'hôte. He was then a fat, short man—short-sighted, and with a sensual mouth. . . . We used to lounge on the end of the pier together, where he told me stories in which fish, mermaids, watersprites, and a very funny old French fiddler with a poodle, who was diligently taking three sea-baths a day, were mixed up in the most fanciful manner, sometimes humorous, and very often pathetic, especially when the watersprites brought him German greetings from the 'Nord See'. . . . He was at Boulogne a month or two, and I saw him often then, and always remembered with great tenderness the poet who had told me the beautiful stories, and been so kind to me, and so sarcastic to everyone else."

3

NOT until late in December, after an absence of more than seven months, did Heine dare to set foot once more in Paris. Even then he did not think it prudent to consider remaining there, and his fixed intention was to move on as fast as possible to Versailles. But he never carried out his intention. He succumbed to his fierce longing for but another glance at the charming grisette —and then dropped all thought of deserting Paris. From that day on, he and Mathilde never parted.

It was rumored in his circle that Mathilde's aunt had demanded three thousand francs for the girl, and the testimony of one of Heine's most intimate friends, Alexandre Weill, seems to substantiate the story. Weill reports that at the breakfast in celebration of the establishment of the joint household, Mathilde said to her lover:

> "I belong to you, for you have bought me; but I also bought you—you know the price—and you are mine now for life."

But if Heine really did pay any such sum for the purchase of Mathilde, it was as nothing compared with what he had to continue to pay to retain her. The girl was costly not merely to his pocket, but even more so to his nerves. Weill reports:

> "Mathilde was in no way a bad character . . . but she liked to make scenes. In a rage she was capable of striking herself with her fists. But two minutes later her wrath ended in tears and sobs. . . . Heine sometimes had to treat her like a badly brought up girl, sometimes like a little pet animal one brings to reason with a slap; but he loved her all the more for that."

There can be no doubt about the depth of Heine's attachment to this empty-headed shop-girl. Soon after he took her into his apartment he began to send her to school. He once told Weill it cost him more than ten thousand francs to have her taught how to read and write. But she proved incapable of education, and remained to her last days quite ignorant of all that was dearest to the man with whom she lived. As he frequently remarked to his friends, he had two sweethearts, his French mistress and his German Muse—but the two were not on speaking terms! Even five years after they first began to live together, Mathilde is reported to have cried:

"They say my Henri is a great poet. Is it not funny that I should know nothing about it?"

But apparently Heine found her ignorance rather charming, and he delighted to show it off to his friends. For instance, Theodore Mundt wrote to Varnhagen a couple of years later:

"We were in his more intimate little ménage in the Rue Cadet, and he was joking with his lady. . . . He told her that Christ had once been Archbishop of Paris—and she really believed it!"

That Heine should have found Mathilde's ignorance almost an attraction, is perhaps explicable only on the ground already suggested. It may have flattered him inordinately to realize that this girl loved him for himself alone, and not for his work or his fame. To us it may seem absurd that so great a man as Heine—and he was by this time one of the foremost figures in the literary life of all Europe—should have been capable of feeling flattered by a grisette's affection. But there can be no doubt that Heine was at bottom not at all certain he was great. He knew well he was a literary genius, and he never hesitated to inform the world of the fact. Even twelve years earlier he had dared to boast:

> "I am a German poet
> In German lands I shine;
> And where great names are mentioned
> They're sure to mention mine."

But he feared this was true of him only as a poet, not as a person. Stripped of his genius, he feared he was no more than a despised ex-Jew, a nervous, sickly, undersized vagabond with a cantankerous, hateful disposition. Already years earlier he had confessed:

> "Oft curiosity has drawn
> Some lovely ladies toward me;
> But when they looked deep in my heart
> They left, and they abhorred me."

Heine was not blind to the defects in his own nature; if anything, the antipathy which he aroused in many people with whom he came in contact, had made him all too conscious of those defects. And this may have been why he could feel so gratified at the affection of Mathilde.

Besides, he was convinced that in her at least there could be no faintest trace of prejudice against him because of his birth. Heine was probably more sensitive about his birth even than most Jews, for he tried more desperately to forget it. Nothing incensed him more than any reference to his origin, as is proved by the manner in which he flung himself upon poor Platen. And by the same token, nothing gratified him more than the company of an individual who was incapable of making such a reference. Now, Mathilde was such an individual, for she never even suspected her lover was by birth a Jew. We have this on the word of Alfred Meissner, who knew the couple intimately during many years. Meissner tells us how one day, while in conversation with Mathilde, he chanced to refer to certain of Heine's friends, among them a cousin named Herr Cohen, as Jews. And he thus describes what followed:

" 'Oh, you're mistaken! Those aren't Jews,' she cried. 'You want me to believe that Cohen is a Jew? But he's related to Henri, and Henri is a Protestant!' . . .

"Like a man who is walking on a frozen sea, and suddenly sees the water welling up through a fissure, I stopped and choked back what was on the tip of my tongue. By chance I had discovered something apparently incredible: namely, that Heine had never told his wife anything about his descent. . . .

" 'You are right,' I hurriedly corrected myself: 'I must have been mistaken about Cohen.' "

Meissner reports this incident as having occurred about 1849, some fifteen years after Heine first met Mathilde. By that time she had already seen most of his relatives, and had even spent a week or more in the midst of his family in Hamburg. Only a colossal stupidity could have made it possible for her to remain still ignorant of Heine's origin. But colossally stupid she was. Meissner says of her:

"Heine to her was not the great poet he was to the rest of the world; no, to her he was what all the world refused to admit: the best, the kindest, the most genuine of men. With tears in her eyes this laughing Frenchwoman would often recount to me the most touching evidences of his generosity of heart. His cleverness and wit she never noticed."

4

BUT though Heine may have found Mathilde's ignorance a charm, he could not but have been repelled at times by her other faults. For instance, there was her personal slovenliness, her frequent neglect to keep herself trim and chic. One contemporary reports "she did not look at all lady-like, but rather poverty-stricken and afraid of water."

Mathilde was slovenly not only about her own person, but also in the way she managed her household. We have several descriptions of Heine's ménage during his first years with Mathilde, and, save for one that was patently colored for German consumption, they all present a most depressing picture. Mathilde was too lazy to do her own housework, and kept a slatternly servant in the flat to make the beds and dust. Whenever possible she cajoled Heine into taking her out to some restaurant for dinner, and thus she escaped the fuss and trouble of cooking. Baron Ludwig von Embden, a nephew of the poet, in his book, "The Family Life of Heinrich Heine," informs us:

> "Heine did not like mutton; therefore, when he returned to the house with a hearty appetite and in good-humor, and asked what there was to eat, she would reply, 'Roast mutton.'" Whereupon he would at once take his hat and say, 'Come, Mathilde, we will go and dine at Vefour's.' If they met good friends on the way, they were asked to come along, and as champagne was an indispensable relish for a good dinner with Mathilde, this oft-repeated trick proved highly expensive."

It was, of course, impossible for Heine to take his mistress out into society, and either because he did not care to go alone, or she did not let him, he had to confine his intimate social contacts almost entirely to his bohemian friends. Among such friends Mathilde was freely accepted, for many of the artists and writers in Paris then were living with their women *sans* the benefit of clergy. In such circles, indeed, Mathilde was even

popular, for although she was intellectually far inferior
to most of the other women, her congeniality and charm
more than made up for the defect. "Her mere laugh
could make one gay," reports Friedrich Pecht.

But this very amiability of Mathilde's sometimes
caused Heine not a few pangs. He was frightfully
jealous of her, and was constantly afraid she might be
unfaithful to him. He watched her incessantly, and
resented the least smile she gave to any stranger. On
one occasion his jealousy got him into a most unpleasant
scrape. One day in a restaurant six French students,
who were sitting at a table near Heine and his mistress,
tried to start a flirtation with the girl. In a rage Heine
strode over to the young men and boxed the most impudent of them on the ear. The result was an immediate
exchange of cards; and, after the seconds were chosen,
all the arrangements were made for a duel. As it happened, the duel was never actually fought, for when the
opponents met in the park at the appointed time, a reconciliation was effected.

Heine came out of the mess rather well. Because of
his popularity with the Parisian journalists, a newspaper declared the next day that Heine had waited until
his opponent had fired and missed him, and then he had
magnanimously shot into the air! . . . But even though
it all turned out so fortunately, one can well imagine
that the affair must have been most distressing to the
nervous and none-too-healthy poet.

It was probably not the only scrape Heine got into
on account of Mathilde. She was forever exciting him

and disturbing his peace. On March 31, 1836, he declares in a letter to Laube:

"How I envy you your loneliness—I, who am damned to live in the wildest whirlpool in the world . . . and am driven crazy with my crying daily needs. . . . How I long for the peace of a German fortress where a warder stands before my door and lets no one in, neither my beloved, nor my other torments—I do passionately crave for silence!"

In another letter a year later, he declares:

"We are both living very happily together: that is, I do not have a moment's peace day or night."

In still another letter he confesses:

"Her companionship is trying because of the dear creature's wildness, which is a constant source of anxiety to me."

In the home Mathilde chattered and sang almost constantly, but that Heine did not mind so much, for her voice seemed very beautiful to him. What he did object to, however, was her squawking parrot, Cocotte, which she insisted on keeping in the apartment all the time. The bird made it so difficult for Heine to work that often he wished it and Mathilde at the other end of the earth. Several times, indeed, he actually threatened to throw them both out. There were scenes: nasty, sordid squabbles between Heine and the woman. Yet, though he often in fury swore to break with her, he never was quite able to do so. She was a heavy burden on him because of her extravagance, and often she caused him bitter chagrin because of the way she insulted the poverty-stricken young writers whom he liked to invite to his table. She sickened him with her shrill complaints because he gave money to every stranded German emigré who came to him for help; and she drove him to desperation with her periodic tantrums. Yet there was something about Mathilde that fascinated him. He was not faithful to her during the first years of their attachment, and apparently made no secret of it. Just how she reacted to his occasional derelictions we cannot be sure. According to some witnesses, she was not at all disturbed, but even allowed him to bring his other loves into their apartment. But according to other, and perhaps more reliable, witnesses, she was as jealous of him as he was of her, and she violently resented his philanderings. "As far as jealousy was concerned," reports Henri Julia, "Mme. Mathilde was anything but easy."

Yet Heine continued to live with her, and to slave away at his writing in order to provide for her every extravagant want. And he did it not out of any sense of duty, but out of a strange irrational attraction which, for want of a more accurate term, we must call love. Despite all her flagrant faults, he liked to have her near him. "Mathilde," he wrote in one of his letters, "brightens life for me with the consistent inconsistency of her whims." He often referred to her as his "goddess," and in many of his letters he speaks of her gayety. "She has a weak head," he confided to his mother, "but a very good heart." He seems to have cherished a strange and very beautiful protective tenderness for her. We can tell this from the way he forever strove to praise her to his mother and sister, and always sought to defend her to his friends. And in addition he was held by a keen, at times even a fierce, physical attraction. As he told Laube:

> "My passion for Mathilde grows more chronic every day. . . . I was lately in her village and experienced the most incredible idyll. Her mother gave me Mathilde's first little chemise, and the tiny piece of linen is at this moment lying in front of me on my writing table. . . ."

THE EXILE IN FRANCE

CHAPTER
FOUR

". . . I am so pressed for money as you cannot imagine.   I am sick with worry. . . . Indeed, I do not know what I shall do. . . ."

IV

Heine seemed a changed man. Saint-Simonism had put an end to the conflict in his spiritual life, and Mathilde had put a partial check on the looseness in his sexual conduct. Neither reform was thoroughgoing or complete, but each was significant and profoundly effective. From 1834 on, Heine seemed definitely a better man; healthier mentally, more stable spiritually, and finer, softer, more tractable emotionally. Had the material concerns of life continued to go smoothly with him, one cannot imagine to what heights his now unharassed genius might have led him. He had discovered his mission in life, and had acquired his mate in love. Now all he needed was an adequate income, and everything bade fair for the future.

But then trouble began again. Heine was one of those hapless creatures who seem inexorably fated never to enjoy rest and plenty. He seems to have been one of those accursed souls for whom "no place has been reserved at the festive-board of life." In part this was certainly the fault of his own temperament; but in larger part it was the fault of the world. Georg Brandes has

characterized Heine as "the thistle in the garden of literature"; and the metaphor is peculiarly apt not only because Heine pricked most people who came near him,
but also because he too was a product of neglect. There
was at least a measure of justification for the complaint
he once made in a letter to his brother Max:

> "All the troubles of my life have come not be-
> cause of any fault of mine, but as a necessary con-
> sequence of my social position and my mental
> gifts."

Certainly the complaint was justified with reference
to the new trouble that came to Heine in 1835. He had
made no overt effort to invite it, yet it came to him
nevertheless. And in its train came a whole series of
other troubles which did not cease until his very last
breath was drawn. Like so many other of the difficulties
that marred Heine's whole life, this which came in 1835
had to do with money. It all resulted from a suppres-
sive law suddenly passed by the German Confederacy,
one of the most preposterous legislative enactments in
all of modern history. It was in effect a blanket proscription of all the books that had ever been written by
any member of what was called the Young Germany
group—*and also of all the books that any such member
might ever write in the future!*

To explain in detail the circumstances leading up to
that monstrous enactment would take us far afield. In
brief the situation was this: a little group of German
writers had become increasingly daring in their utter-

ance of doctrines which the authorities in Austria and Germany considered subversive and dangerous. Those doctrines were not primarily political, though they did have distinct political implications. Primarily they were religious and moral. At their heart lay the alluring idea of the "rehabilitation of the flesh," and out of that sprang the concomitant ideas of feminism, free-love, anti-Christianity, and a new understanding of the rights of the individual. Obviously these notions were all derived from across the Rhine; either directly or indirectly they were all inspired by Saint-Simonism. Indeed, as E. M. Butler declares in his extraordinarily illuminating work on the subject:

> ". . . the statement that Young Germany was a political movement is not comprehensive enough; it should be amplified to include the more important religious and social elements which it contained; and as these elements were Saint-Simonian in their origin, the only satisfactory definition of the school is to call it a Saint-Simonian movement. . . ."

This Young Germany movement was not an organized affair, but rather a vague and muddled attitude of protest articulated by certain young literary men, most of whom did not speak to each other. Far and away the most brilliant of them—indeed, the only truly great figure in the group—was Heinrich Heine. Though he lived in exile, he was virtually their leader, for largely through him had the rest acquired their heresies.

Next to him in point of importance came Karl Gutzkow; then Heinrich Laube, Theodore Mundt, and Ludolf Wienbarg. There were other persons associated with the movement, among them Heine's dear friend, Rahel von Varnhagen; but these played minor rôles. What alone bound them to the writers just named, and what bound these writers to each other, was a common resentment against the established order of things. All of them had been profoundly affected by the July Revolution of 1830, and the cry which had then come to them from the bloody barricades in Paris was still on their lips in Germany five years later. Each in his own way was clamoring bravely against the tyranny, piety, hypocrisy, prudishness, and Romanticism which still obtained in the Fatherland. But though they clamored bravely, it cannot be said that they were able to make much of an impression on the people. Even Heine, who was the most widely-read of them all, was unknown to the masses save as an author of love-lyrics. That is why the panic of the government, manifest in its enactment of the Federal Edict against the Young German writings, appears so ridiculous. A vast machinery was created to destroy a literature which was—save for Heine's part in it—no more formidable than a puff of smoke. The whole affair was preposterous!

Yet it came to pass nevertheless. It was made possible because by 1835 the reaction against the July Revolution was at its height. The German people lay spent, exhausted, after its futile attempt to throw off the yoke of autocracy. And this gave the junker reactionaries

their chance. Young Germany seemed the last spark
left of the last attempt at rebellion—or perhaps the
first spark of the next—and they were determined to
stamp it out now once and for all. Even though the
movement seemed primarily concerned only with moral
and æsthetic standards, the aristocrats were not blind
to its serious political implications. When, however,
they began their agitation to suppress the Young German
literature, the reactionaries based their campaign only
on its supposed immorality, for they knew that thus
could they most easily win the support of the masses.
Nor was it difficult for them to base their campaign upon
such an accusation. In 1835, Gutzkow had published a
novel entitled *Wally, Die Zweiflerin,* which seemed to
some a revoltingly immoral work. Actually it was dull
and childish, and had it not been made notorious by the
attacks of the reactionaries, the book would have attracted almost no notice. It was not in any sense por-
nographic, and it shocked the moralists not because of
its scenes but rather because of the spirit in which its
scenes were described. Gutzkow, it was maintained,
had written a wicked book. He had railed at Christian
hypocrisy, and had advocated unashamed paganism.
His whole work was an earnest plea for the "rehabilitation of the flesh."

This was why the book was made the immediate excuse for the suppression of Young Germany. The agitation was begun by Wolfgang Menzel, whom Heine had
once considered his friend. Menzel's chief point of attack was the immorality of *Wally, Die Zweiflerin,* and

he kept up his denunciations in issue after issue of his *Literaturblatt* until finally the State had to intervene. Gutzkow was condemned to ten weeks' imprisonment, and on November 14, 1835, the Prussian Diet passed an edict proscribing all Young German writings of the past *and the future!* Less than a month later the Bundestag, the Federal Diet, followed suit. And from then on Young Germany as a movement was no more. When Gutzkow was released, his spirit was gone. Laube, who had already suffered imprisonment a year earlier, turned frank traitor to the cause. Mundt held out for a while, but his writing became trivial and cheap; and Wienbarg took to drink and became a patriot. Of the whole group, only Heine did not falter.

2

IT would be difficult to exaggerate the extent to which Heine was disturbed by the Edict. To begin with, it seemed to threaten to end his career as a German writer. Ever since he had begun to write he had had his difficulties with the government censors; indeed, save for his first two books of poetry, every single thing he had ever produced had been more or less mutilated by those gentlemen. But now, under the terms of the Edict, he was made to suffer far more than censorship; now even *expurgated* writings from his pen were not to be printed! At first Heine could not believe that so monstrous an interdict was intended to be taken seriously. "The whole thing," he wrote to Campe, "seems to me to be a false alarm." He at once addressed a syrupy and submissive letter to the Diet, confident that a mere show of docility on his part would at once free him of the proscription.

> "You have accused me," he wrote, "tried me, condemned me, without giving me a hearing on paper or by word of mouth, without anyone being commissioned to defend me, without any summons being sent to me. . . . If, gentlemen, you will not grant me a free conduct to defend myself in person before you, then do you grant me at least the right of free speech in the German Press, and withdraw the interdict which you have placed on everything I may write. These words are uttered not in protest but in petition. . . . As soon as free speech is granted to me, I hope to prove conclusively that my writings are not the fruit of irreligious or immoral caprice, but of a truly religious and moral synthesis. . . . But whatever you may decide, gentlemen, in answer to my petition, you may rest assured that I shall ever obey the laws of my country. The accident of my living outside your jurisdiction will never lead me to use the language of strife, for I respect in you the highest authority of a beloved country. . . ."

But Heine had overestimated the naïveté of the legislators. He had imagined that so gentle a letter from him would melt their hearts immediately. As he assured Campe:

"The Bundestag will be touched. Everyone treats it like a dog, and therefore my politeness and delicate treatment will do it the more good. . . . 'See,' it will say, 'here is a man of human feelings, who does not treat us like a dog! And we wanted to persecute this noble man; we actually thought him irreligious and declared him immoral!' And six and thirty handkerchiefs will be moistened with the tears of the Bundestag. . . . Now we must publish a book which must be very interesting and pleasant, and free of all reference to politics or religion. The book is ready in manuscript . . . and I thought of publishing it under the title 'Salon: Part Three.' . . . Will you be able to publish this book now? And *with my name on the title-page?* . . . The chief thing is that the book should not be subjected to any censorship, and least of all to Prussian censorship. This is a point of honor. If you cannot publish the book uncensored, then you must leave it unpublished. . . ."

We can easily surmise what was Campe's reply, for soon afterwards we find Heine writing to him:

"Your letter of the 15th of March . . . has so filled me with amazement that I cannot collect my wits. But one thing remains clear in my mind. I will not betray the German Press to Prussia; I will not sell my honor for the price of a book; I will not have the least stain upon my good name. . . . If you will not publish the book as it is, then it

will not be published at all; and however bitter it
may be for me, I shall do without the payment
which I had already been counting on. . . . Poor
wretch that I am, I thought to have the pleasure of
another bank draft, for I am so pressed for money
as you cannot imagine. I am sick with worry.
. . . I shall now— Indeed I do not yet know
what I shall do! But first of all I will save my
honor. . . . I want my manuscript back. . . ."

Heine was in a horrid impasse. Here he was,
a writer by profession and instinct, suddenly robbed of
his public. As he wrote with tearful humor in the preface to his next book, the "Florentine Nights":

"I had taken such pains over the German language, with its accusative and dative, and knew
well how to string the words together beautifully,
like pearls. I had found such pleasure in that
occupation, for it shortened the long winter evenings of my exile . . . and made me almost imagine I was home with my mother. . . . And now I
have been forbidden to write!"

All his desire to create was taken from him. "What
is the good of writing," he complained, "when my words
will not be published?"

But this was not the only tragic result of the Edict
for Heine. Even more serious was the fact that it cut
off half his income at a time when he especially needed
funds. A severe attack of jaundice contracted a few

months after the passing of the Edict had depleted his treasury and left him almost penniless. Under other circumstances the poet might have been able to appeal to Campe for help, but as it was, he was left with no recourse save to call on his uncle again. This he did, but in so bitter and complaining a manner, that the millionaire was moved to anger instead of pity, and swore he would cut off even the poet's regular allowance. Salomon Heine had found little reason during the past few years to reverse his opinion about his "unsuccessful nephew." He had heard the most unpleasant rumors concerning the young man's conduct in Paris, and he was more convinced now than ever that money spent on him was worse than wasted. Perhaps the millionaire was glad his nephew's letter had been so impudent, for it gave him a righteous excuse for doing something he may long have been meditating.

3

So now Heine was worse off than before. Not merely did he lack funds at the moment, but in addition he had lost the prospect of ever getting any from his uncle in the future. In his desperate plight he could bethink himself of only one other source of help, his old friend, Moses Moser of Berlin. Heine had broken with Moser several years earlier, when Moser had criticized him for his infamous attack on Platen. In anger he had then written to Moser: ". . . you have never understood my life and work, and therefore our friendship has not come to an end; rather it never really existed."

But now Heine forgot all about that imagined lack of understanding on the part of Moser, and with almost incredible ingenuousness, wrote:

"I have often thought of you, and when I lay very ill in Paris and in my sleepless nights of fever made muster of all my friends . . . I found I could really count only on you and perhaps my brother Max. That is why . . . the friend to whom I have not written for years, now receives a letter from me asking for money. You cannot imagine how desperately I am in need of money, for after the shameful robbery practised upon me by private persons and public governments, I am miles away from the few resources left to me. I love you too much to distress you with an account of my present need. . . . You can do me a tremendous service by lending me four hundred thaler at this, the most bitter moment in the passion of my life. That is all I will tell you today. . . . As for my solvency, I must inform you that my affairs are at present in such a bad way that only a fool or a friend would lend me money now. I broke with my uncle, the millionaire, some time ago; I could not stand his meanness any longer. My French friends in their amiable frivolity have led me into heavy losses. Others have exploited me. I am not allowed to publish anything in Germany but tame

poems and innocent tales. . . . I do not know, my
dear Moser, if I am as much to you as I used to
be. I only know that I have lost nothing of my
own intrinsic value. If it were otherwise, I should
not now be in such terrible need of money. . . ."

It is not known whether Moser replied favorably to
this letter. Even if he did, it could have brought only
slight and temporary relief to the poet. What he needed
was an assured income, for without it he could never
extricate himself from his recurrent money troubles.
And that was why he was driven to a step which in later
days was destined to be almost irremediably costly.
It was an established custom of the French Government
to give pensions to certain of the more distinguished
and needy emigrés who had taken refuge in France. In
character these pensions were really tributes to their
recipients—indeed, tokens of the honor which France
felt at the presence of such distinguished guests. But
to the outside world they took on the appearance of
bribes handed out by the King to secure the favor of
these foreigners.

It was for one of these pensions that Heine now applied. He had freely criticized the rulers of France in
his letters to the German press, but that was evidently
not held against him, for, after the customary delay,
the pension was granted. In essence there was little if
any difference between Heine's willingness to receive
forty-eight hundred francs annually from Louis
Philippe, and Voltaire's willingness to accept six thou-

sand thaler annually from Frederick the Great. Nevertheless, Heine's action did put him in a shady light. Perhaps he himself realized it, for he did not reveal to any except perhaps his closest friends the fact that he was receiving the pension. He realized that his reputation as an independent liberal writer would suffer profoundly if ever it became public that he was being supported by the French Government. So he was discreet, and kept the whole matter a secret.

4

THE look of panic passed from Heine's eyes. Forty-eight hundred francs was hardly enough to support him and his mistress; but at least it was enough to keep them from starving. With a sigh of relief he settled back and finished off an entertaining folk-lore study called "Elemental Spirits" (*Elementargeister*). It was characteristic that in the hour of his greatest stress he should have taken refuge in fantasy. The poise and integration which had marked Heine a year or two earlier were gone now. Once more he was at odds with the world, and could feel at home only in a realm of dreams. Had his circumstances improved, probably he would in time have been able to recapture the wholesome mood which had been in him when he wrote "On Germany." But his circumstances became worse than ever. Hardly had he extricated himself from the difficulties of 1836, than he plunged into far greater difficulties in 1837. For early in that year the news was brought to him that he had incurred a debt of twenty thousand francs!

Just how he had incurred this debt we do not know. Heine himself never vouchsafed more than that it had been "through a friend." Possibly he had endorsed a note for someone in need. Heine had always been generous to those who came to him for help, especially if they were exiled Germans. He had fed them, clothed them, and lent them money even when he himself was in straitened circumstances. Perhaps in this case he had given his name as security for a loan to some friend who had afterwards defaulted. It is not at all incredible, for Heine was quite capable of such reckless generosity. Or perhaps he had incurred the enormous debt through speculating in stocks on the advice of some friend. We cannot tell. All we can say with assurance is that of a sudden Heine found himself face to face with bankruptcy. He could not ask his uncle to settle the debt for him, and he could not hope to pay it off out of his small government pension. Heine knew of but one person, aside from his uncle, who could possibly advance him so huge a sum, and this was his publisher, Julius Campe. But Campe was no easy man to whom to appeal, and the poet realized he would have to make vast concessions to get anything out of him.

And there was the rub: what concessions could Heine possibly make, now that his works were proscribed in Germany? Actually they were many, for the Edict of Suppression was not as absolute as Heine imagined. Campe felt the measure would soon be modified, and perhaps altogether rescinded. And even while it was still in force the publisher knew he could continue to sell Heine's works by stealth. Campe, as we have seen, was a past-master in the art of evading governmental restrictions, and even the sweeping Edict had not put an end to his activities. By shifting his press to the neighboring village of Wandsbeck, which was in Danish territory, he was able to continue printing radical books; and by giving these books false title pages, he was able to ship them into all the states of the Confederacy in the guise of harmless school-primers. It was, of course, a risky business, and required the most elaborate scheming. But Campe, who was an adventurer by instinct, did not rebel at that. The Edict should have affected him more than any other publisher in the whole country, for he had more items of Young German literature on his list than had all the other publishers put together. But actually the Edict had merely added zest to his business.

Heine, however, did not know this. Living far away in Paris, he could have no idea of just what Campe was able to do in Hamburg. Therefore he was ready to make the most inordinate concessions to his publisher in order to obtain the twenty thousand francs he needed. And Campe pressed his advantage to the limit. He finally agreed to advance Heine the money, but only on condition that the poet surrender absolutely all royalties for the next eleven years on everything he had thus far written! And only at such a price was Heine able to save himself from bankruptcy.

5

BUT Heine's difficulties were still not ended. With bankruptcy averted, he found himself confronted with another and even more serious evil. The stress and vexation he had just gone through had gravely affected his whole nervous system, and terrifying things had begun to happen to his body. The paralysis which had appeared in the fingers of his left hand as early as 1832, had advanced until it involved his whole forearm. In July, 1837, he wrote to an intimate friend, J. H. Detmold: ". . . my left hand is getting thinner and thinner, and is withering away perceptibly!" Worse still, he seemed to be going blind. The optic nerves were apparently becoming atrophied, and the lid of his left eye had developed a way of drooping down involuntarily. He told nothing of these disturbances to his old mother in Hamburg; he tried to keep them even from his less intimate friends in Paris. He did not want the world to think of him as incapacitated. The same day he wrote Detmold of the withering of his arm, he wrote to Cotta: "I am in the finest health." He even tried to conceal his troubles from those with whom he came in daily contact. Fortunately this was not impossible, for he had grown quite stout and, by hiding his hand in his pocket and making light of his drooping lid, he could give the less observant an impression of perfect health. A German writer, Ludwig Wihl, who visited Heine in October, 1837, writes:

"I found Heine much stronger and more youthful than I had expected. That is not a man whom the blows of life can shatter; that is an iron, muscular figure, more like a wrestler than a poet."

Théophile Gautier spoke of him as "a fellow like a god," and called him a "German Adonis." And Grillparzer described him as the personification of vigor and the joy of life.

But despite the impression he could give, he himself realized a dread evil was creeping over him. What it was he could not imagine, nor could his physicians inform him. Not until more than twenty years later was the science of medicine sufficiently advanced for such a case to be correctly diagnosed. The ptosis of the eyelid and the growing paralysis in the arm should have been almost unmistakable evidences that Heine was beginning to suffer at last for the indiscretions of his youth. But no one could see that, least of all Heine himself. There were moments when he did have forebodings. In August, 1837, he wrote to his brother Max:

"I am oppressed by the sad premonition that I shall be gone from the world without ever seeing you again. . . I am growing very stout, and when I look at myself in the mirror I am afraid. . . . . I am suffering from headaches again. They have plagued me for three days and make me unfit for work. And new ills have announced themselves. . . . The advance guard of decrepitude has taken up its stand. My youth is gone. . . ."

He spent the summer at the seashore, where he sought relief from his afflictions; but when he returned to Paris in September he was still far from well. To Campe he reported:

"I have been troubled with a soreness of the eyes that grows worse almost every hour. When I arrived here I could see nothing with my right eye and very little with my left. The best oculist, Sichel, has so far restored me that I am able to go out today and to write. But I am not able to see the letters clearly. I am as weak as a fly, I am letting blood every day, and I am able to eat nothing."

For several weeks he felt better, but then the soreness in his eyes returned. His physician forbade him to strain them with protracted reading or writing, and Heine tried hard to obey. But it was impossible, for he simply had to write day after day, and he could not do so satisfactorily with the eyes of another. He did engage an amanuensis—several indeed, one after another. But he could not get used to dictating his material, and invariably he had to correct with his own hand every other word in the secretary's manuscript. Yet this did not deter him, and he continued his literary efforts without cessation. It is indeed amazing to see with what assiduous industry Heine devoted himself to his writing in spite of all his afflictions. Like almost every other writer, Heine did not enjoy the actual labor of writing. He far preferred to chat in cafés, or saunter along the boulevards, or loll in little fishing-

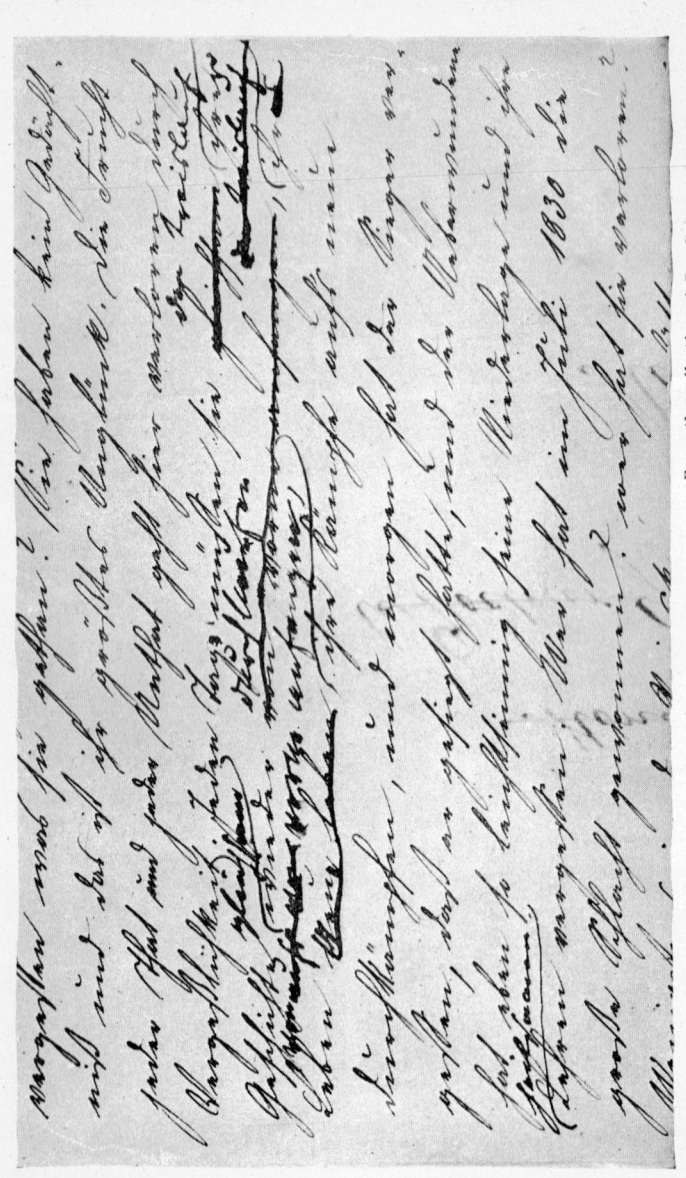

From the collection of Dr. George Alexander Kohut.

Fragment of dictated Mss. showing corrections in Heine's own hand.

boats afloat on gentle seas. But though he did not like to write, he could not be happy without having written. . . .

Most of what he now produced, however, was either violent diatribe against his enemies, or else plain hack-work. The latter he hated, for it went against his grain to write to order. But he could not avoid it, for the pension he received from the French government was not nearly sufficient for his needs. The worst of it was, however, that no matter how much hack-work he turned out, he still could not make up the deficiency. For a whole year he struggled desperately, and then he gave it up. Once more he began to make overtures to his uncle, using Max as intermediary. On August 5, 1837, he wrote his brother a long letter to explain the precise circumstances of the quarrel with the banker in 1836:

"At a time when I was brought to bitter extremity by sickness (I had jaundice as well) and by misfortune that was not of my fault, I wrote to Uncle in a tone which should have called for pity rather than anger. It only excited rage in him, however. . . . The few thousand francs that I cost him hardly justify him in complaining of me, he, the millionaire, the greatest millionaire in Hamburg, whose generosity—enough! You know that I loved this man as my own father, and now I must —but enough! What hurts me most of all is that the world cannot explain my Uncle's hardness save

on the ground that I did some scurvy trick which
my family knows but keeps from the public . . .
Ah! If I were to play a scurvy trick or two, I
should now stand well with the whole world and—
enough!"

Max in his reply to this letter must have urged Heinrich to apologize to the millionaire—advice which elic-
ited the retort:

"By God, it is not Uncle but *I* who have cause
to complain. . . . After all, with what can he reproach me except disrespect in words?"

Nevertheless, Heine did write conciliatingly to his
uncle. He tried to explain that he had addressed him so
disrespectfully a year earlier, simply because he had
been almost out of his wits at the time.

". . . it was a period when the most unmerited
misfortune had cruelly embittered me, and my
dreadful sickness, jaundice, had changed my whole
being and had inspired me with fears of which you
can have no suspicion. . . . You know that in our
family, with our frank and quick-tempered character, angry words do not mean much, for they are
always regretted the next moment—if not entirely
forgotten. Who can know this better than you,
my dear Uncle, at whose angry words one would
die were not one assured that they came from
. . . a heart full of kindness, gentleness, and
magnanimity."

Thus Heine went on, conciliatingly, caressingly. He rehearsed his troubles once more, told of his superlative gifts, lamented the "curse which falls upon all men of great genius," and finally rounded off his letter with the appealing query:

"Tell me why the man who is so gentle, so compassionate, so full of pity for strangers, should treat his own nephew with such harshness?"

That letter, so mollifyingly phrased, had its effect. The millionaire let it be known that he was not unmoved by his "unsuccessful nephew's" petition, and a reconciliation was effected. But the allowance was not at once renewed. Salomon Heine thought it well to keep the repentant scapegrace on tenterhooks for a while yet, and refused to say a word about money. So the poet, in despair again, began to look elsewhere for help. It occurred to him there might be some profit in publishing a German paper in Paris, and eagerly he went about in search of some person able and willing to finance the project. He found such a person after great difficulty, but then he discovered that the undertaking could never yield any monetary returns unless the paper were permitted to circulate in Prussia. That, of course, put an end to the scheme. Even though Varnhagen, at Heine's behest, used all his influence in Berlin, and Heine himself promised the paper would offend against none of the accepted standards, the Prussian government refused out of hand to promise toleration of any journal at all associated with the poet's name.

So now there was nothing left for Heine but to return to his hack-work. By this time, fortunately, the Edict against the Young German writings had been somewhat modified, and he was once more given the right to publish in the Fatherland, though only under the strictest censorship. He hit off a preface for a new edition of "Don Quixote," and he wrote a whole series of critical studies entitled "Shakespeare's Women and Maidens" (*Shakespeares Mädchen und Frauen*). But he had no high opinion of those products. Of the Don Quixote preface he confessed to Campe, "It is the worst thing I have ever written. . . . I did it for money"; and of the work on Shakespeare he wrote, "Between ourselves, it is no masterpiece." Still, they had their value, for at least they helped keep a roof over the head of their author and his mistress.

Finally, however, Salomon Heine softened and with showy benevolence came to the rescue. On a business trip to Paris sometime in 1838, he saw his nephew, took pity on him, and renewed the allowance of four thousand francs a year. And thus at last Heine's most pressing financial difficulties were ended.

6

BUT the three years of torment had left their mark on the poet. They had broken him physically and had poisoned him spiritually. Gone altogether was the last vestige of the spiritual integration he had attained in his middle thirties. Now he was left more embittered

against the world and more remorseless to his foes than
ever he had been before. Save for the essays and prefaces he had been compelled to write for money, all of
his products after 1836 had been vituperative assaults
on those whom he considered his enemies. In 1837
he had flung himself on Menzel, who had precipitated
the war on Young Germany. The next year, 1838, he
belabored Pfizer, and the others of the Swabian School
of poetry who had dared to speak slightingly of his
genius. In 1839 he turned—not without justice—on
his own publisher, Campe, and on his former co-work-
ers, Gutzkow and Wihl. And finally in 1840, he quite
lost control of himself and wrote a brilliant but malicious and indefensible book against his old and now
dead enemy, Ludwig Börne.

Of all the sorry mistakes ever committed by Heine,
the writing of the book against Börne was certainly the
sorriest. Its underlying thesis was valid, and indubitably deserved publication. As Dr. Ras contends:

> "Heine's book on Börne is more than an act of
> vengeance; it is the apologia of a poet-publicist who
> realized he knew the great 'watchword of the fu-
> ture' . . . and who championed the cause of the
> 'war for human liberation' with greater vision and
> therefore in a more revolutionary way than was sus-
> pected by the Liberals with their bigoted party
> spirit."

But though its thesis was valid, the tone of the book
was deplorable. One can explain it only on the ground

that his nerves were so raw from incessant vexation, and his body so poisoned by disease, that he did not really know what he was doing. The book purported to be a character sketch of Ludwig Börne, who had died three years earlier. As we have already seen, the relations between Heine and the great radical leader had been strained from 1832 on. During those years Börne had taken occasion again and again to attack the younger man, denouncing him for his shameless immorality, calling him a renegade from the cause of liberty, and even hinting he was in the pay of the reactionaries. To all these attacks and insinuations Heine had never once replied in print. Even in private conversation the poet seems to have been rather restrained in his comments about Börne. Indeed, from first to last, Heine revealed a patience and a discretion which redounded highly to his credit. If at times he was tempted to write against Börne, the memory of the Platen incident may have kept him from yielding. He was still suffering from the popular reaction to that onslaught, for many people now laid to it the blame for Platen's untimely death. But Heine could not remain silent forever, for with the passing of the years Börne's extremist ideas seemed to be gaining in popularity, and the poet felt it was his bounden duty as a liberal to make some protest.

But as soon as his book appeared, the cry went up that the author had waited until Börne was dead, only out of cowardice. Heine might have guessed this would happen, but the bitterness long pent up in him had ren-

dered him incapable of reasoning. He had not heeded
even the anxious warnings of his closest friends. Heinrich Laube tells us:

> "I advised him against it, for such a work could
> only hurt the liberal cause. . . . It became the
> subject of daily argument between us . . . never-
> theless, he did write the book, and when he brought
> me the manuscript he exclaimed with a triumphant
> air: 'Read and remain master of your senses. It
> is remarkable!' I did remain master of my senses,
> and said the book was empty and annoying. I told
> him he ought at least erect a mountain in the midst
> of his low invectives, a mountain which would re-
> veal loftily his own higher and broader view of
> the world. That might excuse all the polemical
> matter in the book. . . . And Heine replied, 'You
> are right about the mountain. I shall erect it.'
> And then, day after day, he would report: 'The
> mountain is begun! It is growing! It arises!' "

What is perhaps most bewildering in connection with
this sorry book is the absurd valuation Heine put on
it. To be sure, he did write it with inordinate care,
revising it more than once, and striving to fill it with
his most mordant wit. But even that does not explain
how he could say of it, as he did to Campe:

> "I believe my 'Börne' will be recognized as the
> best work I have yet written. . . . It will have an
> enduring historical value, as well as the charm of

a humorous book of entertainment. Certainly it
will be far more enjoyed by the people of our own
day than my purely fantastic writings."

A madder prophecy was never made. Most people,
far from preferring it to his other works, considered
it one of the most unfortunate ever written by any
author.

Most of the critics conceded that the book was superlatively clever and witty, but all of them insisted it was
inexcusable nevertheless. Gutzkow in the *Telegraph
für Deutschland* said: "Heine pretends to be a poet, but
writes like a gamin." Rosen in the *Literaturblatt* declared: "Heine shows here all the ugly qualities of an
alien race we shall not mention: deceit, presumption,
cowardice, and shamelessness." The *Mainzer Unter-
haltungsblätter* called the author a "chattering washer-
woman," and his book merely "gilded mud." The
Elberfeld Zeitung concluded: "The final judgment is
'Pfui!'" And the *Didaskalia* declared:

"For years we've seen a man go through the
streets with gloomy eye, dissipated face, and an ef-
feminate smile, his hands always in his pockets
because they pay the cost of sin that shuns the light
of day . . . and spattering the passerby with mud.
. . . Börne, like the Savior, was betrayed by the
kiss of Judas."

The comments were obviously vindictive. The critics had long awaited an opportunity such as this, for

Heine seemed utterly indefensible now and they knew
they could pounce upon him and rend him with impu-
nity. "Heine has dealt himself the death-blow," they
cried gleefully—and immediately the jackals fell to
tearing at his flesh.

What made "On Börne" especially diabolical was its
pretense of impartiality. Heine did not condemn whole-
sale, but, with a great show of gracious justice, he admitted Börne had his qualities. For instance, he spoke
quite glowingly of Börne's patriotism.

> "Yes, this Börne was a great patriot, perhaps
> the greatest that ever sucked sweet life and bitter
> death from the breasts of Germania, his step-
> mother."

And Heine made it very clear that he considered
Börne's ancestry a thing to his credit.

> "It used to amuse him," Heine wrote, "when his
> enemies could find nothing worse to say of him than
> that he was a descendant of a race that once had
> filled the world with its glory, and, in spite of all its
> degradation, had never altogether lost its sanctity.
> . . . Indeed, the Jews are of the dough whereof the
> gods are kneaded. If today they are trampled
> under foot, tomorrow they are worshipped; while
> some of them creep about in the filthiest mire of
> commerce, others ascend to the highest peaks of
> humanity—for Golgotha is not the only mountain
> on which a Jewish God has bled for the salvation

of the world.   The Jews are the people of the spirit,
and whenever they return to their spirit they are
great, splendid, and put to shame and conquer their
rude oppressors. . . . It is remarkable, how striking are the contrasts!   While among the Jews there
is to be found every possible caricature of vul-
garity, there are among them also the ideals of the
purest humanity.   Just as they once led the world
into new paths of progress, so the world has perhaps still to look for leadership from them."

It is obvious, of course, why Heine should have
grown so rhapsodic in speaking of Börne's Jewish origin.
He could hardly do otherwise, for any attack on Börne
as a Jew would have been an attack on himself as well.
The only qualities in Börne which he dared to assail
were those which he himself lacked.   For instance,
there was Börne's willingness to make fellowship with
beer-drinking, tobacco-smoking unwashed artisans.
That had always been beyond Heine's comprehension,
for his olfactory organs alone made the company of
those ragged revolutionaries impossible.   But yet, it
was not to his own squeamishness in this regard that
Heine attributed the disfavor with which the other
had long regarded him.   No—

". . . all his [Börne's] animosities were funda-
mentally nothing but the petty jealousy which the
little drummer feels for the great drum-major.
Börne envied me my great plume which waved so

bravely in the air, my richly embroidered uniform . . . my skill in balancing the great baton, and the loving glances which the wenches cast at me and which I perhaps returned with some coquetry. . . ."

But such reflections on Börne were as nothing compared with the remarks directed at his gentle platonic friend, Frau Wohl. In making these Heine sank to a depth of caddishness which even the spirit of his generation, the intensity of his grudge, and the state of his health, cannot quite explain. Heine's description of the lady was alone enough to condemn the book. Madame Wohl was, he wrote,

> . . . a thin person whose yellow-white, pock-marked face resembled an old piece of matzoh . . . and whose voice creaked like a door on rusty hinges."

And this ugly woman, Heine freely insinuated, was far more than merely a platonic friend to Börne. When the poet had stopped over in Frankfurt in 1827 and asked where he could find Börne, the answer was: "Where Dr. Börne lives we do not know—but Frau Wohl lives on the Wollgraben. . . ."

> "One did not know [continued Heine] just what her relationship with Börne entitled her to be called, whether his sweetheart or merely his wife. Their closest friends firmly maintained for a long

time that Mme. Wohl was secretly married to him, and would make her appearance one fine morning as Frau Doktor Börne. . . . But then we were all astounded by the sudden news that Mme. Wohl had married not Börne but a young merchant from Frankfurt. All three lived together for a while [in Paris]. Yes, they say the young husband only married the woman to get in closer touch with Börne, and he stipulated that the earlier relationship should remain unchanged. I was informed he played the servant in the house . . . a useful messenger for Börne, whose reputation he peddled around. . . . If I am to tell the truth, I must admit I saw in this household of Börne's an immorality that revolted me . . . Mme. Wohl actually joined him under cover of marriage with a ridiculous third person!"

Heine regretted that last passage the moment the book appeared, and he expunged it and most of the other references to the lady from the second edition. But by then it was already too late, and adequate amends could never be made. As William Sharp comments in this connection in his little biography of Heine:

"After one throws a stone through a stranger's bedroom window, it is not sufficient restitution to voluntarily pay the glazier's bill."

Heine was destined to have to pay more than that, far more, and involuntarily, for the crime he had committed. First of all, he lost the regard of many of his most loyal admirers. Even those who had disliked Börne could find little excuse for the character of this onslaught. And Heine suffered further because Frau Wohl (now Straus) immediately replied by publishing all that Börne had written to her about *him*. In a small measure that helped Heine, for it revealed how vilely he had been pelted by his enemy before he attempted to retaliate. But in far greater measure it hurt Heine, for it left him publicly covered with mud.

7

BUT there was still more for Heine to pay. Frau Wohl had been able to retort by publishing a book; but her husband, the "ridiculous third person," sought satisfaction in a directer manner. According to his account, he one day confronted Heine on the street and boxed him on the ears. The act was intended, of course, to provoke Heine into a duel; but, although cards were exchanged, Heine did not wait for the arrangements to be made, but fled at once to the Pyrenees. At least, such was the story Straus told to the newspaper reporters; and he claimed he had several witnesses to substantiate it. But he lied at least with regard to the last detail, for actually he had no witnesses at all. According to Heine, Straus's whole story was a gross fabrication.

"Not a word of it is true [he wrote his friends]. I am certainly not the lamb who suffered insult in

the street in the heart of Paris, and the individual
who boasted of it is certainly the very last of the
lions who would dare do such a thing! The whole
encounter consisted of a few stammering words with
which that individual tremblingly approached me,
and which I laughingly brought to an end by giving him my address and the information that I was
on the point of setting out for the Pyrenees. . . .
That is the whole story of the encounter. There
were no witnesses, and I give you my word of honor
that in the whirl of business with which I was bur-
dened the day before setting out on the journey,
the whole affair almost slipped my memory. . . .
I have to deal here with the flower of the Frankfurt
ghetto and a vengeful woman. . . ."

But it was useless for Heine to try to explain what
had happened. The German press had caught up the
story avidly and had carried it throughout Central Europe. Ten weeks later, when Heine returned to Paris,
he saw he would never be done with the nasty affair
until he shot it out with Straus. But now Straus was
most reluctant to meet Heine, and found every possible
excuse for putting off an encounter. Heine, however,
pursued him indefatigably. "He must meet me," he
declared, "even if I have to pursue him to the Great
Wall of China!"

Finally, on September 7, 1841, the duel was fought.
Heine's account of the meeting, given in a letter to
Campe, is as follows:

"The day before yesterday at seven o'clock I had at last the satisfaction of meeting Mr. Straus. He showed more courage than I had credited him with, and he was remarkably favored by circumstances. His bullet struck my hip, which is at present still very swollen and as black as coal. I have to stay in bed, and shall not be able to walk properly for some time. The bone was not injured, but has suffered a concussion which I still feel. The affair has gone off well for me—physically, not morally." . .

THE EXILE IN FRANCE

CHAPTER
FIVE

"On the 31st of August I married Ma-
thilde . . . with whom I had previously
quarreled daily for more than six
years. . . ."

V

HOSTILITY, disgrace, scandal, a duel, a swollen hip—all these were part of the price Heine had to pay for his attack on Börne. Yet, compared with the rest he had to pay, these were petty costs. Hostility and scandal he was accustomed to; the swollen hip he could survive. But the gravest consequence of the imbroglio dogged the poet to his dying day, for as a direct result of the encounter with Herr Straus, Heine married Mathilde!

He had been driven to take this step by concern for her future. Heine had feared that in the event of his death, she would be left almost penniless if she were not his legal wife. His main source of income, aside from the French pension, was the allowance given him by his uncle, and this, Heine had felt, would never be continued for Mathilde if she did not bear his name. Accordingly, about a week before the time fixed for the duel, the poet took his mistress to the Hotel de Ville and made her legally his wife. And because Mathilde, who was a most devout Catholic, had not considered herself sufficiently married by this civil ceremony, Heine had gone with her later to St. Sulpice and had there suffered the union to be solemnized by the Church. And thus, at the age of forty-four, Heine had at last become a respectable married man!

We cannot be sure whether or no Heine enjoyed his new rôle; probably he was not sure himself. Certainly he entered into the union with bitter misgivings, as we can see from the way he reported the event. To his sister he wrote:

> "On the 31st of August I married Mathilde Crescentia Mirat, with whom I had previously quarreled daily for more than six years. Yet she has a most noble and pure heart, and is as good as an angel."

To August Lewald, he declared:

> "This matrimonial duel, which will not end until one of us be slain, is certainly more dangerous than was the short combat with Solomon Straus of the Frankfurt Judengasse."

To his friend, Caroline Jaubert, who wanted to tell the musician, Rossini, about the marriage, Heine said:

> "But tell him that my happiness was decided with a pistol at my throat!"

And to Alexandre Weill he jokingly declared:

> "That horrible Frau Wohl has taken a cruel revenge . . . but I have avenged myself in turn. When, after leaving the church, I made my will, I

bequeathed everything to my wife. But I stipulated one condition: that she marry immediately after my death. You see, I have thus made sure that there shall be at least one man on earth who will regret my passing! . . ."

A stranger and worse mated couple than this poet and his shop-girl wife, would have been difficult to find. Mathilde had not changed greatly with the passing of the years. At twenty-five she was still a wild, irresponsible, reckless creature, thoughtless, ignorant, and irrepressibly gay. Of course, at times she could be delightfully gentle and generous; but such times were none too frequent, and never very prolonged. Our most detailed reports concerning Heine's ménage come from his friend, Alexandre Weill, and although these seem often suspiciously high-colored, on the whole they are probably not untrustworthy. Here is a characteristic anecdote for which Weill is responsible:

" 'What do you think of the pike?' asked Madame Heine at dinner one night. 'I bought it myself.'

" 'It smells,' I replied. But the words were hardly out of my mouth before Mathilde, picking up the platter on which the pike was swimming in its gravy, threw it in my face! She might have broken my nose, had not the fish softened the blow. I was speechless.

" 'Weill,' said Heine, 'she must love you very much to let herself go so far!' . . .

"And Mathilde wiped me off with her napkin, laughed, and asked my pardon for her liveliness. *That* was the sort of thing she called liveliness!"

The anecdote sounds incredible; yet there is sufficient testimony by other witnesses to convince us that Mathilde was capable of such conduct. But Heine, who had always had a preference for volatile people, seems not to have objected to the woman's excitability. Other of her traits, however, could not but have made her company almost unendurably trying. The worst of these was her continual noisiness. She had a delightful voice, and several of Heine's friends have commented on the way the poet would often pause in the midst of whatever he was saying, to listen to her carolling in another room. But there must have been hours when the sound of her voice tormented him unspeakably. Heine was not one of those facile writers who could hit off their poems or essays while lounging in cafés. He needed utter stillness, for he wrote with exacting pain. And the continual presence of Mathilde must therefore have been agonizing. If she herself was not talking, her irrepressible parrot, Cocotte, squawked at the top of its shrill voice. Mathilde was almost morbidly attached to the bird. She had other pets—a cat, a canary, and some goldfish—but from first to last the dreadful parrot was her favorite. She thought more of it than of her husband, and frankly admitted as much. If, after a quarrel, she stamped out of the apartment and did not return in time for dinner, Heine's first concern was to see if the parrot was still in the kitchen. As long as the bird was there, Heine knew his wife had not deserted him. Mathilde always took the bird with her whenever she went on a long journey, and when, many years later, it was secretly done to death by the exasperated poet, she was prostrated for days.

But the parrot and cat and other pets were not the only disturbing elements that Mathilde brought into Heine's home. In addition there were shop-girl friends to whom she liked to chatter for hours on end. One can hardly blame Mathilde. She *had* to have some sort of companionship during hours when her husband sat at his desk and wrote. In the afternoons she would often go out and stroll on the boulevards or shop for bargains in the *magazins*. But in the forenoons, and on rainy days, she could not remain in her room alone. Another woman might have been able to while away the hours in reading or housework; but Mathilde could not read and would not work, so she was forced to seek diversion in the company of her parrot or her friends.

Heine must have realized this, for he complained very little of the disturbance caused by those visitors. Perhaps on the whole he was better satisfied to have his wife make a noise at home than get into mischief abroad. For he was fearfully jealous of his pretty Mathilde, and always worried when she was away. Having seduced her without difficulty, he was never free of the fear that another man might find the feat as easy. So he encouraged her to remain at home as much as possible. Not merely did that keep her out of sight of the boulevard philanderers, but also it kept her away from the shopkeepers. Like many another girl reared in poverty, now that Mathilde had money she could not resist the temptation to spend it. She was forever buying dresses and hats and linens and trinkets, cluttering up every closet in her apartment with laces and bric-à-brac. Next to her noisiness, her extravagance was perhaps her greatest fault. Heine had to labor and fret incessantly to pay for her foolish expenditures.

There were still other faults in Mathilde. She lacked entirely all sympathy with her husband's work. She could not even understand what he was doing, let alone inspire him. Mentally and spiritually these two lived in utterly different worlds; they spoke two different languages. And what made it worse, the grisette resented this even more than the poet. It angered her that most of her husband's acquaintances paid almost no attention to her, and she did her utmost to make it uncomfortable or even impossible for them to call on him at his home. As a result, of all the many contemporaries who have left us any record of the Heine household, only one reveals any particular sympathy for Mathilde. That person was Caroline Jaubert, a funny little Frenchwoman who was one of the very few persons who never wavered in loyalty to the poet. With an understanding which, under the circumstances, only a woman could have had, Mme. Jaubert writes:

"It was hard for this young, lively, childless wife
. . . to endure the life they led, and one can only
praise her conduct towards Heinrich Heine . . .
To go walking on his arm, to show herself openly,
were pleasures of vanity which she had rarely enjoyed. Before he grew too ill, she used to drag him
to concerts. This was an opportunity for her to see
and be seen, and thus we several times met the
couple; but it always seemed to embarrass Heine.
He seemed to want to act like a bachelor and yet
not abandon his wife."

There is ample reason for believing that Heine was
indeed secretly ashamed of his wife when in company.
Usually he went out alone, and when people called on
him at his apartment, he seems to have kept her out
of the way. Hans Christian Andersen tells us that
when, on his first visit to Paris, he sought out the great
poet, he was not introduced to Mathilde—who was in
the next room, playing with some children from a
neighboring house—until he had assured the poet that
he did not intend to publish an account of the visit!
Heinrich Börnstein, a German journalist who visited
Heine, reports:

"Heine was greatly embarrassed when any
stranger from Germany looked him up directly at
his home. Then he usually said he was ill or not
at home, had the stranger leave his address, and
the next day wrote and gave him an appointment
at a café of the Palais Royal or the Tuileries."

Yet nothing is more obvious than that Heine loved Mathilde with a deep and sincere passion. One cannot on any other basis explain the patience with which he bore all her vagaries, or the anxiety with which he sought to protect her. It is not enough to point out, as has already been done here, that Heine found her lowly origin and her naïve ignorance peculiarly satisfying to his harried ego. Quite clearly he felt for her an attraction that must have been rooted in the very chemistry of his being. The newer psychology can offer at best only a hint as to the origin of that attraction. It can suggest that children often repeat the sexual histories of their parents, and it can point out in this instance that since Peira van Geldern had been moved to marry a "love-object" beneath her socially and intellectually, her son was psychically predestined to do likewise. But that is hardly enough to explain the vast patience and tenderness and unflagging passion with which Heine clung to the vain, extravagant, lazy baggage whom he made his wife. No matter how much technical jargon one may dragoon into service on this matter, it still remains a perplexing and perhaps insoluble mystery. Heine *loved* his wife—and that is all the explanation one can give.

2

THE most striking evidence of Heine's affection for Mathilde is to be seen in the way he spoke of her to his mother and sister. The poet wrote to Hamburg on an average of once a month, and his letters reveal a side of Heine's nature one would never suspect from his other writings. To the world that man was a veritable demon, a fiendish creature who scoffed and scorned and destroyed without qualm; but to his old mother he was as tender, as considerate, as a son out of fiction. She was in her seventies now, a sad, broken old lady, dwelling alone in a ramshackle house by the city wall. Life had not dealt generously with her. She who once had been so proud and ambitious, was now left a pauper dependent upon the bounty of her rich brother-in-law. Of her four children, only one, Charlotte, lived near her in Hamburg. The rest were all living far away. Max, the physician, was in St. Petersburg; Gustav, now a cavalry officer, was in Vienna; and Heinrich, the poet, was in Paris.

Of all her children she seems to have loved Heinrich the most, as one might well expect, seeing he was the one who had all along brought her the greatest concern and grief. She worried about him constantly, for she feared his mad ideas and his pain-racked body would bring him to no good end. And Heinrich, who knew this, made every effort to dispel her fears. When he wrote to her it was always gaily, as though he had hardly a trouble in the world. If at times he complained, it was always lightly and with some witticism. He lied extravagantly about the state of his health, and about the circumstances of his life in Paris; and almost always he spoke of his wife in terms of the highest praise. Here, for instance, is a characteristic passage:

"As for my marriage, there has been no change in it. On the contrary, my wife becomes every year more reasonable and pleasant, and I have never regretted having married her. That is saying much in these days, and especially in Paris, which swarms with wretched marriages. Indeed, good ones are so rare that they ought to be preserved in alcohol!"

Quite clearly he did not want the old lady to know the true state of affairs. Once, long before, when she wrote that she yearned to see him and planned to come to Paris, he hastily forbade her to do so. Indeed, he jokingly threatened to flee to Egypt if she persisted in carrying out her intention. But she continued to dwell on the matter until Heine, for fear she might come despite his adjurations, now finally went to see her in Hamburg. He set out on the journey suddenly and secretly. In Hamburg, which was a "free city," he knew he would be fairly safe from police molestation, but to get there by land he had to pass through Prussian territory, and there he was still liable to arrest. So he let none save his mother know of his intentions. At the end of October, 1843, Heinrich Heine suddenly turned up in Hamburg. After an absence of more than twelve years, the Prodigal Son was home once more.

Heine has left us a delightful account of that homecoming in a long, semi-humorous poem entitled "Germany—a Winter's Tale" (*Deutschland ein Winter-*

märchen). His old mother was transported at the sight of him, and, in the manner of all good Jewish mothers, immediately began to ply him with food and questions. She made him sit down before a table loaded with stuffed-fish and roast duck and other such viands, and then, seating herself by his side, began at once to ask:

"My darling child, in your foreign home
    Are you carefully served and tended?
Does your wife understand how to keep a house?
    Are your shirts and stockings mended?"

To which Heinrich could only reply evasively:

"Dear little mother, the fish is good,
    But fish is a risky diet;
You so easily choke on a bone if you speak;
    Just leave me a moment in quiet."

But the dear old woman was not to be put off. Insistently she continued:

"My child! And what are at present your views?
    Is your interest still as hearty
In politics as it used to be?
    What is your creed? Your party?"*

Heinrich, according to the poem, still did not answer directly. He knew his old mother, and was certain she

* This version is by Gilbert Cannan, and is taken from his translation of Gustav Karpeles's work: "Heinrich Heine's Memoirs."

would never understand if he told her the truth. As he wrote in the first of his letters to Mathilde:

"I found my mother much altered. She is very weak and feeble. She has shrunk under the weight of her sorrows and her old age. Being anxious as she is, the smallest trifle can excite her. Her great misfortune is pride. She never goes out because she has not the means to entertain visitors in her own house."

Heine spent most of his time with his mother in her two little rooms, allowing her to show him off to her cronies, entertaining her with fabulous tales of his life in Paris, telling her how beautiful and kindly was his wife, and otherwise striving to bring her joy. Continually he joked and chaffed, discovering in everything a hidden absurdity at which she could not but laugh. When, for instance, he saw one of her friends, a sere old Jewess in wig and mittens, he chucklingly pointed out that she would be entrancingly beautiful if only her face did not disfigure her so! Heine realized that his poor old mother had laughed all too little in the seventy years of her life, and he determined now to have her make up for it. With a love and tenderness almost inconceivable in a man who could have written the "Baths of Lucca" or "On Börne," Heinrich devoted himself to filling the life of the aged woman with cheer.

3

BUT he could not remain at home with his mother all of the time he was in Hamburg. As soon as his presence became known in the city, he was allowed very little quiet. For by now he was recognized as one of the most famous men that had ever lived in Hamburg, and (next to Klopstock!) certainly the greatest poet. Accordingly he came in for not a little lionizing, especially on the part of the few residents of Hamburg who had any love for the arts. Even his rich old uncle, Salomon, was cordial to him. The old man was quite ill at the time, and in such pain that he could hardly feel in a generous mood. Yet he seems to have gone out of his way to assure Heine that he no longer considered him his "unsuccessful nephew," or a "stupid boy." And, if we are to accept the opinion of Elster, Heine received a reception even more than cordial from his cousin, Therese. And there is evidence in such poems as *"Alte Rose"* and *"Wiedersehen"* to substantiate Elster's idea.

There can be no uncertainty, however, as to the manner in which Heine was received by his publisher, Julius Campe. One of the express reasons for the poet's journey to Hamburg had been his eagerness to see this man. For twelve years now he had been carrying on all his negotiations with the publisher by mail or messenger, and matters had not gone smoothly. Heine felt he ought to come to some definite terms with Campe as to the future. He realized he was Campe's most valuable author; that, indeed, his works were the pillars upon which the whole firm of Hoffmann and Campe rested. And now Heine was determined to get a little of the profit for himself. He wanted Campe to pay him—or Mathilde, should she survive him—a fixed annual subsidy. The sum was not to be considered in the nature of an advance against his royalties, but rather a retainer. Heine did not ask that it be a huge sum; he hoped for about three thousand francs, no more. But that much—well, almost that much, at least—he was utterly determined to get.

Campe, knowing even better than Heine how deeply he was indebted to the poet for the present position of his house, was ready to be tractable. He was almost excessively cordial to the visitor, arranging little parties in his honor, and generally putting himself out in order to show his friendliness. Apparently he was quite sincerely pleased with Heine, for in a letter to Gutzkow he wrote:

> "I find Heine unchanged—without the corpulence and all the foolishness people have reported. But changed he is in this—that he is thirteen years older, quieter, more thoughtful, more manly, less exacting—in short, pleasant and entirely amiable."

But though he was thus favorably impressed with Heine, the close-fisted publisher was by no means willing to accede immediately to the poet's demands. Some sort of retainer Campe knew he would have to give; but he hoped to haggle the amount down to considerably below

Heine's figure. Campe, who was not a Jew, was yet a master at the art which Christian tradition so blandly credits exclusively to the Jew; indeed, at bargaining Heine was not even remotely a match for him. The poet did not know how to hem and haw, how to seem aggrieved when he was secretly satisfied, or simulate finality when he was ready to compromise. Besides, he was pressed for time. Despite the pleasant way in which he was being treated in Hamburg, he wanted to get away. The horrid climate of Hamburg made his head ache, and filled his whole being with wretchedness. And —what was even harder to bear—he was worried about Mathilde. Evidently his old jealous distrust of her still lingered in his heart, for in his every letter he adjured her to "be prudent and stay at home." In one letter he reported to her:

> "Karl Heine makes fun of my jealousy, and is surprised that I was ever able to resolve to leave you in Paris. You are my poor, beloved wife, and I hope you are well behaved and sensible. I pray you not to show yourself too much in public."

In his next letter, three days later, he wrote:

> "I am thinking only of you, my dear Nonotte. It was a great resolve to leave you alone in Paris, that fearful abyss! Do not forget that my eyes are always upon you. I know everything you do, and what I don't know I shall learn later."

And again three days later he wrote:

"You are always in my thoughts and I cannot be at ease. Vague and melancholy fears torture me day and night. You are the only joy of my life—don't make me unhappy."

And he goes on:

"Adieu, my angel, my dearest, my poor child, my good wife! . . . My God! My God! I haven't heard you twitter for two weeks."

Thus did he write to his wife again and again, always telling how dearly he loved her and revealing how deeply he distrusted her. He was consumed with passionate jealousy, and he would have hastened back to Paris almost immediately had it not been that he was determined not to let Campe cheat him entirely out of his rights. Even as it was, he could not hold out to the bitter end. By the end of November he could stand the separation from Mathilde no longer, and he modified his demand. Thereupon a contract was immediately signed, and then Heine wrote to his wife exultingly:

"My affairs with my publisher have been cleared up. Everything is arranged, even for the future. I have given him the right to publish my works for all time. . . . And he is to pay me in return a life annuity of 1200 marks banko—that is about twenty-four hundred francs. If I die before you, this annuity will pass to you. . . . This is the basis of our contract. It is a great secret which I shall tell to no one; but as you wish to hear details from me,

I shall not keep from you this new arrangement, which, four years from now, gives me two hundred francs a month more for our livelihood. At the same time it is an undertaking to assure your income after my death—which will not occur so very soon, for I am in excellent health. It is the duty of every man to provide for his wife in the event of his death, and to see that his widow is not exposed to difficulties. *This is no merit in a man, but duty.* . . . My Uncle is better. My family is quite well. I never cease talking about you. . . ."

Once the contract was signed, Heine left immediately for Paris. From Bückeburg, on the way, he dispatched a final letter which is worth quoting:

"I am sure you do not know where Bückeburg is, even though it is a very famous town in the annals of our family. But that does not matter; the main thing is "that I am on my way, I am well, I love you with all my heart, and I shall probably embrace you on Saturday. I am tormented with anxiety about you. To be so long without news of you! God, how terrible! I am exceedingly angry with you, and when I arrive I shall give you only five hundred kisses, instead of a thousand!"

4

BACK again in Paris, Heine at once settled down to work. He was in excellent spirits now, for he felt almost at peace with the world. He was more relieved now mentally than he had been for years, and he could give himself to verse with a freedom he had rarely before enjoyed. Already the year before, in 1842, he had been able to produce a work of poetry. It had been a long epic poem in which he had satirized the current world-saving idealisms of both the Communists and the German-Christian Burschenschaft members. "Atta Troll" he had called it, after the name of a bear who was the hero of the epic. Atta Troll, a runaway dancing bear, sits in the forest, surrounded by its ursine family, and holds forth in a delicious, childlike, monotonous growl concerning the rights of man, religion, and the future of the world. And through these ineffectual growlings, Heine had made sport of all the narrow, bigoted, humorless dreamers of his time. Elster agrees in characterizing it as "the last, free, wood-song of Romanticism," and Fürst, as "the swan-song of a vanishing period." Portions of it, especially the descriptions of the wild hunt, were later recognized as among the most brilliant poetic presentations in the German language. Heine had been in fine fettle again. The Muse had returned to him—as it almost always returned when the wolf was not too close to his door—and once more he had been able to lift his voice in song.

And the Muse was still with him now that he was back from his successful visit to Hamburg. Almost immediately he began to write another long poem, this time in rhyme. It was that long, humorous narrative epic, "Germany—A Winter's Tale," from which quotation has already been made. Its satirical jabs, particularly at the Prussian police, were rather too blunt and violent to make good verse; but in Heine's own opinion, the poem was one of his finest achievements. When he had finished it he wrote Campe: "It will arouse a greater furore than the most popular pamphlet, and will yet have permanent value as a work of classic poetry."

But Heine was not ready to remain idle until such time as his prophecy might be fulfilled. As soon as "Germany—a Winter's Tale" was completed, he returned to prose for a short while. He wrote several articles for the *Allgemeine Zeitung*—the old ban against his press reports was forgotten by now—and hit off prefaces for certain of his earlier works which were now to appear in new editions. Then once more he veered back to poetry, making a collection of all the lyrics he had written since his first coming to Paris. "New Poems" (*Neue Gedichte*) he planned to call the collection, and only when he had prepared the entire manuscript did he begin to think at last of taking another holiday.

He was overcome by a desire to visit Hamburg again, for he longed for another look at his dear ones there. Besides, he had had a long and unsatisfactory correspondence with Campe concerning his "New Poems," and he wanted to see the work through the press himself. But this time Heine took his wife with him. During his first visit he had, as he expressed it, "spied out the land" in Hamburg, to see whether it was safe for his wife to come there. But the lively interest in Mathilde expressed by all his relatives reassured him, and he felt certain she would be well received in their midst. So, with Mathilde by his side, and Cocotte, the parrot, on his lap, he set out once more for Hamburg.

They arrived in the city one day in July, 1844. In order to avoid passing through Prussian territory, where Heine was still a man with a price on his head, they had travelled by water; and his sister and her family came out to meet the couple at the dock. Almost immediately there was trouble, for Herr Embden, Heinrich's clumsy brother-in-law, chanced to drop the box which contained Cocotte, and Mathilde screamed with angry terror. But her fury soon passed when she saw her pet was uninjured, and for a while all went pleasantly. The visitors were made comfortable at the home of Heine's sister until, about a week later, they moved to a small apartment of their own. Mathilde impressed her husband's relations quite favorably, for, after the momentary outburst on her arrival, she managed to control herself to perfection. They thought her beautiful and charming, and she thought them elegant and kind. From all indications the visit promised to be hugely delightful for all concerned.

But in a day the whole situation changed. Shortly after their arrival, Heine took his wife to dine at the house of his uncle; and then the difficulties began. Tyrannical old Salomon Heine, who knew nothing but German—and spoke even that with ghetto carelessness —would never allow any foreign tongue to be used at his table. As a result, Mathilde had to remain silent throughout the long meal—a torment she could not endure. She gave vent to her resentment the moment she got out of the millionaire's house. Never again, she swore, would she enter that place! Heine tried to reason with her. He tried to make her see that if she offended his uncle, the chances of their being remembered in the old plutocrat's will would be seriously jeopardized. But it was in vain. Once Mathilde had made up her silly mind, nothing on earth could move her to change it. There was naught for the poet to do, therefore, but send her back to Paris. He told his uncle that Mathilde's mother had suddenly become ill and demanded her presence in France; and then he hurriedly packed her off, together with her parrot, and prepared to spend the rest of his time in Hamburg alone.

For a while he was busy watching over the publication of the "New Poems," which included "Germany—Winter's Tale." Then his mind was kept busy noting its reception by the critics and the public. The volume achieved immediate notoriety because it was prohibited in Prussia, and almost as immediate renown because it won the praise of most of the more daring critics. It was undeniably brilliant; even Uncle Salomon enjoyed it. Indeed, the old man was put in such good humor by it that he renewed his promise to care for Heine and Mathilde during all the rest of their lives. And Heine, confident that the renewed promise would be mentioned in the millionaire's will, felt immensely relieved. With his retainer from Campe, his pension from the French government, and now this legacy from his uncle, he and Mathilde were assured of a livelihood even though he sold not another line of verse or prose. It was a triumphal moment for him. All his life Heinrich Heine had strived for financial independence; and at last it had come.

5

EIGHT weeks had passed since Mathilde had left, and Heine could remain in Hamburg no longer. He would have liked to protract his stay for his mother's sake, but his concern about Mathilde was too intense. He had been writing to his wife almost daily, and always with anxious, passionate, jealous love. "I always think of you," he told her, "and I have a thousand things to say to you. The most important . . . is that *I love you to distraction,* my dear wife." He used such phrases repeatedly. In letter after letter he called her "darling," "dear lamb," and other such pet names, and continually he begged her to write at least once a week. Evidently she did not obey, as we can tell from his frantic pleadings. Again and again he assured her he did not care how badly or carelessly she wrote, so long as he might have word from her. But no answer came. Days passed, weeks, before she replied; and Heine could not bear it. In an agony of apprehension he packed his bags and flew back to Paris.

Mathilde was still there when he arrived. Heine gratefully accepted what lame excuses she offered for her failure to answer his letters from Hamburg, and con-

vinced himself she had been true to him while he was
away. Happy over his new financial security, and con-
tented with his wife's protestations of faithfulness, he
settled down now to enjoy the leisure he had so long
awaited. His health was improved, and he felt extraordinarily strong and cheerful. Almost he felt as in the
first days of his early manhood, when he had been able
to write: "I feel as though I could devour all the ele-
phants of Hindostan, and then pick my teeth with the
spire of Strasburg Cathedral!"

But ill-fortune, which had plagued him all his life,
was still not done with him. Hardly had his fingers
closed on security when it was snatched from him once
more. A few weeks after his return to Paris the news
reached him that his uncle had passed away. That in
itself was bad enough, for though Heine had fought
with his uncle for years and had called him every imag-
inable unflattering name, he yet had loved the old man
profoundly. But three days later, even worse news
came: *the will contained no mention of an allowance for
Heine!* The millionaire had left him merely a bequest
of some sixteen thousand francs—nothing more. And
Karl Heine—that same Karl whom the poet had nursed
through the cholera epidemic of 1832—in communi-
cating this information, added that, as the chief heir,
he could allow the poet no more than two thousand
francs a year. And what was more: this reduced allowance would be granted only on the condition that Heine
promise never to publish anything about the dead man
without the express permission of the family! . . .

Alexandre Weill reports that when the poet read the letter containing the news, he actually fell unconscious to the floor. And when Heine came to, he seemed an utterly broken man. He shook with impotent fury, and hot tears welled from his eyes—"the only tears," remarks Weill, "that I ever saw him weep."

It is no wonder Heine was so affected by the news. Not merely was he chagrined at his uncle's forgetfulness, but even more he was shocked at Karl's meanness. In high indignation he wrote to his cousin *demanding* that his annual allowance of forty-eight hundred francs be continued. But Karl was obdurate, and, finding nothing could be done by direct negotiation, Heine called in the aid of intermediaries. First he wrote to his publisher, Campe, begging for his vigorous intercession to keep the matter from being dragged into the courts.

"You will see," Heine wrote, "that I am beginning a fight to the death, and will win public opinion as well as the courts to my side if Karl Heine does not give in. I shall have my rights even if I have to set the seal on them with my death."

The very next day Heine wrote a second letter, this time to his Hamburg friend, Dr. J. H. Detmold.

"Perhaps they expected me to come to them with supplication . . . but I expect to exercise a greater effect by threats. . . . My action at law is no empty threat. I can conduct it quite well. But if I show how far I intend to go, they will be frightened and give in. The press must do its best to

help in this work of intimidation. I therefore leave
it to your prudence to insert a series of short articles in the papers which are read in Hamburg. It
will be easy to win public opinion to the side of a
poet against millionaires."

If only he had been well enough, Heine would have
picked up and gone storming to Hamburg in person.
But this wretched affair, coming on him so suddenly,
had brought on a return of his nervous disturbances,
and he did not dare risk the journey. There was nothing left for him, therefore, but to remain at home in
Paris and fume in impotence. His mind was much too
distraught for him to be able even to think of continuing
his literary work. The only writing he could do was
of violent letters to any and every friend he could think
of. Varnhagen, Meyerbeer, Lassalle, Prince Pückler,
Alexander Von Humboldt, and many others were asked
to intervene in an effort to bring pressure to bear on
Karl. Heine had discovered by this time that legally
he had a very poor case against his cousin. He had
been assured of this by no less an authority than Cré-
mieux, possibly the foremost lawyer in Paris at the
time. So his only hope was to plague Karl with pro-
tests and complaints until at last the latter could be
made to give in. As the poet told Campe:

"I shall clamor unceasingly in the newspapers,
write memoirs, invoke God and the world as witnesses. . . . He [Karl] will not be able to endure
it. He will beg me in God's name to desist."

What Heine expected of Karl he made clear in one of his letters to Campe. First, he wanted his legacy of sixteen thousand francs without any condition whatsoever; then he asked that his annual allowance of forty-eight hundred francs be legally assured him for life, and half that sum be assured Mathilde in the event of her surviving him. In return, Heine was willing to promise never to write a line that might injure Karl's family.

"This promise," he wrote Campe, "may be drawn up as stringently as they please. . . . If I can secure peace, I shall be as tame and tractable as I am wild and rough when I have to wage war."

But then immediately he added:

"It does not matter much how binding you make it. *I shall never, at any price, deliver up anything that I write to the censorship of my relations;* but I am quite ready to swallow my private grudge, and write nothing about the pack of rascals. Let them rejoice peacefully in their obscure existence, and rest confident of a complete oblivion after death. . . . I have better people to write about. . . ."

Such were the demands Heine made on his cousin, and he fondly imagined that with the aid of his friends and their influence he would soon have his way. But he underestimated Karl's stubbornness. The more this man was plagued, the more obdurate he became. Heine was

beside himself. He fretted and stormed until he thought
he would go mad. The illness which had been creeping
over him for years became immeasurably aggravated.
His eyesight grew weaker than ever, and the paralysis
began to spread to his legs. His physicians urged him
to go south to the Pyrenees and try to regain his strength
in the sunshine there; but he lacked the funds for the
journey. The most he could do that summer was go off
to Montmorency near Paris, and live there in a little
cottage with Mathilde and her parrot. He began to tire
of the fight with Karl, began to tire even of life itself.
"Once my life was very sweet," he wrote to Campe,
"but now it is dreary, and I long for death."

He still continued to write letters of complaint against
Karl, but no longer with any great passion. When he
returned to Paris in the autumn, he tried to make up
for the loss of his allowance through gambling on the
stock exchange. His friend Rothschild, the Paris
banker, had made him a present of some shares in a
new railroad, and that started the poet on a career of
speculation. For a while he seems to have won, but in
a very little while he lost again. He even managed to
run through the sixteen thousand francs which by then
had been paid to him out of his uncle's estate. When
the new year, 1846, opened, he was practically penniless, and he dared put off literary work no longer. Hurriedly he wrote a short ballet which the director of His
Majesty's Theatre in London had ordered; and then he
wrote several short poems. But he could never write
enough to make up for the loss of the allowance, and

he was compelled to take up again his battle with Karl.
His first thought now was to obtain some immediate relief for his paralysis, so that he might be strong enough
to go right up to Hamburg and press his claims there.
But he knew of only one man who might be able to give
him such relief, the famous Dr. Dieffenbach—and he
lived in Berlin. Before Heine could ever consult him,
therefore, he had first to obtain a pardon from the Prussian government. Accordingly Heine appealed to Alexander von Humboldt, who was known to have considerable influence at the Prussian court.

"I turn to you, Herr Baron, with the request that
you use your influence to gain assurance from the
authorities that I shall not be called upon during
my journey through the Royal Prussian State to
answer any accusations concerning the past. I
know very well that such a request is not in accord-
ance with the administrative customs in Prussia;
but at a time which is in itself somewhat exceptional, it ought to be possible to enrich the old records with a rubric for exceptional contemporaries."

But von Humboldt could do nothing. The Prussian
minister, von Bodelschwingh, peremptorily declared that
if Heine were ever caught on Prussian soil he would
immediately be arrested and imprisoned for *lèse
majesté*. So the whole plan had to be dropped. Heine
had to remain on in Paris and conceive some means of
pricking the hide of Karl from the distance. The only

such means he could imagine was to write another of those attacks for which he had already become notorious. He had not yet ceased to regret the slanderous assaults he had once made on Platen and Börne; but so consumed was he with anger that he could not restrain the impulse to make a similar assault on his cousin, Karl. By February he was already at work on it. As he told Campe:

"I regard my allowance as lost, and I am therefore ready to run any risk. I have not long to live, as my doctors, Dr. Roth and Dr. Sichel, have told me out of friendship, and because they know I am a man whom death does not terrify. My wife will then go into a convent, and will live on the meagre income which you will give her."

Heine was not exaggerating his condition. He was indeed seriously ill and apparently not far from his end. The paralysis had crept down his face to his mouth.

"I kiss," he wrote to Ferdinand Lassalle, "but feel nothing, so much are my lips affected. My palate and a part of my tongue are also touched, and everything I eat tastes like earth."

And to Campe he reported:

"My organs of speech are so paralyzed that I cannot speak, and for four months already I have not been able to enjoy eating because of the difficulty of chewing and swallowing, and the complete loss of taste. . . . I look like a skinny, one-eyed Hannibal. . . . I know I am past saving. At the utmost I can last out in wretchedness and agony but another year or two."

That this was really so, is borne out by the testimony of those who saw the poet at the time. For instance, Friederich Engels in a letter dated September 16, 1846, writes to his fellow-Socialist, Karl Marx:

"The poor devil [Heine] has gone to the dogs. He has grown thin as a skeleton. The softening of the brain has spread, and it has paralyzed all his face. . . . He is in full mental vigor, but his appearance, all the more queer because of his graying beard (he cannot be shaved) is enough to make anyone who sees him feel wretched. It is dreadfully distressing to see so fair a chap die away bit by bit."

The unhappy poet had apparently reconciled himself to his fate. As he confessed in the letter to Lassalle:

"I am miserable and wretched as I have never been before, and were it not that I should be leaving a helpless woman behind me, I would very gladly take my hat and say good-bye to the world."

And as he declared to Campe:

"But it does not matter to me that I shall soon be dead. . . . Between ourselves, that is the least thing to be feared. The horrible thing is dying, not death—if there be such a thing as death. Death is perhaps the last superstition. . . ."

6

BUT when, through a false report, the German newspapers suddenly announced that Heine actually was dead, he was greatly disturbed. The report brought home to him the gravity of his condition. He could not afford to die now, he realized, for he had not yet provided for Mathilde. Therefore he wrote testily: "The report has not amused me. At another time I should have laughed at it; but not now."

As it turned out, however, this false report proved a fortunate mishap for Heine. Overnight it made him almost a hero in Germany, bringing him expressions of sympathy and admiration from every corner of the land. The news of the poet's grave condition had shocked all who knew him into a sudden realization of his genius. Even Karl Heine was moved to write to him in a friendly spirit. And when, the following February, Karl came down to Paris, he frankly came forward and asked for a reconciliation with the stricken poet. It is highly probable that from the beginning Karl's motive in refusing the allowance had been to get Heine completely in his power, for he was never free of the dread that the poet might write something ridiculing the family. Heine had often spoken of certain "Memoirs" he had begun, and what prompted Karl to seek a reconciliation now, was the fear lest the poet should suddenly die and leave these "Memoirs" to appear in a collected edition. Eagerly, therefore, Karl now agreed to continue the old allowance of forty-eight hundred francs a year, and agreed also to give half of this sum annually to Mathilde should she survive her husband. And Heine for his part promised never to publish any attack on Karl or his family. And thus was the harrowing war brought to an end.

THE EXILE IN FRANCE

CHAPTER
SIX

"I am no longer a divine biped . . . no longer the Great Heathen No. 2 . . . smiling down gaily on the melancholy Nazarenes. I am now only a poor sick Jew. . . ."

◆

The long and bitter struggle over the inheritance was ended at last—but Heine, for all that he had won his point, had lost fatally. The excitement and fear and anger which had seethed in him incessantly during those years had wrecked him utterly. A body congenitally weak and in addition racked for years by distress and dissipation, never well nurtured and now decayed with disease, could hardly stand up under the strain. Indeed, only the inordinate strength of his spirit now kept the poet alive. Despite all his protestations of disgust with life, his will to live was indomitable. It blazed in his eyes, hidden though they were beneath paralyzed lids; it galvanized his fingers, twisted though they were on his paralyzed arm. So tremendously virile was his mind, indeed, that it could actually make fun of his body. Heine could still laugh, and laugh uproariously—even at his pain. He had always been a neurotic; but now that he seemed literally at the door of death, his strongest impulse was not to whine but laugh. The sense of the comic, that imperious quality which had buoyed him up amid the floods of discrimination and hate, was still

with him. It kept his head high above the waters of
pain, lifting him up so that those twisted lips of his
could still be seen smiling sardonically at fate. He did
not hesitate to confess in what agony he existed; but
always he tried to veil the confession with a witticism.
For instance, his characteristic way of describing his
constitution was to say it was even worse than that of
Prussia!

He was dying—this he knew full well. But for the
present he was still alive—and naught else concerned
him. Despite pain and discomfort he continued to write
almost as in the days of his fullest bodily vigor. He
kept up with his Parisian friends, inviting them to
dinner-parties, and attending theirs. In Germany so
many conflicting reports had been published about him
that he had become almost a legend; but in Paris he was
very much of a reality. Balzac dedicated one of his
stories to him, proclaiming him the "sweetest representa-
tive of the French spirit in Germany, and of German
poetry in France." Gautier, in the preface to one of his
works, took occasion to make numerous flattering references to Heine. And in several of the memoirs of the
time the poet was depicted in a manner which leaves no
doubt as to the way he impressed the people who saw
him. For instance, K. M. Kertbeny in his memoirs
gives the following poignant description:

"One day in a fearful snowstorm I was about to
take shelter in the reading room of the Palais Royal
in the Galerie Montpensier when I noticed someone

feeling about the glass on the door, as though trying to take hold of the knob. To my terror I recognized Heine. I reproached him for going out in such weather; and, like a child, he let himself be scolded. Plaintively he sought to excuse his act on the ground that he had sat at home all alone for several days, and could not stand the monotony. I . . . went out to call a fiacre to take him home . . . but when I came breathlessly running back, I found him laughing gaily with some grisettes. He was making a lot of clever witticisms, and the ladies were all calling him 'Mr. Einé'!"

Here is another telling quotation—this from the memoirs of Stephan Born:

"One of the reading rooms in the Palais Royal had French, English, and the most important German papers, and also a rather large library. . . . Suddenly an unusual movement in the quiet room. A man apparently of advanced years had entered, and half a dozen people hurried to be of assistance to him. Someone took his arm, led him to a comfortable chair . . . gave him the *Allgemeine Zeitung*. I watched him, astonished and full of pity. One of his eyes was closed, and the other seemed motionless, for instead of following the words on the paper, the paper itself was moved back and forth in front of it. . . ."

And that man was Heine!

2

Thus did the poet manage to drag himself about during all the rest of 1847. Still he smiled sardonically at the world and himself; still he crawled through the Paris streets to the reading rooms where he could find his beloved German papers; still he smiled at grisettes, and made love to his wife, and wrote with unflagging mordancy.

But it could not last long. By February of the next year, 1848, he was already so broken in body that he had to be taken to a hospital. Mathilde and a servant —and of course the parrot—came along with him, and there, in a private sanitarium conducted by one of his friends, he had to linger many weeks. But he could not be idle. Ill as he was, he yet managed to continue his writing. He composed several news-letters for the *Allgemeine Zeitung,* and busied himself also with translation.

It was while Heine was at this hospital that the Revolution of 1848 broke out in Paris. There was fierce fighting in the barricaded streets, great terror and confusion for days and nights—and then an ominous lull. The trumpery monarchy of Louis Philippe was overthrown, and the republic established at last. And then the flame of revolution swept from Paris to blaze in half the other lands on the Continent.

But Heine did not react to this conflagration as he had to the one of 1830. He did not leap up and cry ecstatically: "I am the sword and the flame." For he was no longer the young enthusiast he had been eighteen

years earlier. He was an old man now, sick and disillusioned; he had learned a great deal about this revolution after eighteen years of unhappy fellowship with
those who had sought to bring it on. Most of all he
knew that it was doomed to be futile. He had never
been a partisan of the dethroned king, and in his letters
to the German newspapers Heine had prophesied again
and again that the Communists would inevitably sweep
the poor weakling out of power. Even though Heine
was receiving a pension from Louis Philippe's government, he had rarely hesitated to foretell the doom of the
régime. Especially had this been true between 1840
and 1843, when Heine had again contributed regularly
to the *Allgemeine Zeitung*. He had then indirectly been
of inestimable value to the Communists, for he had informed them, scattered and hounded as they were, just
how strong they could be. From his letters they had
learned just how wide-spread they were, how common
were their aims no matter in what land they dwelt, and
how certain was their ultimate triumph. He had compared them to the *ecclesia pressa* of the first century,
and had openly called them "the only party worthy of
decided attention."

Yet now that those very Communists had fought their
way to victory, he was not happy. As he told Alfred
Meissner in a letter written a week or so after the
Revolution:

"The present doings, and the hopes of the world,
are quite foreign to my heart. . . . I should like

to flee from the terrifying tumult of public life and take refuge in the eternal spring-tide of poetry."

Did one not know the consistent inconsistency of Heine's character, one might conclude he had gone the way of all flesh, and had renounced in his fifties the self-same ideals for which he would have died in his thirties. But actually Heine, even in his repudiation of this second revolution, was not in any real sense turning tail. As he had always declared, he had never been one of the Communists. He had favored them in his articles only because he had seen in them the most dangerous enemy of the aristocrats. But he was almost as loath to see them in power as the princes whom they were bent on destroying. As he wrote in later years:

"I can think only with anxiety and terror of the time when these dark iconoclasts will have gained power. With their horny hands they will heartlessly smash the marble statues of beauty so dear to my heart. They will destroy the fantastic toys and spangles of Art which the poet loved so much. They will cut down my grove of laurels and plant potatoes in their stead. They will tear from the soil of the social order the lilies that toil not nor spin. . . . The same fate will befall the roses, those idle brides of the nightingales; the nightingales, those useless singers, will be driven out—and alas, my 'Book of Songs' will be used by the grocer to make little paper bags in which he will wrap coffee or snuff for the old women of the future."

Even had Heine actually believed in Communism, he would not have been able to grow enthusiastic over the new revolution, for he saw it was superficial. By this time he had learned that a real revolution demanded a change not merely in the form of government, but rather in the heart of man. Therefore he wrote in bitter wisdom:

"This republic is nothing but a change of name. . . . How could this corrupt and soft society change its heart so quickly?"

So during the Revolution of 1848 Heine was not to be found among the insurgents. During all the confusion and shouting, while the whole world seemed to be reeling, Heine lay there in the sanitarium and patiently labored at his writing. What mattered it to him that the whole earth trembled beneath the thunderous march of the revolutionary rabble? He knew the earth had trembled many times before, and would tremble many times again. Liberty, he now realized, was a relative thing, and its attainment could never be complete. Only Beauty, he told himself, was absolute, and only the pursuit thereof could bring enduring reward. Therefore he closed his ears to the shouting of the Marseillaise, and tried to keep his mind fast on literature. For, as he explained to Meissner: "I have this in common with all other artists: I do not write for the moment but for centuries, not for a country but for the world, not for a party but for humanity!" . . .

3

But no matter how little Heine cared to interest himself in the revolution, it was destined to affect him gravely nevertheless. One of the first things done by the victorious republicans once they swept into power, was to make public the archives of the defeated government —and this entailed the revelation of the fact that Heine had been "in the pay" of the monarchy. The whole matter was exposed in one of the Paris journals, and at once the scandal spread across to Germany. In April, 1848, an anonymous letter was published in the *Allgemeine Zeitung*, making public the fact that Heine, who had been for years its Paris correspondent, had been receiving a regular subsidy from the French government. No mention was made of the precise nature of this subsidy, but the inference was openly drawn that it had been a bribe. Even the editor of the paper, in commenting on the letter, admitted he thought the subsidy might have influenced Heine at least to suppress unfavorable comments about the government of Louis Philippe!

Heine could not contain himself when he saw the letter. Immediately he wrote a long reply, making quite clear the circumstances under which the pension had been granted him.

"The support I got from the Guizot Ministry was not a tribute; it was merely support. It was—let me give it its proper name—the alms which the French people gave to many thousands of foreigners who had been more or less gloriously compromised in their native countries by their zeal for the cause of revolution, and who had taken refuge beside the hospitable hearth of France. I applied for this charity shortly after the deplorable decrees of the Bundestag had appeared—those decrees which tried to ruin me financially because I was the choir leader of a so-called Young Germany."

He had had to take the pension from the French government because the German rulers had tried to starve him into silence. His acceptance of it in no sense entailed agreement with Guizot's policies, or defense of his acts. He had received his subvention as an artist, not a newspaper correspondent. It had been given him in order to keep a poet alive, not to keep a radical silent. Such pensions were being granted by France to all sorts of great individuals who had fallen on hard times.

"Among the men whom we find on that list . . . are exiles from every quarter of the globe, refugees from Greece and San Domingo, from Armenia and Poland, from Bulgaria and Spain. The high-sounding names of barons, counts, princes, are among them, and of generals, ex-ministers, even priests, forming as it were an aristocracy of poverty."

Long and emphatic was the letter Heine wrote that day in reply to the attack in the *Allgemeine Zeitung*. He realized the accusation was serious, and he was determined to scotch it at once. He went out of his way to make it quite clear that, despite the far greater generosity of the French government, he had never forsworn his Germany nationality.

"My marriage to our dear Lady Germany, the blonde idler, was never happy. I remember lovely moonlight nights when she held me tenderly to her large bosom . . . but always toward morning there was an inevitable boredom and coldness, and then began the incessant scolding. In the end we had to live apart in both bed and board. But it never came to an actual divorce. I could never find it in my heart to renounce my domestic cross."

This last was in the nature of a revelation, for he had never before denied the common assumption that he had become a naturalized Frenchman. It might have been far better for him if he had indeed changed his nationality, for as a French subject he might easily have obtained some government position, and with it an excellent income. But he had been incapable of taking the step.

"It was a bit of idealism from which I could not free myself. I have ever been a free-thinker with regard to what is usually called patriotism, but I could never have escaped a certain horror had I dared to do anything that might have appeared in any degree a renunciation of my Fatherland. . . . Naturalization may do for other people. A drunken lawyer, or a blockhead with a brow of iron and a nose of copper, may very lightly give up his

Fatherland—which knows nothing of him, anyway —in order to snap up a schoolmaster's job. But such conduct is not fitting for a German poet who has written the most beautiful German songs. It would be a horrible thought for me, quite mad, did I have to say to myself: I am a German poet and at the same time a citizen of France."

4

BUT though Heine was so coherent and cogent in his apologia for accepting the French pension, he quite failed to be convincing. The accusation that he had accepted bribery was spread and believed throughout Germany. It put an end to his writing for the *Allgemeine Zeitung*, and for every other German newspaper, for his standing as a correspondent was discredited. And the disgrace was not without its dire effects on his already shattered nerves. Early in May he had felt sufficiently recuperated to leave the hospital and return to his apartment; but by the end of the month he was worse than ever. For several weeks he could not even leave his house, and when one day he became desperate and did venture out into the street, he came quickly to grief. The excitement of the Revolution was not yet subsided, and there was a great rushing to and fro in the streets. The poor, half-blind, half-paralyzed man could not stand it. In agony he stumbled along, seeking some place where he could take refuge. Fortunately he was not far from the Louvre, and somehow he managed to keep up until he got there. But then he could remain on his feet no longer. With his lame hand he felt for a chair, and then, in exhaustion, he collapsed. He was so dazed that he was not conscious of his whereabouts. Not until several moments had passed was he able to look about him. And then he saw that, of all places in the Louvre, he had collapsed at the very feet of the Venus de Milo. There she stood towering over him, beauteous and bewitching as ever, but now somehow ineffably pathetic. The sick man was overwhelmed at the sight of her; a flood of hot tears streamed down his shrunken cheeks. He lay there at her feet almost in a faint.

"At her feet I lay for a long time," he declared later, "and wept so as to move a stone to pity. And the blessed Goddess of Beauty, our Dear Lady of Milo, looked down on me with mingled compassion and desolation, seeming to say: 'Dost thou not see that I have no arms, and therefore cannot help thee?'"

It was the last time Heine ever walked out on the face of the earth. From then on he had to remain forever in his room, either lying on a cot or sitting propped up with cushions in a chair. Thus began for him the final and bitterest phase of his Passion. Daily his body withered away until at last it looked as thin and shrunken as that of a child. His eyes became more and more blind; his legs, his whole body, became nerveless. Only the mind remained alive. And this, the survival of his mind, was the greatest of wonders to those who knew him. Suspecting the nature of his disease, they had all along imagined it would be his brain which would go first, and that he would become a maniac or an imbecile. But no —if anything, his mind became even more brilliant, even more quick and clear and creative, than ever it had been before. And his whole soul took on a new quality. Now in his great pain a new understanding came to him.

"I am no longer a divine biped," he confessed; "I am no longer the 'freest German since Goethe,' as I was called in better days; I am no longer the Great Heathen No. 2, another vine-crowned Diony-sus, excelled only by my colleague, No. 1, to whom was given the title of Grand Duke Jupiter of Wei-mar; I am no longer a joyous Hellene, sound in body, smiling down gaily on the melancholy Nazarenes. I am now only a poor sick Jew. . . ."

When he had taken that last walk and had fallen at the feet of the "Divine Lady of Milo," Heine had bidden farewell forever to the old pagan gods. He knew now that those beautiful idols could no longer be of any use to him. They were armless, and could not help him as he lay there on his bed of pain. As he told some friends who came to call on him one afternoon: "For my part I am convinced that the sick and the healthy need two entirely different religions." Once upon a time, when he had been strong and full of daring, the laughing heroes of the heathens had seemed the only gods for him; but now that his strength had left him, he could believe only in the God of his fathers.

"I became bankrupt of all earthly happiness by the loss of that immeasurable good which is health. But then I found in my heart a quiet spot where the treasure of religion had rested unnoticed, and through it I am saved from despair."

Heinrich Heine had completed the cycle of faith. Through Catholicism, Paganism, Protestantism, Atheism, and Saint-Simonism, he had at last returned to his starting point: that battered, despised, but (for the Jew) apparently inevitable religion called Judaism.

We have already seen how Heine in his middle thirties became a convert to Saint-Simonism. He had taken up the religion with all the fervor of an evangelist, and, inspired by it, he had written his two most significant prose works. But the fervor had not lasted. Soon he discovered this benignant pantheism was altogether too benignant—and vacuous. Airily it promised it could harmonize spirit and flesh, could merge Christianity and Paganism—but it never fulfilled the promise. So, after but a few years had passed, Heine had once more begun using the phrases of Paganism. In his book on Börne he had bluntly declared it was vain to seek a harmonization of those two tendencies which tore the whole world in two. There were what he called the "fat" among souls, and the "lean"—and they were two races so disparate and foreign to each other that no miscegenation between them could be effected. As for himself, he belonged to the "fat." He loved flesh and color and all else the Hellenes had included in the one word Beauty. He was, he declared, unalterably a Pagan. And in that conviction he had written all of those ballets and folk-lore studies which occupied him—when he was not committing literary assaults on his enemies—between 1836 and 1847.

But in 1848 he once more experienced a change of heart. He did not return to Saint-Simonism, for he still saw it to be sterile and vapid. Most of the professing Saint-Simonians had tired of their utopian idealism and taken to very practical financial scheming. Enfantin and his fellow-warriors in the great crusade for "human liberation," had become the builders of railroads. Those martyrs no longer bore a cross, unless it were, as Heine remarked, the cross of the Legion of Honor. No, it was not to pantheism that the poet now turned for salvation, but to simple, intuitive, personal deism. From Jupiter he went over to Jehovah, and stricken there on his "mattress grave" he of a sudden confessed that he had become one of the faithful again.

5

ACTUALLY the final conversion did not come to Heine of a sudden. Already for several years before 1848 he had been dissatisfied with Paganism. But he had been loath to admit this even to himself. He had continued to write in the Pagan vein about the gay old gods and demons, for all the world as though he still believed in them. As he himself facetiously suggested, he had wanted his conversion to take even God by surprise!

But by the middle of 1848 he no longer made a secret

of his change of heart. He was still reluctant, however, to have the fact of his return to God bruited about in public. When he was asked to announce his conversion in the newspapers, he refused. "What can it matter to the great elephant of the King of Siam," he said, "whether a small mouse in the Rue d'Amsterdam in Paris believes or disbelieves in his grandeur and wisdom?"

But the story leaked out nevertheless, and then it swiftly spread throughout Germany and the rest of Europe. And in its train there sprang up the absurdest exaggerations. It was even declared that Heine had actually gone over to Rome and become a Catholic!

This displeased the poet intensely. At once he tried to scout the wild tales, writing to his friends to deny them categorically.

"Do not believe the rumors going around that I have become a pious lambkin. The religious upheaval which has taken place in me is purely spiritual: more an act of my reason than of holy feeling. And my sick bed has had very little to do with it. I have come by great, exalted, terrible thoughts— but they were thoughts, flashes of light, not the phosphorescent vapors of hysterical faith."

To prove how far he was from acceptance of any of the established faiths, he made public the fact that he wanted neither priest, minister, nor rabbi to officiate at his funeral. He did not hesitate to scoff at the churches as bitterly as ever he had done. One day he assured

Meissner that if he could walk out on crutches he would go straight to a church; and when his friend stared at him incredulously, Heine explained: "Where else should one go—with crutches? Of course, if I could walk out without crutches I'd prefer to stroll along the lively boulevards or go to the Bal Mabille!" To all others who came to inquire of him as to his new beliefs he indulged in similar raillery. Heine had returned to God, but he had brought his mocking smile with him. He still could be ironic, even at the expense of Him whom he now recognized as his Creator. Even while lying there at the door of death, this temeritous man refused to tremble before his God. Indeed, he seemed to feel it necessary to apologize for even believing in Him. "If the German people in its need could accept the King of Prussia," he would argue, "why should it be a crime for me to accept a personal God?" He was always talking in such a vein about his new faith. "The heathen Gods would not treat a poet in this way," he liked to complain; "only our own Jehovah would be capable of it. For look: He has actually paralyzed my lips so that I can't kiss!" Frequently he threatened to lodge a complaint against God with the Society for the Prevention of Cruelty to Animals for the way he was being ill-treated! He had no illusions as to the help he might get through religious offices. One day his old friend, Princess Belgiojoso, brought him a priest to pray with him. But, as Heine later reported, "since that priest left I've decided to go back to my poultices. The relief is prompter!"

Heine was still Heine, still a man doomed never to *belong*. All his life he had been thwarted. So it had been when, as a youth, he had tried to become part of a Holy Germany; and so it was now when, as a dying man, he tried to give himself to the Holy God. The curse had fallen on him in the very cradle: he could not *belong*.

CHAPTER
SEVEN

"God will forgive me—that's His business."

CHAPTER
SEVEN

"God will forgive me—that's His business."

———◆———

THE horrible thing is dying, not death. . . ." So Heine had declared in 1846, and as the slow years dragged by, the full truth of the remark became ever clearer to him. And not merely pain made his slow sinking to·the grave so horrible, but even more the worry and despair occasioned by the lack of money. The loss of the government pension affected him seriously. He needed more money now than ever, for there were physicians and nurses to pay, and vast quantities of drugs and medicines to buy. In October, 1851, he wrote to Campe:

> "I quite forgot that this is the day when the rent should be paid, and when Mlle. Pauline [the servant] looked in my desk to see how much was there, she found that fortunately there was enough to pay the rent and leave thirty-three sous over. Now let anyone tell me I am no poet!"

In his plight, Heine had no other recourse than to go begging. First he appealed to certain of his own relatives. There lived in Paris two wealthy bankers by the name of Fould, who were his own cousins by marriage. They had never befriended him during all his years in the city; indeed, they seemed to have been openly hostile to him, probably because at some time or another he had insulted them. Quite possibly Karl's attempt to deprive the poet of his stipend in 1845 had been partly due to the enmity of these same Foulds, for Karl had married the daughter of one of them. But so desperate was Heine's situation now that he did not hesitate to appeal even to these men for help. He sent his friend Alexandre Weill to approach them on his behalf, and Weill thus reports the success of his mission:

"I had hardly spoken of the purpose of my visit, mentioning Heine's illness and his embarrassment, before Benoit Fould escorted me to the door and said: 'I shall be glad, Monsieur Weill, to be of service if *you* need anything. But for that scoundrel, that *canaille* of a Heine—I must beg you never to mention his name in my house. If he ever dares to show himself here I shall have him thrown out like a dog!'"

Weill never told Heine what occurred. He simply reported that the Foulds were unfriendly and seemed unwilling to be of assistance. So now Heine sent Weill to Meyerbeer, the musician, who was a man of considerable wealth. Here the messenger was received in quite another spirit. "What?" cried Meyerbeer; "the greatest lyric poet of Germany in *such* need?" Immediately he gave Weill a thousand francs to take to Heine, and with it the humble request to be permitted to call on the sick man the next day. The gift relieved Heine, but only temporarily. In an effort to retrench he had already moved to a smaller and more modest apartment which Mathilde found in the Rue d'Amsterdam near the St. Germain station. It was a small apartment in the rear of a paved courtyard, and only two of its windows gave upon the light. It was a dark and cheerless hole, literally a grave for Heine, for the two flights of stairs leading to the flat were so narrow that once he was up there, he could not easily be carried down again. Nor was this the worst about the place. Mathilde had chosen it because, being so far back from the street, she had imagined it would be quiet. But she had not troubled to find out whether there might not be other and worse than street-noises to contend with. As it turned out, several young girls in the house were learning to play the piano, and the stillness of the dingy court was continually being shattered by the sound of labored hammering at the keys. When Heine first moved in, the embryo musicians were still struggling with Czerny's finger exercises; but the improvement was slow, and four years later the musicians had still not progressed beyond banal pieces like Shulhoff's "Longing for Kiev." Yet the girls practiced daily, banging away with unflagging patience, and driving the poet almost mad.

2

ONCE Heine had been moved to this new dwelling place, however, he could not bring himself to make

another change. At least the apartment had the virtue
of being cheap, and this was a cardinal consideration
with him now. He tried to cut down all his other expenses, employing a secretary who demanded little pay,
a slatternly maid-of-all-work, and one nurse. But still
he was unable to meet his bills. Only in part was this
because of the vast doses of drugs, and the bizarre and
elaborate "burnings" and "pumpings," which his physicians in their ignorance prescribed for him. His im-
poverishment was due in far larger measure to his wife's
extravagance. Great as were her many other faults, im-
providence was the greatest. Even Heine had to admit
that of her, no matter how blindly he defended her
against every other charge. Even in his letters to his
mother and sister, in which he was forever trying to describe Mathilde in the best light, he could not keep
from calling her his "little spendthrift." His letters to
Hamburg are replete with little admissions revealing
how sorely he was tried by his wife's extravagance. For
instance:

"My wife . . . consoles and delights me, but
sometimes she unconsciously breaks my heart by
her incurable extravagance. It cannot be helped:
that is really my greatest worry. This fever continually to spend money is dreadful."

Or again:

"My spendthrift has got herself a green silk dress
which I call the Vitzliputzli robe, because I have

estimated that it cost just what I got for the poem, 'Vitzliputzli,' in the 'Romancero.' We live in the greatest harmony, in the most beautiful and expensive peacefulness."

Or again:

"My wife is tolerably well. She complains that she is no longer as pretty as she used to be, and that she must therefore dress the more beautifully. But I disagree with her—because of the extra expense."

Or again:

"She is very amiably inclined, and will make fewer New Year's presents than usual this season— which is indeed a great improvement."

Or still again:

"My wife is well, and is at this instant extremely happy because I have expended a considerable sum in buying linen for the household. Linen stuff pleases her better than fine clothes—which, you will agree, is very praiseworthy. We live harmoniously —that is, I yield in everything."

Thus does Heine betray himself into veiled complaint in letter after letter. Perhaps he would have been able to suppress even such reflections on his wife, had he not felt it necessary to excuse himself to his relatives for being in financial straits. So hard pressed was he for funds that he was not above accepting money now even from his mother. Poor as she was, she sent him a thousand francs in the spring of 1850, begging him to indulge in a few luxuries during his illness. He returned the gift immediately, for he knew how little she could afford it. But less than a year later he wrote and asked her to send him the money after all!

Heine borrowed also from his brother Gustav, who by now had become a wealthy newspaper publisher in Vienna, and also from Max. He had tried desperately to have himself reinstated as a pensioner of the French government, but in vain. Finally there was nothing left for him but to turn once more to his cousin Karl. Humbly Heine begged that his annual allowance of forty-eight hundred francs be increased, and Karl, touched by the plea, agreed to make it eight thousand.

The generosity of his cousin relieved Heine greatly; but still his income was not large enough to supply his wants. He appealed to his friend, Rothschild, and received a little help. Then he wrote to another friend, Pereire, who had been one of the leading Saint-Simonians twenty years earlier, and who was now a great railroad magnate. But this time he was less fortunate, for Pereire did not even deign to reply to Heine's letter, but merely sent him a paltry twenty shares of stock in a company which the financier happened to be floating at the moment. Heine's pride was outraged, and he did not soon again try to beg help. Instead he tried, ill as he was, to earn what he needed by writing. For hours on end he scrawled away on huge sheets of paper, or, when that was too much for him, dictated with labored breath to his secretary.

One does not recall a single chapter in all the history of letters quite so heroic and sad as this of Heine's last years of literary creation. One eye was totally blind, and the other, already very weak, he could use only when he held up the lid with his fingers. His lips were so paralyzed that, as he himself used to say, he could not hiss even at one of Scribe's plays. His limbs had shrunk till they were no larger than a child's, and he could stir them hardly an inch. Through repeated burning with poultices and irons, his back had become one great open wound into which opium had to be sprinkled repeatedly to deaden the pain. "I have suffered more tortures," he once complained, "than the Spanish Inquisition could ever invent." Yet day after day he continued to labor at his writing, never permitting himself to succumb to despair. He could quite easily have put an end to his torments, for he always had a bottle of opium within reach, and also a dagger which he still had sufficient strength to use. But he refused to die. Strangely enough, the less life seemed to hold out for him, the more bitterly he fought off death. "Miserable as I am," he told Adolph Stahr and Fanny Lewald, "I should like to live a long time. For the most miserable earthly existence seems to me far preferable to heavenly joys."

3

AND in all his great pain he seems to have received but slight comfort from Mathilde. He loved to have her near him, for her gayety cheered him greatly; but she would not stay with him for long at a time. Yet she resented it when anyone complained of her conduct. One day, after she overheard Heine's consulting physician, Dr. Wertheim, telling the sick man that he needed better nursing, she waylaid the doctor outside the room and struck him in the eye with her fist. Fortunately he did not attempt to retaliate, for the woman was so furious that she might have strangled him. Naturally enough, Dr. Wertheim refused to continue with the case, and only after the invalid had pleaded with him in many pitiful letters to forgive "the madness of a beloved one," did he consent to come in again even for occasional consultation. He allowed another physician, Dr. Gruby, to take complete charge of the case—and he could hardly have left it in worse hands. Dr. Gruby had already been attending Heine for several years, and Heine's desperate condition now may have been in part due to that doctor's incompetence. Gruby was very largely a charlatan, and practiced methods which properly belonged to medieval torture-chambers. He dosed the patient with strychnine, bored setons in his neck, covered him with leeches, seared his back with hot irons, and used a score of other such barbaric therapies. Several times Heine declared he thought any country doctor in Germany would have been able to handle his case more successfully than this fashionable Paris healer. And more than once Heine in exasperation swore to have done with Gruby and every other physician. As he wrote to his mother on one occasion:

"With doctors I will have no more to do. I observe that all the people who died here this winter had medical attendance!"

But as his case became more and more desperate, the power to rebel left him. Above his head hung several ropes which he could grasp when he wished slightly to change his position; otherwise he was incapable of movement. Yet he never became petulant; he never nagged or became maudlin. He did not complain even at the way his wife neglected him. She seemed always to be out when he needed her, excusing herself on the ground that the odor of the sick-room nauseated her, and that she had to take exercise to keep down her fat. Each day she came back exultant with some new vanity purchased "at a bargain," and always she pouted and scolded if the invalid did not share her pleasure. She made no effort to help him in his torment; indeed, by her extravagance and quick temper she only added to it. She seemed far more devoted to her pets than to her husband. Meissner reports that one day Heine greeted him with the cry:

"Oh, what a night we had! I was not able to close an eye. We had an accident in our house. The cat fell from the mantelpiece and scratched its right ear. It even bled a little. That gave us great sorrow. My good Mathilde remained up, and applied cold poultices to the cat all night long. She never remains awake for me."

Yet Heine loved Mathilde. Always he managed to find some kind word to say of her to his mother, even if it was no more than: "very few fat women could be so lovable in this hot weather!" He was not altogether blind to her faults, but seemed grateful they were not even more egregious. Apparently he never doubted her faithfulness to him, though why he should have been so confident it is difficult to imagine. There is reason to suspect she may have been carrying on a clandestine affair during a good deal of her husband's invalidism. We know, at least, that she disappeared the moment her husband breathed his last, and did not return until after his funeral. And we know also that at the time people said she had run off with her *maquereau*. Even so cautious a person as Karl Marx repeated this story in his correspondence. . . . Yet it would be unfair to imagine that Mathilde cherished no affection for the poor bed-ridden man who slaved to pay for her extravagance. At least she could be jealous of anyone who threatened to supplant her. She was almost unfailingly churlish to all who came to visit her husband, especially if they were women. She even resented the presence of a nurse who was particularly attractive. Henri Julia, who became Mathilde's legal adviser after Heine died, and who therefore can hardly be accused of especial prejudice against her, reports:

"The poet, who liked to see young and attractive faces about him, enjoyed being nursed by Marietta, who was very charming to look at, and had a most pleasant manner. But unfortunately Madame Heine would not have her about . . . although the girl did her duty and conducted herself blamelessly. Dr. Gruby replaced her with an old ugly mulatto woman, whom the poor poet could not endure, and of whom he spoke with wrathful resentment even years later."

But in this way almost alone did Mathilde show any affection for her dying husband—yet he loved her.

Arsène Houssaye, director of the Comédie Francaise, reports that once the sick man explained to him:

"Do you know why you still find me here alive? Juliette holds me here with all her might. She loves me so much, and when I am about to die she cries so wildly, that I wake up again to drink her tears."

At times Heine spoke of having himself carried back to Hamburg, so that he might die among his own people. But it was the thought of Mathilde, his "Juliette," that kept him from carrying out the idea. "What would she do there?" he once asked. "It is very sad, for I have no Fatherland here, and she has none there."

4

IT is all strange and perhaps inexplicable, this tenderness and patience wherewith the tormented man spoke of Mathilde. He, who in earlier years had demanded everything of the world, was now glad to receive even the most fleeting attentions from the vain, selfish creature who was his wife. Only because of her did he have to keep scribbling so assiduously day after day. Perhaps he would have continued to create his songs even had she not been there to drain his purse, for the born artist does not lightly turn from his work. But then he would have written out of love, not goading necessity. As it was he had to work almost like a slave at the galleys—day after day, week after week, furiously, restlessly, with unremitting desperation.

It is astounding how much work Heine managed to do during those years of his living death. And even more astounding is its high quality. "Like a dead man, the living poet was nailed in his coffin," wrote Théophile Gautier; "but when we bent over him to listen, we heard poetry ringing from under the pall." Between 1849 and 1851 Heine dictated a whole volume of verses, the "Romancero," which proved to be the apogee of his poetic achievement. Every phase of his extraordinary genius was revealed in it. The verses were by turn imaginative, tender, bitter, graceful, grossly cynical, and exquisitely delicate. And they were of a metrical virtuosity nothing short of prodigious. When one realizes that the work was produced by a half-blind man who was almost visibly rotting away to a cadaver, one is overcome with awe. Karl Hillebrand, who was Heine's secretary during this period, informs us:

"His suffering was so intense that in order to get any rest—at most four hours of sleep—he had to take morphine in three different forms . . . [yet] it was during those sleepless nights that he dictated his most wonderful songs. He dictated the entire "Romancero" to me and then he polished it for hours. . . . He asked me about its sound, cadence, and clearness; he decided with precise care between the present and the imperfect tenses, examined each archaic or unusual word . . . cut out every unnecessary adjective, and corrected every minute error."

When Campe heard that Heine had a new volume of poems ready for the press, he immediately rushed down to Paris to negotiate for its publication. He had been neglecting the poet unpardonably of late. Irritated by something Heine had written to him, Campe had left all the invalid's letters unanswered for three years. But now that the goose had laid another golden egg, the business-like publisher was all affability again. He flattered and cajoled and wheedled extravagantly—and finally bought the complete rights to the new book for the insignificant sum of six thousand marks.

The "Romancero" created an inordinate stir almost as soon as it was published. Wolff declares the book had "a success such as lyric poems had never had before in Germany, or have ever had since." It sold more than twenty thousand copies within the first two months; and the profit it brought Campe would have been more than enough to keep the hapless author out of money difficulties during all the rest of his short life. But Heine never got a penny more than the six thousand marks for which he had sold the book, and he had still to fret about finances. But the success of the "Romancero," if it did not make Heine rich, at least did give him courage to continue writing verse. There had been a time when he had imagined his genius as a poet was gone from him entirely. But now all that was changed.

> "Rosy-cheeked boys come leaping to me, and, placing the old harp in my trembling fingers, they cheer as they cry: 'Thou hast been long silent, thou lazy gray-beard! Sing us again the songs of thy youth.' "

So once more he became a poet. "Poetry has remained my best friend," he told one of his friends: "She is not frightened away by my sickness. On the contrary, she has followed me to the edge of the grave, and is fighting for me with death."

He did not, however, confine all of his literary work to verse. He wrote new prefaces for one or two of his earlier works which were being republished, and also several new volumes in prose. The first of these new works was a long prose fantasy entitled the "Gods in Exile" (*Götter in Exil*), and was translated into French for publication in the *Revue des Deux Mondes*. It at-

tracted wide and favorable attention there, and promised
to bring the author considerable profit once it was ren-
dered into German. But before he could even begin
to translate it into his native tongue, some anonymous
scrivener in Germany got hold of it and hastily brought
out a clumsy version in a pirated edition. There was
no law of copyright to protect Heine, and he was left
without any means of redress. There he was, tormented
by pain on a bed that was virtually his grave, neglected
by his wife, maligned by his enemies, pressed for money,
at odds again with his publisher—and in addition, here
treacherously robbed of the few marks his book might
have earned him in Germany. It was too much!

Yet he did not give in. Despite all the torments and
terrors which fate seemed to be piling on him with
devilish profligacy, he never for a moment threw down
his pen. For hours each day he dictated to his secretary, uttering a sentence, recalling it, phrasing it anew,
recalling it again; and finally, in exasperation, blurting
out something and letting it stand until, later on, he
could rewrite it entirely with his own hand. It was
galling labor, for at times his throat was so affected that
it was difficult for him even to whisper his dictation.
And, in order to revise what he dictated, he had to go
through the most excruciating torment. Propped up
in bed, or in a large easy chair, he had to hold open
the lid of the one eye not yet blind while he scrawled
with a lame and twisted hand. Yet he was able to get
through a vast amount of work nevertheless. In the year
1853 he wrote not only the "Gods in Exile," but also

a number of poems and the first half of an autobiographical essay which he entitled "Confessions." He
ended this essay abruptly the next year, finding it apparently too tedious a thing to round out. As he left
it, it was no more than a fragmentary account of his religious conversion, his exile, his intimacy with Hegel,
his attitude toward Judaism and the Jews, and finally his
Passion on the "mattress grave." It was an inchoate
document, without plan or order; but it was dazzlingly
brilliant and devastatingly ironic. Here, for instance,
is one of its paragraphs—perhaps as tragically temeritous as any to be found in all literature:

"Ah! God's mockery weighs heavily upon me.
The great Author of the Universe, the Aristophanes
of Heaven, shows me, the little German so-called
Aristophanes of the earth . . . how pitifully I
lag behind Him in humor and the making of colossal jokes. Yes, the biting contempt which the Master pours down upon me is horrible; dreadfully
cruel is His jest. Humbly do I acknowledge His
superiority; I bow to the dust before Him. But
though I be lacking in such great creative force,
there is yet in me the light of eternal reason, and
I can bring the jest of God before that court and submit it to respectful criticism. And I dare there
express the most humble opinion that this cruel
jest with which the Master is chastising His wretched
pupil is too long drawn out. It has already lasted
for six years, and is become tedious. Then I should

like to permit myself the deferential observation that the jest is not new, and that the great Aristophanes of Heaven has already made use of it on another occasion, and has therefore been guilty of self-plagiarism! . . ."

Thus did Heine dare to write with a mockery that was half reverence, in the death-bed document which he called his "Confessions."

5

But at last there came an interruption in Heine's labors. The cholera had broken out once again in Paris, and was ravaging particularly in the district where Heine dwelt. It was a serious thing to attempt to move the invalid, but he was tired of living in his wretched little flat, unable ever to see the sun or green grass. Almost six years he had been immured there, tortured daily by the banging of the amateur musicians across the court. Death was almost preferable to so wretched a life, and therefore he made no complaint when his wife insisted on their moving. He gritted his teeth and endured the agony of being lifted down the narrow stairs and out into a conveyance. He was even able to stand the torture of the long rough ride beyond the city limits to the new apartment Mathilde had rented in Batignolles. But when he arrived there at last, he was almost at an end of his strength. Half-unconscious, he lay back on his padded bed and struggled almost in

vain to keep breathing. The end seemed at last to have
come.

But it was not the end—not yet. He recovered again,
and once more was able to smile at his own pain. And
when he dictated his regular letter to his old mother,
he still could not keep from lying to her about his condition. All the six years he had been moribund, he
had kept the gravity of his illness from her. He knew
she did not read the newspapers, and he forbade his
friends and relatives in Hamburg to tell her anything.
And in his regular letters he lied to her consistently,
always claiming that only the weakness of his eyes made
it necessary for him to resort to dictation. Even now,
after the serious relapse which followed his moving
to the new apartment, he was capable of writing to her:

> "You can have no idea, dear Mother, how much
> fresh air and sunshine benefit me—and I had none
> of these in my last dwelling-place. Yesterday I
> felt much improved, sitting under the trees in my
> own garden, and eating the fine plums which almost
> fell into my mouth!"

A more extravagant lie he could hardly have told. Actually the new apartment was most undesirable. It was
damp and Heine contracted a severe throat infection
only a little while after he was brought there. He could
hardly whisper, and the pains in his ears and head became intolerable. So a second time he had to be moved,
this time to a small but really quite pleasant apartment
on the Avenue Matignon, just off the Champs Elysées.

It was on the fourth floor, and one had to mount more than a hundred steps to reach it. But it was the most pleasant place he had been in since first he took to bed. His room, though small, had a little balcony on which he could sit and bask in the sunshine. Nearby were the spreading trees of the Champs Elysées, and at his feet strolled the fashionable throng. It was the first gay sight he had witnessed in fully six years, and he was almost overcome by it.

"You can't imagine how I felt," he told Adolph Stahr. "After all those years I was able once again to look out upon the world—even though with only half an eye! . . . I took my wife's opera glass and looked with unbelievable delight at a little baker's boy who was offering his cakes to two ladies in crinoline, and at a little dog standing against a tree. But I had to close the glass; I did not want to see any more—for I envied the dog!" . . .

Once he was settled, he returned again to his labor. He had just produced a new book, "Lutetia," a collection of the newspaper reports he had written for the *Allgemeine Zeitung* between 1840 and 1843. But his pay for the volume had already been used up to defray the expense of moving. Heine therefore immediately set to work with a collaborator to prepare a French version of the work. The preface to this version was an extraordinary document, for it revealed how strong were the passions still burning in the burnt-out frame. Heine was still Heine, and the old sureness of thrust was yet within his power. Here, for example, is a passage taken almost at random from the preface:

> "I confess frankly that Communism, which is so inimical to all my interests and inclinations, yet exerts a magic influence over my soul. . . . Two voices move me in its favor, two voices which will not be silenced, and which in their essence may be quite diabolical. The first is logic . . . and the second . . . is hate—the hate which I feel for . . . the so-called Nationalist Party in Germany. . . . I have detested and fought the latter all my life, and now, as the sword falls from the hand of the dying man, I feel myself consoled by the conviction that Communism . . . will give them the *coup de grâce*. It will, however, be no blow with a club, but rather a crushing beneath a giant's foot. Communism will tread on aristocracy as one treads on a vile toad. . . . Out of hatred for the champions of nationalism I could almost love those Communists. . . . Howl away, ye nationalists! The time will come when the fatal tread of the giant's foot will grind ye to dust! With this conviction I can calmly leave the world. . . ."

With "Lutetia" published in German and French, Heine rested for a while from his labor He was too tired to begin a new book; and besides he was now receiving many visitors. During the previous two or three years he had been almost completely deserted. Mathilde had succeeded in driving away most of his old friends, and Heine was a little afraid to trust himself with strangers. But in 1855 the World's Fair brought a particularly large influx of German tourists to Paris, among them many of his old companions. It became almost the fashion to pay a visit to the little apartment on the Avenue Matignon where Germany's greatest living poet lay outstretched in his living tomb. Heine liked to say he had at last become a holy saint, for people came as reverently to his room as pilgrims might come to a shrine. Or else he spoke of himself as one of the side-shows of the Fair!

Among those who visited him during this year were several of the friends of his youth—most prominently, Dr. Leopold Zunz, who had been one of the leaders of the Union for Jewish Culture and Learning in Berlin. Zunz's visit was a particularly pleasant one for the poet. It recalled to him his student days and his short-lived enthusiasm for the cause of a reformed Judaism; and eagerly he inquired of Zunz how matters were progressing in Israel. He joked in Yiddish, and asked what he could read to get an understanding of the old Cabbala. For Heine's mind was still alert, and he was still eager to learn.

Many other Germans, great and small, came to call on the bed-ridden genius; and hardly a week passed but that some German journal carried an account of such a visit. Not all of the accounts were friendly, for Heine was still cordially hated in the reactionary circles in the Fatherland. And he, curiously enough, was still capable of being furiously exercised over unfavorable reports. He still labored under a delusion of persecution, and he retained an old Jew in his employ for the sole purpose of keeping informed as to what was being written about him in Germany and Austria.

But though a few of those who came to see him brought him eventual distress, the majority afforded him only undiluted pleasure. Especially was this true of his own relatives. They came, it must be admitted, with shameful infrequency; but Heine was grateful nevertheless. Gustav visited him in 1851; Max in 1852; Therese —but only for an hour, and in company of her brother —in 1853; and Maria, his niece, in 1854. Maria, now Princess della Rocca, was Charlotte's daughter, and had long been a favorite of the poet. Her description of the last hours she spent with her uncle is well deserving of quotation:

"I sat with him the evening before I left the city. He had told me of his youthful years, of his battles with mankind, and of his adventures in love; and I listened in silence. He was weak, and lay almost lifeless. The sickroom was but badly lighted by a lamp that burnt dimly behind the screen. . . . I did not dare to disturb his repose, and sat immobile in my chair. And then, of a sudden, he made an effort to change his position. . . . He was attacked with agonizing pains, and groaned in the most terrible manner. . . . I imagined the end had come. Pauline, his faithful nurse, endeavoured to

quiet him, declaring it was but a passing pain, and
that she had often seen him in such a state. But I
could remain no longer in the room. I ran away
sobbing, and saw him again but once, for an
instant, to take leave of him. . . . It was for
eternity!"

That had been in the spring of 1854. But in the autumn of the following year he was still alive, and this
time Maria's mother came to see him. One wonders that
she had not come sooner. Next to his wife and mother,
Heine had loved his sister more than any other person in
the world. Indeed, he had always expressed such affection for her in his letters that a Freudian interpreter
would be tempted to hypothecate the most extravagant
of fixations. Yet never once in all the years that Heine
lay dying in his bed did this sister come to visit him.
Only now, in 1855, did she at last appear. Yet he
harbored no resentment. When Charlotte arrived he
was transported with delight. She herself thus describes
their first meeting:

"He held me long in his arms without uttering
a word. . . . He would not let me leave his bedside except for meals. . . . After what I had previously learned as to the illness of my brother, I
feared the first sight of his suffering would shock
me terribly. But as I saw only his head, which
smiled at me with a wondrous, transfigured beauty,
I could abandon myself utterly to the first delight

of seeing him again. But when, later on, his nurse carried him in her arms to a chaise-longue in order to make the bed, and I saw the shrunken body from which the limbs hung down as if lifeless, I was compelled to summon all my energies to endure the terrible sight. My bed was next to the sickroom, and during the first night it was agonizing to hear how he suffered from protracted pains in the chest and head. Similar attacks returned every night, and when I hastened to his bed and laid my hand on his forehead, he seemed to get immediate relief. My brother often said that I possessed a rare magnetic power which he felt the moment I stepped, though ever so softly, into his room."

But before many weeks had passed Charlotte was called back to Hamburg because of the illness of one of her children. She promised to return the following spring, confident that her brother would still be living. The doctor had informed her that the patient would probably be able to survive another two or even three years, and, accepting the prognosis, she did not feel she was bidding a final farewell.

6

No other relative ever visited Heine after that; nor did very many acquaintances come either. His dearest friend, Gérard de Nerval, had died in a mysterious manner. Balzac, too, was dead. Weill, who had been

Heine's intimate companion for years, had been driven away by Mathilde. Alfred de Musset, Rahel, Engels, Marx, Lassalle, and a host of other great men and women who once had been wont to visit him regularly, had either left the city or forgotten about him. Once the poet Béranger, now well in his seventies, climbed the four flights to call on Heine; Gautier came once or twice, as did also Dumas. But save for these infrequent visitors, Heine was left largely alone. Yet he did not whine because he was thus neglected. Heine's body had shrunk till there seemed nothing left of him save a voice—but he was still Heine. He still could find a way to laugh off his tragic condition. Once, when Berlioz suddenly appeared, the sick poet cried, "What! Someone is actually visiting me! Ah, but Berlioz always was original!"

Thus, with some witty phrase that quite concealed the catch in his voice, he greeted all who came to call on him. He was always ready with some *bon-mot* wherewith to repay his visitors for their long climb up to his chamber. Often his witticisms were directed at the world; for, as Berlioz put it, Heine stood like a ghost at the window of his own tomb and could not but mock the world in which he had no further part. But more often Heine's witticisms were directed at himself and his own plight. When people asked him, "Are you really incurable?" he would answer "No, I shall die some day." And sometimes he would add, "But I shall have to apologize to the worms for offering them nothing but bones." . . . When, in order to make his bed each day, his nurse would pick him up bodily and carry him over to a sofa, he would remark to any bystanders: "Do you see how they carry me about on their hands in Paris?" . . . "No poet ever had such a lucky chance before," he loved to cry. "Many a one has survived his own immortality; but I—I survive my own death!" . . . Because he was forced to keep to a strict diet which consisted almost entirely of spinach and other greens, he sometimes signed his letters: "Nebuchadnezzar the Second—Formerly Atheist to his Prussian Majesty." . . . He spent much of his time studying ing the nature of his own ailment, spelling his way through the gruesome treatises by Hesse, Albers, Andral, and other such authorities. And when anyone asked him why he occupied himself thus, he used to answer: "My studies will probably not help me much, but I'll be able to give clinical lectures on my ailment in Heaven." . . . He seems to have known rather certainly the origin of his sickness. When some benignant visitor told him that people were saying he had broken down from excess of work, Heine is reported to have replied: "Well, it *was* excess at any rate!"

But as the months dragged by, fewer and fewer became those to whom he could thus relieve himself in bitter wit. There had been a time when he had been able to complain that his visitors tired or bored him. On one occasion he greeted a visitor with the words:

"Ah, you find me now utterly stupid!"

"Ill, you mean," the other suggested.

"No, stupid," the invalid insisted. "You see,

Alexandre Weill was just here, and we exchanged ideas!"

But that had been years earlier, when he had not yet exhausted the patience of his friends. Now he literally hungered for company as he lay there alone on his pile of mattresses; he ached for someone to whom he could talk.

7

AND then, as it were miraculously, such a person appeared. She was a young German girl who went by the name of Camille Selden, and she seems to have come at first, sometime in 1855, to bring Heine some music from one of his admirers in Vienna. She was not especially beautiful, but there was a fineness about her, a sympathy in her spirit, a richness in her voice, and a delicacy in her German pronunciation, which won Heine to her at once. Camille Selden had been born in Germany but reared in France. Though still quite young, she had already endured much suffering. She had been married, robbed, and deserted by her scoundrel of a husband, and when she first came to Heine she was eking out a living by tutoring in German. Yet, though in such straits, she refused to become a paid secretary to the poet. She desired rather to be his friend, and she visited him as frequently as his condition permitted. From the very beginning Mathilde was jealous of the attractive German girl, and she took pains to make her jealousy obvious. Whenever Camille appeared, the fat, over-dressed, foolish woman would stalk out in high dudgeon, refusing even to greet her. But despite the insults of Mme. Heine, Camille continued to visit the sick man week after week. She had admired his work from her early girlhood, and she felt, as did Heine himself, that there was an intellectual bond between them. Sometimes the girl served as his amanuensis; at other times she read to him in German or in French; and often she simply sat by his bedside and held his frail hand while he whispered of his tender love for her. For he did love her, and more tenderly perhaps than any other young woman he had known in all his life. "The last flower of my mournful autumn," he called her: "my good fairy," or "my kind, delightful Mouche."

"I do not know why your dear sympathy does me so much good," he once wrote to her. "I am a superstitious creature, and I imagine a good fairy has visited me in my hour of travail. Or are you an evil fairy? I want to know soon. . . . My kind, delightful Mouche, come and buzz about my nose with your little wings. I know a song of Mendelssohn with the refrain 'Come soon!' The tune is forever running in my head: 'Come soon!' I kiss your two dear little paws, not together but one after the other."

But she could not always come, for Heine was often too ill to receive her. At moments he was furiously resentful at the low way fate seemed to be treating him. The irony of it, that he should fall in love now—now when he was almost a corpse! . . . Yet rarely did he voice his resentment to those who came near him. Instead he gave vent to it in writing. He was still writing, even in this, the eighth year of his invalidism. He was occupied once again with his "Memoirs," with the reminiscences of all he had suffered in life. We shall never know just what he wrote in that, his final work. Only a fragment of it has ever been made public, a fragment narrating with irresistible humor and tenderness the events of his boyhood days. The rest of the book is gone. It was either destroyed by his relatives after he died, or else was concealed where none now can find it. Even the fragment which has survived is not without its lacunae. We know that once when his brother Max managed to lay hands for a moment on the manuscript, he hastily tore out a number of pages and threw them into the fire. No doubt other relatives did likewise, for there was much in the book which they must have found shockingly offensive. Stretched out there on his bed, lonely and full of bitterness, he had given vent to his emotions with a freedom even he had never before dared indulge. Camille Selden, in her reminiscences of Heine, speaks of the almost ghastly glee with which he wrote those "Memoirs." Again and again when she came to see him she would find him propped up on his mattresses, scrawling away on the great white sheets of paper. At last he was having his final fling. He was clawing at his enemies, mauling them, trampling them, rending them limb from limb. "I have them!" he cried one day to Camille as his pen dug away at the paper. "Dead or alive, they can't escape me now!"

The dying man loved to talk about those "Memoirs." He refused to show them to a soul, but he never ceased to gloat over what was contained in them. Whenever anyone came to see him he would point exultingly to the iron box in which he kept the manuscript. There was enough toxin in that box, he used to say, to poison every one of his enemies. He spoke of himself as the Great Exterminator, and boasted that when the book would be published all his foes would be stricken like so many bed-bugs destroyed by an insecticide. Some of his visitors thought he was only half in earnest. They imagined he was seeking merely to frighten his relatives and make his opponents feel ill-at-ease. But Heine was not jesting. The fact that his relatives took such pains later to get rid of the manuscript proves how vitriolic must have been its contents. Heine was taking his final vengeance in this work. "Heine does not die like one of the mob," he once told the Mouche. "The tiger's claws will rend and tear even after the tiger is dead!"

Vengeance was not the only motive, however, for the writing of the "Memoirs." Almost as impelling was his fear for Mathilde's future. The poor man was terrified lest Karl break his promise and refuse to contribute to Mathilde's support once he himself was gone. That was why Heine guarded the pages of his final work so carefully. So long as the woman could threaten to publish this work, so long Karl must stand in terror of her. And knowing this, the dying poet found all the more reason for making the work superlatively malicious. Day after day he forced his twisted fingers to

hold the crayon and write. Fierce was the ache in his
eyes and head, excruciating was the pain in his back.
His poor legs were so crooked that when they dangled
limp the heels would hang in front. To breathe was
itself a torment; to cough seemed more agonizing than
death. The color was gone from him entirely, and as
he lay there he seemed more an image of wax than a
living being. His face, wan and pallid, had somehow
taken on an aura almost of spirituality. A veritable
Christ he appeared to many who came to see him—a suffering Christ stretched out on a tomb of straw. But it
was only his features and his bloodless skin that gave
him this appearance. His eyes, though nearly blind,
could still shine with fire, and when he wrote he seemed
more like Mephisto than the Nazarene. For not even
with death already on him could the liveliness of his
spirit be subdued. Heine was still Heine. A man of
sorrows he was indeed, but meek, poor in spirit, broken
or contrite?—*never*.

8

So did Heine living out his last days of life. All through
the autumn of 1855 he continued laboring furiously at
his "Memoirs." But as the winter came on he notice-
ably sank, and by the beginning of February, 1856, it
was evident that the end had come. Heine himself knew
this, and whenever a visitor came, the sick man promised he would be accommodating and would not delay
his death much longer. Breathing became unendurably

painful, and he found it impossible to lie back on his pillows even at night. His nurse, a woman named Catherine Bourlois, could not leave him even for a moment. Yet on Wednesday, the thirteenth day of February, he actually worked six hours! The nurse begged him to rest from his labor, but he refused. "I have only four more days to work," he told her, "and then I shall be done." The Mouche came to visit him a day or two later. She had been kept in her room for over a week by a cold, and when she appeared she found him broken and melancholy. "At last you have come," he cried to her. She burst into tears because of the reproach in his voice. She could hardly tell him, stricken as he was, that she had had to drag herself from her bed to come to him. All she could do was sob in silence. He called to her to come near, and she sat on the edge of his bed. "Take your hat off, that I may see you better," he whispered. She obeyed, and then, without a word, she sat and gazed at him. He lifted his withered hand and laid it on her head as though in benediction. Then he let it fall, and remained immobile.

It was the last time Camille Selden ever saw him alive. As she was leaving she heard him call weakly: "Tomorrow—do you hear? Don't delay." But, either because she was too ill or did not care to meet Mathilde's angry glances again, she did not come on the morrow.

Then began the final agony. His head ached so frightfully that he could not possibly write, and all day long he reproached himself because he had not sent a letter in several weeks to his old mother. "I shall never be able to write to her again," he mourned.

The next day his condition became even worse. Early that morning the nurse sent for Dr. Gruby, but he was not at home. Not until the afternoon was she able to get some other physician, an old practitioner who lived in the neighborhood. He ordered a half-cup of orange-blossom tea, and vichy water with a drop of laudanum, for the invalid. Dr. Gruby did not arrive until evening, and then immediately countermanded the other physician's prescription. There was a fleeting improvement, and the patient was even able to speak a little. "I am so happy," he told the nurse, "that I saw my dear sister once more—for I am a dead man." Some friend rushed in to see him that evening, and, according to the story, asked Heine whether he felt he had made his peace with God. Whereupon the dying man's paralyzed lips curled just a little, and he sighed: "God will forgive me—that's His business!"

All that night the nurse sat up with the patient, for she feared death might come at any moment. Yet she did not once call Mathilde, for she knew Mme Heine's lack of control would be an added torment for the dying man. The next morning the patient was still alive, but his condition had become even more despairing. Under the influence of drugs he managed to doze fitfully for a few hours. Then, sometime between four and five in the afternoon, he awoke and began to mutter words which his nurse could not at first make out. She realized the dying man was struggling to tell her something, and to placate him she nodded her head and said, "Yes, yes."

But he was not satisfied. With all his might he strained to make her understand what he wanted.

"Write—write!" he finally managed to gasp. "Paper . . . pencil!"

Hurriedly the woman brought him what he wanted, and, weak as he was, he succeeded in taking hold of the pencil. But almost immediately it fell from his grasp. Frightful convulsions set in, and his thin white face was distorted with the agony of the last moment. Then the rigidity passed, and his face became calm once more. The fires died down in his eyes; the bloodless lips no longer curled. The smile of Mephisto was gone, and only the sweet benignity of the Nazarene suffused the face of the poet. For at last Heinrich Heine was at rest. *"Olav ha-shalom,"* his brethren in Israel could now say of him: "Peace is upon him!" For his exile was ended, he was at home at last—he *belonged.*

BIBLIOGRAPHY

HEINE'S WRITINGS

German:
Heinrich Heines sämmtliche Werke, ed. Adolf Strodtmann, I-XXII, Hamburg, 1876.

Heinrich Heines sämmtliche Werke, herausgegeben von Ernst Elster, Leipzig und Wien, Bibliographisches Institut, 1898.

Heines Werke in Einzelausgaben mit Bildern aus seiner Zeit, herausgegeben von G. A. E. Bogeng, Hamburg-Berlin, Hoffmann und Campe Verlag (with introductory essays by G. A. E. Bogeng, Jakob Schaffner, Alfred Döblin, Georg Brandes, Eduard Engel, Herbert Eulenberg, Oskar Loerke, Oskar Bie, Alfred Kerr and Erich Loewenthal).

Heinrich Heines Briefwechsel, herausgegeben von Friedrich Hirth, Bd. I-III, München, G. Müller, 1914-20.

English:
The Works of Heinrich Heine, translated by C. G. Leland (T. Brooksbank and M. A. MacDougall), London, W. Heinemann, 1891-1900.

Heinrich Heine's Memoirs, ed. by Gustav Karpeles, English translation by Gilbert Cannan, New York, John Lane Co., 1910.

The Family Life of Heinrich Heine, 122 family letters, etc., by Ludwig von Embden, from the German by Ch. DeKay, New York, Cassell Publishing Co., 1892.

The Memoirs of Heinrich Heine, with an introductory essay by Thomas W. Evans, London, Geo. Bell and Sons, 1884.

The Poems of Heine, translated into the original metres by Edgar Alfred Bowring, London, G. Bell and Sons, 1884.

Poems of Heinrich Heine, selected and translated by Louis Untermeyer, New York, H. Holt and Co., 1917.

Poems Selected from Heinrich Heine, with an introduction by Kate Freiligrath Kroeker, The Walter Scott Publishing Co., London, New York.

The Prose Writings of Heinrich Heine, edited, with an introduction by Havelock Ellis, London, W. Scott, 1887.

* * *

BIOGRAPHICAL REFERENCES

German:

Bartels, Adolf: *Heinrich Heine: Auch ein Denkmal*, Dresden,
    C. A. Koch, 1906.

Beyer, Paul: *Der junge Heine; eine Entwicklungsgeschichte
    seiner Denkweise und Dichtung*, Literarhistorische Gesell-
    schaft, Bonn.

Bieber, Hugo: *Heinrich Heine Gespräche*, Welt-Verlag, Ber-
    lin, 1926.

Bienenstock, M.: *Das jüdische Element in Heines Werken*,
    Verlag für Literatur, Kunst und Musik, Leipzig, 1910.

Börne, Ludwig: *Ludwig Börne's Urtheil über H. Heine; als
    Anhang: Stimmen über H. Heine's letztes Buch, aus Zeit-
    blättern*, Frankfurt am Main, bei Johann David Sauer-
    länder, 1840.

Brandes, Georg: *Hauptströmungen der Literatur des 19ten
    Jahrhunderts; Das junge Deutschland*, Erich Reiss Verlag,
    Berlin, 1924.

Brauweiler, Ernst: *Heines Prosa*, G. Grote'sche Verlagsbuch-
    handlung, Berlin, 1915.

Eckertz, Erich: *Heine und sein Witz*, Berlin, Verlag von Emil
    Felber, 1908.

Elster, Ernst: *Heines Leben und Werke*, Bibliographisches
    Institut, Leipzig und Wien.

Fischer, Hans R.: *Heinrich Heine im Lichte unserer Zeit*,
    München, Verlag von Dr. E. Albert und Co.

Fürst, Rudolf: *Heinrich Heines Leben Werke und Briefe*,
    Tempel Verlag, Leipzig, 1910.

Heine, Maximilian: *Erinnerungen an Heinrich Heine und
    seine Familie*, Berlin, Ferd. Dümmler's Verlagsbuch-
    handlung, 1868.

Houben, H. H.: *Gespräche mit Heine*, Rütten und Loening,
    Frankfurt am Main, 1926.

Houben, H. H.: *Jungdeutscher Sturm und Drang*, F. A. Brock-
    haus, Leipzig, 1911.

Houben, H. H.: *Verbotene Literatur*, Dessau, Karl Rauch
    Verlag, 1925.

Hüffer, Hermann: *Aus dem Leben Heinrich Heines,* Berlin, Verlag von Gebrüder Paetel, 1878.

Jaubert, Madame C.: *Heinrich Heine. Erinnerungen aus den letzten 20 Jahren seines Lebens (1835-1855),* autorisirte Uebersetzung von Luise Welter, Paris und Leipzig, 1884, Commissionsverlag von H. Le Soudier.

Karpeles, Gustav: *Heinrich Heine. Aus seinem Leben und aus seiner Zeit,* Leipzig, A. Titze, 1899.

Kaufmann, David: *Aus Heinrich Heines Ahnensaal,* Breslau, S. Schottlaender, 1896.

Key, Ellen: *Rahel (Varnhagen von Ense),* E. Haberland, Leipzig.

Keiter, Heinrich: *Heinrich Heine,* Köln, 1891, Verlag J. P. Bachem.

Kohut, Adolph: *Heinrich Heine und die Frauen,* Berlin, 1888.

Krienitz, Elise: *Heinrich Heines letzte Tage; Erinnerungen von Camilla Selden* (pseud.), aus dem Französischen, Jena, Costenoble, 1884.

Meissner, Alfred: *Die Matratzengruft,* Verlag von Robert Lutz, Stuttgart, 1921.

Meissner, Alfred: *Heinrich Heine. Erinnerungen,* Hamburg, Hoffmann und Campe, 1856.

Meissner, Alfred: *Geschichte meines Lebens,* Wien und Teschen, 1885, Verlag Karl Prochaska.

Moos, Eugen: *Heine und Düsseldorf,* Marburg, 1908.

Nassen, J.: *Heinrich Heines Familienleben,* Fulda, 1895.

Nietzki, Max: *Heinrich Heine als Dichter und Mensch,* Mitscher und Röstell, Berlin, 1895.

Plotke, Georg J.: *Heinrich Heine als Dichter des Judenthums,* Dresden, C. Reissner, 1913.

Proelss, J.: *Das junge Deutschland,* Stuttgart, 1892, Verlag der Cotta'schen Buchhandlung.

Proelss, Robert: *Heinrich Heine,* Stuttgart, Rieger'sche Verlagsbuchhandlung, 1886.

Puetzfeld, Carl: *Heinrich Heines Verhältnis zur Religion,* G. Grote'sche Verlagsbuchhandlung, Berlin, 1912.

Rahmer, S.: *Heinrich Heines Krankheit und Leidensgeschichte,* Berlin, Verlag von Georg Reimer, 1901.

Ras, G.: *Börne und Heine als politische Schriftsteller,* J. B. Woeters' U. M.-Groningen, den Haag, 1927.

Springer, Brunold: *Die genialen Syphilitiker*, Berlin-Niko-
lassee, Verlag der neuen Generation.
Strodtmann, Adolf: *Heinrich Heines Leben und Werke*, Ber-
lin, F. Duncker, 1873-4.
Treitschke, Heinrich von: *Bilder aus der deutschen Geschichte*,
Bd. II, Leipzig, Verlag S. Hirzel, 1908.
Wendel, Hermann: *Heinrich Heine: Ein Lebens und Zeitbild*,
Kaden und Comp., Dresden.
Wolff, Max J.: *Heinrich Heine*, E. H. Becksche Verlagsbuch-
handlung, Oskar Beck, München, 1922.

French:

Selden, Camille: *Les Derniers Jours de Henri Heine*, Paris,
Calmann Lévy, Éditeur, 1884.

Italian:

Bonardi, Carlo: *Enrico Heine nella letteratura italiana*, Liv-
orno, Raffaello Giusti, Editore, 1907.
Perticone, Giacomo: *Arrigo Heine*, A. F. Formíggini, Editore
in Roma, 1925.

English:

Butler, E. M.: *The Saint-Simonian Religion in Germany*,
Cambridge, University Press, 1926.
Francke, Kuno: *Social Forces in German Literature*, New
York, Henry Holt and Co., 1896.
Freud, Sigmund: *Wit and its Relation to the Unconscious*,
New York, Moffat, Yard and Co., 1916.
Monahan, Michael: *Heinrich Heine*, New York, Michael Ken-
nerly, 1911.
Philipson, David: *Old European Jewries*, Jewish Publication
Society of America, 1894.
Sachs, Henry Baruch: *Heine in America*, Philadelphia, 1916.
Sharp, William: *Life of Heinrich Heine*, London, Walter
Scott, 1888.
Sybel, Heinrich von: *The Founding of the German Empire*,
Vol. I, New York, Thomas Crowell and Co., 1890.
Whitehouse, H. Remsen: *A Revolutionary Princess*, London,
T. Fisher Unwin, 1906.

* * *

CRITICAL ESSAYS

German:

Becker, Godfrid: "Heinrich Heine, eine biographische Skizze," *Heine*, 7 vols., Verlag von Schäfer und Koradi, Philadelphia, 1868.

Berg, Leo: "Heine, Nietzsche, Ibsen," "Heine und Nietzsche," *Essays von Leo Berg*, Berlin, Concordia Deutsche Verlagsanstalt, 1908.

Eulenberg, Herbert: "Heinrich Heine," *Schattenbilder*, Berlin, Verlag von Bruno Cassirer, 1922.

Hebbel, Friedrich: "Buch der Lieder von Heinrich Heine," *Sämtliche Werke*, XII, Max Hesses Verlag, Leipzig.

Hirth, Friedrich: "Heinrich Heines Aphorismen," *Zeitschrift für Bücherfreunde*, Leipzig, 1919.

Karpeles, Gustav: "Heinrich Heine und der Rabbi von Bacharach," *Freien Blattes*, Wien, 1895.

Lange, Georg: "Heine und Nietzsche," *Oesterreichische Rundschau*, Wien, 1920.

Linden, A. v. D.: "Das Heine Grab auf dem Montmartre," Leipzig, Verlag von H. Barsdorf, 1898.

Meissner, Alfred: "Letzte Erinnerung an Heinrich Heine," *Schattentanz*, Verlag von Cäsar Schmidt, Zürich, 1881.

Meissner, Alfred: "Heine's Mouche," *Kleine Memoiren*, Verlag von R. Lesser, Berlin.

French:

Bourget, Paul: "L'enfance de Henri Heine," *Revue Critique des idées et des livres*, Plon-Nourrit et Cie., Paris, 1912.

Drumont, Édouard: "Henri Heine," *Les tréteaux du succes: figures de bronze ou statues de neige*, Paris, 1901.

Faure, Gabriel: "Goethe et Heine en Italie," *Revue politique et littéraire*, Paris, 1918.

Gautier, Théophile: "Henri Heine," *Portraits et souvenirs littéraires*, Paris, 1881.

Heine, Gustave: "Les dernières années de Henri Heine; notes inédites de son frère," *Revue de France*, Paris, 1924.

Hennequin, Émile: "Henri Heine," *Études de critique scientifique*, Perrin et Cie., Paris, 1889.

Launay, Robert: "Heine," *Figures juives*, Nouvelle librairie nationale, 1921.

Mirecourt, Eugène de: "Henri Heine," *Les Contemporains*, G. Havard, Paris, 1856.

Italian:

Croce, Benedetto: "Heine," *Poesia e non Poesia*, Gius. Laterza e Figli, Bari, 1923.

Fanciulli, Giuseppe: "Heine Profetta," *Rivista d'Italia*, Milano, 1918.

English:

Arnold, Matthew: "Heinrich Heine," *Essays in Criticism*. Macmillan Co., New York, 1924.

Butler, E. M.: "Heine and the Saint-Simonians," *Modern Language Review*, Cambridge, 1923.

Dowden, Edward: "Heinrich Heine," *Essays Modern and Elizabethan*, New York, E. P. Dutton and Co.

Ellis, Havelock: "Heine," *The New Spirit*, Boni and Liveright, New York.

Eliot, George: "German Wit: Heinrich Heine," *Essays and Leaves from a Note-Book*, Edinburgh, William Blackwood and Sons, 1884.

"Heinrich Heine. Emotion and Irony," *Edinburgh Review*, London, 1908.

Howells, William Dean: "Heine," "Heine, George Eliot, Hawthorne, Goethe," *My Literary Passions*, New York, 1895.

INDEX

411